With Our Compliments

IMS

The Institute for
Management Studies

*Over Twenty Years of Excellence
in Executive Development*

Corporate Headquarters:
4600 Kietzke Ln., I-205
Reno, Nevada 89502
702/826-8686

Go for Growth!

Go for Growth!

*Five Paths to Profit and Success—
Choose the Right One for
You and Your Company*

Robert M. Tomasko

John Wiley & Sons, Inc.

New York ■ Chichester ■ Brisbane ■ Toronto ■ Singapore

Library of Congress Cataloging-in-Publication Data:

Tomasko, Robert M.
    Go for growth ! Five paths to profit and success—choose the right one for you and your company / Robert M. Tomasko.
        p.   cm.
    Includes bibliographical references and index.
    ISBN 0-471-13290-X (cloth : alk. paper)
    1. Reengineering (Management)   2. Success in business.   I. Title.
HD58.87.T66   1996
658.4'063—dc20   95-44836
                                                                              CIP

To Laura, Julia, and William

Contents

Key Ideas Guide

1. The Growth Imperative

Today, the term multinational doesn't refer to a particular type of company; it denotes a dimension of growth attractive to many American businesses. Increasingly, though, contemporary frontiers are not geographic; they are intellectual and technological. **p. 4.**

The main benefits of cost-cutting are past. **p. 5.**

Cost reduction may help keep the wolf at bay, but it alone won't take a business anywhere. **p. 5.**

Cost reduction is a tactic, not a business objective. Downsizing and reengineering can masquerade as a plan, but they alone won't necessarily provide top-line growth—or a future for the business. **p. 7.**

Outsourcing is no substitute for growth. **p. 12.**

Growth is an essential lubricant for many change programs. **p. 14.**

Strategies and organizations only exist to help channel people's efforts. Debates about the future that lead to new insights about the marketplace occur among people. New ideas are created, nurtured, championed, and even squelched by people. The Herculean efforts required to crush a sales target or produce and ship a critical rush order come only from people. Change happens only when people change. Growth happens only when people grow. **p. 17.**

2. Growth Isn't What It Used to Be

Keep productivity growing by increasing the revenue part of the equation, **p. 19.**

Many seasoned executives have very outmoded views of how to grow a business. **p. 21.**

Many more junior managers and employees have never had first-hand experience in organizations that were doing anything but contracting. **p. 21.**

Having your business grow in sales without increasing at the same rate the value added to customers will only create opportunities for competitors to move in. **p. 27.**

Too many companies have put a too-narrow definition of growth on too high of a pedestal. **p. 29.**

Growth managers have the ability to deal with events that are separated in time. They know there is often a long wait between the time something happens and the time its consequences are apparent. **p. 30.**

Businesses hoping to grow through team efforts are making sure the greatest rewards are flowing to high performers who expend effort upgrading the skills of their team-mates, p. 33.

The belief that momentum drives growth and that growth comes from a rapid succession of victories is deeply ingrained in the American business psyche. p. 34.

A string of wins will accumulate a massive number of these obstacles-in-waiting. p. 34.

Success sets you up for failure, which really isn't all that bad. Sustainable, real growth is driven much more by failures than successes. p. 34.

3. One Size Never Fits All

Reengineering is being used the way "quality" or "strategic planning" were in the past—as a general purpose, cure-whatever-is-ailing solution to a business's problems. p. 43.

Just when a majority of the employees seem to be "getting with the program," the game plan shifts, and a new direction is announced. p. 45.

Reengineering is something done to a machine, not to a living, breathing, forward-moving enterprise. p. 49.

Trying to use an organization successful for yesterday's growth journey to carry it on tomorrow's. p. 52.

Each growth type has a distinct personality, corporate character, or core competence. p. 54.

There is no one best way to organize and manage a business. But, for a given situation, some ways are much better than others, p. 54.

As the marketplace and competition change, a company's structure and management practices must also evolve. p. 54.

4. Breaking the Rules

The compromise and accommodation central to their functioning make it hard for them to serve as vehicles to challenge the wisdom of their parents. p. 66.

Rule Breakers seldom need to take time away from work to attend team-building programs; an exciting, shared mission serves that purpose even better. p. 67.

The real danger is that the up-and-coming Rule Breaker diverts so much attention and energy resisting encroaching bureaucracy that not enough is left to develop new ideas. p. 73.

Constantly staying on the cutting edge can become a tiring and expensive position to maintain. p. 80.

5. Playing the Game

Game Players, like Coke and Pepsi, thrive when their competitive actions serve to expand their markets, not to destroy each other. p. 94.

Game Players that miss the long-term dynamics of their markets—demographic shifts, technological discontinuities, globalization, and the like—may find themselves with an increasing share of a shrinking market. p. 101.

6. Making the Rules

Although seldom publicly admitted to, a Rule Maker's greatest fear is that of being overtaken. p. 116.

Rule Makers take good advantage of the flywheel effect—that is, once a wheel is moving rapidly, it takes more energy to slow it down than to speed it up. p. 117.

The shrewdest moves Rule Makers make are those that obsolete themselves on an ongoing basis. p. 119.

Visions that grow businesses are rooted in reality. At their core is a belief about what customers will want and an illusion-free appreciation of what the business is good at delivering. p. 120.

For Rule Makers, the product exists more as a vehicle for the company

8. Improvising

Improvisers make up for a lack of concentrated effort with an organization built around speed, cunning, and flexibility. **p. 182.**

Planning in a way that surprises and throws the competition off balance has a lot to recommend to it, **p. 186.**

It is easy for an Improviser to stumble when it is too adapted to its situation. **p. 186.**

While it is vital to roughly align organization with marketplace dynamics, too close a coupling with an industry lacking clear direction can become very debilitating. **p. 189.**

In pressurized situations, teams begin to value their own cohesion over dealing directly with the conflicts that naturally arise from differing perspectives and opinions about courses of action the business needs to consider. **p. 197.**

Not all shared visions are good shared visions. **p. 198.**

Eisner did not attempt to become the "new" Disney, replacing one cult figure with another. Instead, he led by holding the company to applying its founder's values in a way relevant to the company's current situation. **p. 200.**

It is not so much their habits and traditions that give them problems, it is that these old mind-sets have become disconnected from their original context. **p. 201.**

The trick to successful change is not so much to abandon the past (an impossibility, anyhow) but, to reinterpret it to serve the needs of the present:, **p. 202.**

Improvisers are good at creating variations, wary of ultimate solutions. **p. 205.**

Ghosh kept changing his division's form, observing the ensuing reactions, and took them into account in planning his next change. No single form was right or wrong, each was just a tool to create a temporary balance between conflicting needs. **p. 208.**

The larger an organization becomes, relatively fewer people are spending time connecting the business with the outside world, **p. 209.**

Change, for pragmatic Improvisers, is a welcome source of unexpected opportunities. **p. 211.**

9. Keeping the Focus on Growth

What was not realized, he admitted, was, how much that growth would change the character of the company. **p. 222.**

No single measure of growth is appropriate for all businesses. **p. 225.**

Growth stumbles when companies become, over adapted, either to yesterday's market realities or to the internal struggles that take place within every organization. **p. 225.**

Growth failures frequently occur when, rather than moving toward other paths, a company meets adversity with a renewed commitment to do more of the same. **p. 227.**

Sustaining growth over the long haul, across decades for example, requires skill at changing course. **p. 227.**

Growth during the medium term, a stretch of time ranging from 5 to 15 years, can be accomplished for many companies through a combining of paths. **p. 227.**

In the short run, over the next year or two, assuming a good match has been made between path and situation, the primary growth issue is one of focus. **p. 227.**

What can more easily be manipulated is the link between the two; a company's organization. **p. 228.**

Organization works the same way a vehicle does. It performs three critical functions:, **p. 229.**

Sound plans are the result of intensive fact-based debate about alternative courses of action. **p. 232.**

The best time to draft a corporate mission is immediately after a major business victory. **p. 236.**

Mission statements can be most effective for communicating and reinforcing a direction already chosen. **p. 237.**

The more people there are in a company who can imagine what it can become, the more likely it is to get there. **p. 241.**

Our employees are the customers of our management, **p. 242.**

Culture is something that managers cannot put their hands around. It is not something that can be directly managed. **p. 242.**

A company is positioned for growth when its people are. A growth-oriented organization is one in which its three functions are working in tandem to focus employees' attention on, and direct actions toward the requirements of the path it has chosen. **p. 243.**

Common visions only come to life when a structure is present to support them. **p. 244.**

Structures alone are confining prisons of daily drudgery when they lack a source of direction and energy to bring them to life. **p. 244.**

It is never possible to change just one part of an organization. The three functions (Direction, Propulsion, and Stability) are completely intertwined in the minds and behaviors of most employees. Making changes in a disjoined manner only sends mixed signals that dilute focus. **p. 245.**

A company with all employees marching forward in lockstep can be a disaster if they are headed toward the edge of a steep cliff. **p. 246.**

10. Changing Course to Sustain Growth

When organizing businesses with diverse growth paths under one corporate umbrella is not to try to tightly integrate things that are not meant to be tightly integrated, **p. 251.**

Ongoing management attention is required to operate businesses on divergent growth paths under the same corporate structure. **p. 252.**

Some species just cannot turn into others, **p. 253.**

After becoming well established, businesses do not grow by successive minor changes in strategy and organization but by large-scale transformations that involve the corporation as a whole. **p. 254.**

Golub believes, for American Express and its competitors, that every business is destined to ultimately go out of business. The only issue, as he sees it, is if the wounds are to be self-inflicted, by American Express changing its product mix, or suffered at the hands of competitors. **p. 254.**

Most major reorganizations—essential in any shift from one growth path to another—are handled very poorly. This is often because all the attention is given to figuring out what comes next, and too little time is devoted to closing the books on the past. **p. 257.**

Companies obsessed with winning every game find it very hard to learn a new one, **p. 258.**

The existence of deviations or performance shortfalls is used to question the original assumptions behind the appropriateness of the performance targets. **p. 259.**

Individuals in these jobs would spend more time worrying about what the company is not doing than what it is doing. **p. 260.**

The bottom line of any organization is how well it positions its employees for growth. Organizations shape the way people interact. **p. 261.**

Epilogue

Can you become more of a grower, less of a pruner? What new skills need to be acquired or rediscovered, and which old habits need to be withdrawn from center stage? Spend a minute thinking about where you have most excelled over the past five years. What are the three or four accomplishments for which you have received the most recognition? What is the nature of these achievements? Did your efforts focus on improving the company's inner workings, or was attention directed more outward, at customers, competitors, and markets? How much practice have you had at growing the business, or have you been more of a platform builder? What do you need to focus on now? **p. 264.**

Employees are linked to market demands through the kind of organization the business has chosen. **p. 265.**

This is where overly smug managers fail to set aside resources for future growth and are too content with the status quo to prepare the business for renewal. **p. 267.**

It's amazing how many businesses attempt to make radical shifts in

strategy but assume they can leave the team that provided past success in place. **p. 268.**

These five growth path categories are abstractions. **p. 269.**

The important point is that there is more than one way company can grow. **p. 269.**

The purpose of the five is to provide a common language, a vocabulary to label what path is being taken to growth, **p. 269.**

Look hard for the pros and cons of potentially useful techniques. Both are always present. Then look hard at where the practice worked and understand why it worked in that particular situation. Never try something until you find an example of it failing, and be sure you know what was behind the failure. Then ask how similar—or not—is your business's situation to these others. Finally, list the adjustments you will need to make to the new idea to increase its likelihood of success. **p. 270.**

Don't put any company too high on a pillar. **p. 271.**

Choosing the wrong path can lead to ineffectiveness, creating the wrong organization will cause inefficiency, but attempting to grow with the wrong people is likely to result in disaster. **p. 274.**

Companies sustainably grow only when the people who work in them do. **p. 275.**

Introduction

The observation that in business, you are either growing or dying is true now more than ever. This book is about growing a business. It is more a what-to-do guide than a how-to-do-it manual. It is written for managers and professionals tired of retrenching; for those who want to see their companies and careers grow, not contract; and for those who want to build, not destroy.

To keep focused on for whom this book is intended, I talked with managers from several hundred companies and over a dozen industries and asked them where they wanted to see their companies headed. With almost a single voice, they said they wanted their businesses to grow. If all their comments could be pulled together into a note from a prospective reader to the author, it would read something like this:

> I want to take this business to the next level. I'm tired of cutting back and squeezing. I want to see this company grow again.
>
> We're a bunch of smart people. We've been around the track. We know how to make things happen. Give us something to read that will stimulate our thinking and give us a sense of how to approach growth. Just don't fill it with a rehash of business school jargon; another ten-phase, multiyear program; or some one-size-fits-all gimmick of the month.
>
> Don't insult our intelligence by oversimplifying or sugarcoating reality. Instead, give us some principles, some lessons, and some do's and don't's. You've watched companies grow, and you've watched companies stumble. What have you learned?
>
> Tell us what we need to do to position this business to grow. How do we select the *right growth path* for us? How do we organize the business so our people's attention is focused on that strategy—

not on last year's game plan or what made us famous decades ago? And what kind of people do we need to get us where we want to go?

Right now some of us are chafing at the bit to move forward, and some of us are still ducking for cover in fear of the next round of cutbacks. There's got to be a better way to sort out who will be happiest here; who will have the most to contribute; and who will do better, with our help, to relocate their career.

Please don't tell us to imitate Jack Welch, Bill Gates, or Herb Kelleher. They're all good, strong leaders. But they're them; I'm me. I need to figure out what will work for *me.*

Give me an outline I can flesh out, a road map. Give it to me in digestible nuggets. Tell me what questions I've got to ask. Provide alternatives, with the pros and cons of each. Help me find a unique path to growth. Help me find my place on it.

That is a tall order, covering a lot of subjects. The next three chapters make a case for growth having priority over internal improvements. Although for many managers it has been years since their business was in a growth mode, the world is different now. The rules for growth have changed. Companies, as never before, need to customize their growth plans.

Because different people contribute in different ways, the five chapters that follow provide various baselines from which alternative growth paths can be plotted. At the end of each of these five chapters, first-person descriptions are provided of what it is like to work in businesses on each growth path.

The last two chapters describe how organization can be used as a tool to focus everyone's attention on the business's growth objectives. Sustaining growth over the long haul usually requires a change in trajectory. Accomplishing this through organizational change is the subject of the last chapter. Finally, the epilogue pulls these ideas together with some comments on how to apply them to your situation.

We've got a lot of ground to cover, so let's get started.

Build, Don't Destroy

You Can't Save Your Way to Prosperity

1

The Growth Imperative

isten to two managers, each describing the high points of their past week:

It's been a real roller coaster. Monday started with great fanfare as two new reengineering projects were announced. The PR hype that went out with them said they were going to create enough economies to save the division. I've been assigned to both. The only problem is that I have the quality project and two other task force assignments and—did I mention—my regular job. I'd be lost without that new meeting-scheduling software. By Thursday, my mood darkened as end-of-month results were released and rumors of further job cuts spread like wildfire. Looks like more work for me—I'm on the outplacement committee, also. At least I've got some measure of job security; I'm on too many projects for them ever to let me go.

What a week! I've spent half the time fighting a voice-mail battle to free up funds to build a new prototype part that a customer asked for ASAP. Bottom line: no money; it's been a rough year. That's okay; I've got some funds salted away behind some accounting codes no one from headquarters ever bothers to look at. No customer goes away unhappy on my watch. . . . The rest of the week was spent at an off-site with a bunch of hotshots from our new European sub-sidiary. We're all battling the same Japanese competitor, and now we've got a coordinated plan of attack. Number-one market share position, here we come. There's been a rumor going around that I'm on the list for promotion. Promotion? Me? That will be the day. I'm too busy to be promoted.

Referring to the two different weeks described above:

- Which week would you prefer to experience?

- Which company would you like to work in?

- Which business is likely to have the brightest prospects?

A Call to Arms

Grow or die—it's a call to arms spreading throughout America's corporations. *Growth* is appearing at the top of many management meeting agendas. It's prominently featured in glossy annual reports and confidential strategic plans, it's optimistically discussed with investment analysts, and its pros and cons are quietly debated around the water cooler and on the E-mail—and none too soon.

American businesspeople have always preferred growth to contraction. It is an idea deeply ingrained in the culture. Maybe it's something in the water, or maybe it's lingering memories of manifest destiny, an idea once studied in an otherwise forgettable history class.

The frontier has always played a big part in American history. Horatio Alger's rags-to-riches tales are entrenched in our folklore. We are a nation of immigrants, people attuned to breaking away from something old, to looking for something better. When we filled the continent and expanded our living space through acquisition and annexation, we focused offshore. **Today, the term *multinational* doesn't refer to a particular type of company; it denotes a dimension of growth attractive to many American businesses. Increasingly, though, contemporary frontiers are not geographic; they are intellectual and technological. These will be the drivers of future growth and expansion.**

Our business heroes—Henry Ford, Akio Morito, Sam Walton and others—are all people who have taken an idea, or a technique that embodied it, and grown it. They made something happen where before there was nothing. That is the kind of challenge that gets the adrenaline moving and the morale up. It's what makes waking up in the morning exciting and makes you again as eager to come to the office as you were when you started your career. It's an excitement that is easily appreciated, regardless of whether it's driven by a personal vision or fueled by a team project whose goal is bigger than what any of its members could accomplish alone. It's a challenge sorely needed after a decade of dispiriting downsizing and making do with less.

Build, Don't Destroy

The main benefits of cost-cutting are past. Operating from a low-cost position is something many in business have come to take for granted. It's a minimum requirement, an admission ticket to the competitive arena. **Cost reduction may help keep the wolf at bay, but it alone won't take a business anywhere.** At some point, it also becomes very hard to generate any enthusiasm for the next round of downsizing.

Downsizings inevitably eliminate the wrong people. Bright, aggressive, self-confident, and independent employees are usually among the first to accept voluntary severance or early retirement offers. This result leaves the company, unfortunately, with a higher percentage of people with exactly the opposite traits—not always the best foundation for the future.

Mobil Corporation, like others in the restructuring-prone petroleum business, worries about the dearth of new blood. "Most of us have stopped bringing in young talent in adequate numbers to replace the talent that will be retiring over the next five to ten years," laments Rex Adams, a Mobil vice president. This is a real danger of the contraction mind-set. Most downsizing is done very myopically. Today's cuts go to tomorrow's bottom line, but their positive impact can be too easily reversed by serious skill shortages lying just over the horizon.

In contrast, if you have a chance to visit very long with Wayne Calloway, PepsiCo's chief executive, you are bound to hear him implore, "You can't save your way to prosperity." Growth is one of his favorite subjects and for good reason. PepsiCo's sales have grown at an annual compound rate of 17 percent. He'd probably call it "the real thing" if that phrase hadn't been usurped by another beverage company.

Growth is moving higher on the agendas at hardware as well as soft drink companies. Honeywell is a one-time troubled computer maker that recently rediscovered that the gateways to its future are the businesses that always have been at the core of its history: controls and sensors. To mark the end of its old restructuring- and downsizing-dominated era, its chief executive, Michael Bonsignore, announced, "The chain-saw days are over. We're shifting to growth." With their vision sharpened by removing the distractions of being an also-ran computer company, Honeywell's employees are more focused and motivated than ever to grow the part of the business they know well and in which they are strong.

It's getting harder and harder to justify mega job cuts with vague references to "staying competitive" or "overseas competition." How, *specifically*, do you plan to compete? How are your organization changes really going to support that plan? Is the size of your payroll the biggest impediment to its success? Or, as is increasingly becoming the case, are your employee's contributions the key to the business's future? The only valid reason to prune a business—short of saving it from bankruptcy or liquidation—is to generate fuel for its expansion.

The Limits of Cost-Cutting

A recent study sheds some light on this issue. The U.S. Census Bureau closely examined the performance of over 100,000 plants during the past decade of downsizing. What they found contradicts much of today's conventional wisdom. According to their research, the companies increasing productivity *and* employment are the ones that also do the best job growing the value they pass on to their customers. These growth-oriented upsizers had more than five times as great a difference between their manufacturing cost and price they received as did those suffering from downsizing myopia. They weren't slackers in productivity growth, either—it was almost as high as those who relied exclusively on painful cutbacks to increase efficiency.

A Boston-based consulting firm considered the same issue from a different angle. They examined how well the stock market values growth and found that the chronic criticism Wall Street receives for being shortsighted may be a bum rap. After studying 800 public companies, the firm found that not all profit dollars are equally valued. According to the stock market, those generated by cost-cutting count only half as much as those derived from higher sales. The stock price of companies that achieved better-than-average earnings from better-than-average revenue growth grew *twice* as fast as those whose ahead-of-the-pack profits came from internal economies. Cost-cutting may seem easier, but the benefits of growth last longer.

Many businesses are coming to appreciate that "lean and mean" is a slogan, not a strategy. It's also a slogan that, if overapplied, can result in a company better characterized as "lean and lame." **Cost reduction is a tactic, not a business objective. Downsizing and reengineering can masquerade as a plan, but they alone won't necessarily provide top-line growth—or a future for the business.**

Managing as if the Future Really Mattered

The future is what growth is all about. Industry has worked overtime in the last decade to earn more money by being more productive. From here on, for many of us, earnings growth is going to have to come from revenue growth. In the long run, growing profits by cutting people and costs is—by definition—a dead end. It is even self-defeating. As a company becomes better and better at cutting, it eventually runs out of things to trim. It's not just that the business runs out of what productivity experts like to call "low-hanging fruit"; eventually there is no fruit left at all, no more processes left to reengineer. It is possible, if care is not taken, to work very hard to fine-tune a source of diminishing payback.

If managers lack a clear understanding of what really creates value for their customers, both today's and tomorrow's, they may find themselves in a very dangerous situation. They can fall into the trap of mindlessly lopping off expenses, all the time strangling the business's ability to generate new revenue.

Consider the plight of Zenith Electronics Corporation. This U.S.-based television manufacturer has been under siege for years from Asian consumer electronics producers. After a decade of downsizings, the company halved its payroll. Was this a necessity for survival of the business? It possibly was, but it also resulted in Zenith leaving money on the table when demand surged for its new hot product, flat computer screens. Compaq and other personal computer makers were left looking for other suppliers when Zenith's chronic cutbacks left its manufacturing operation too lean to fill all its customers' orders. In 1995 Zenith finally threw in the towel. It sold itself to a Korean company, Lucky-Goldstar.

Kodak is another company that strayed from its growth path. Its core business, photographic film, was plagued by offshore competition. In response, wave after wave of costly job cuts were implemented. To compensate for revenue losses in its core business, Kodak acquired a marginally related (at best) drug company. The bottom line from all this frenzy: profits only slightly larger than they had been during the previous decade and a lackluster stock price. Eventually the importation of a chief executive from growth-oriented Motorola was required to bring Kodak back to the path to growth through doing what it knows best.

Bausch & Lomb, a corporate neighbor of Kodak's in Rochester, took a similar approach to reenergizing its endangered contact lens and sunglass businesses. The company's first move was to acquire growth-seasoned leadership. The painful but realistic realization that "we can't get to where we want to be from where we are" prompted Bausch & Lomb to recruit a new chief executive, Daniel Gil, from Abbott Laboratories.

At Abbott, Gil was steeped in the tradition of making money by making wise investments. This simple philosophy, neither novel nor arcane, has fallen into disfavor in many American businesses where penny-pinching is king. But when Gil carefully applied the invest-to-grow mentality to Bausch & Lomb's cash-starved businesses, miracles occurred. Innovations, focused acquisitions, and product extensions broadened the company's scope, first from optical products to overall eye care. Eventually the Bausch & Lomb brand appeared on a wide variety of personal health care products, from hearing aids to electric toothbrushes. In the past decade, sales soared from less than $500 million to $2 billion annually.

Changing leadership at the top is a drastic remedy to slow-growth stagnation, and it's also fraught with many perils of its own. A better solution may be for a business's managers to light a fire under their chief executive. All it takes is a leader with enough self-confidence to be able to listen to their concerns or maybe one bold enough to regularly ask what's on their minds. It also takes followers with the courage to speak their minds without fear of being seen as disloyal. A rare combination? Perhaps, but when present, it's one that can quickly galvanize major change.

Emerson Electric's About-Face

Has your boss ever asked you to tell him or her what he or she was doing wrong? If you had dropped in on a recent meeting of Emerson Electric Co.'s 15 most senior managers, you would have heard Chuck Knight, their chief executive, do just that. Emerson makes a lot of mundane electrical products: garbage disposals, pressure gauges, refrigerator compressors, and power tools. But it is not a mundane company. Emerson is one of the few companies mentioned in Tom Peter's book, *In Search of Excellence* (Harper & Row, 1982), whose performance would warrant a place in the book's sequel. *It has had an unbroken string of 36 years of increased earnings.* This rare track record stands despite Emerson being in global markets so hotly contested that customers haven't allowed significant price increases in over ten years. In short, Emerson is one of America's productivity superstars, and Chuck Knight's forceful leadership is one of the chief reasons behind its success.

He is a very direct man and expects very direct answers from his managers, so when he asked them for criticism, they didn't hold back. While acknowledging that Emerson is already more productive than its Japanese competitors, their forecasts indicated that further gains from cost reduction would be marginal at best. They felt pride in profit margins far higher than the industry average, but revenue growth was stalling—because Knight was directing all their attention to the bottom line. This was *wrong*, they said. Where was the business going, they wondered? Was the path that served it well in the past the right one to take it safely into the next century?

Focus on the Top Line

Knight quickly got the message. No laggard in the vision department (he started worrying about overseas competitors nearly a decade before most U.S. manufacturers), he quickly realized that productivity *was* yesterday's battle and that his management team was right about where Emerson's future advantage lay. He soon announced a company-wide top-line growth program. Noting that Emerson had invested more than $300 million in the past five years in restructuring and cost reduction, Knight pledged—in the company's annual report—that an equivalent amount would be earmarked over the next five years for growth programs. Specifically, Emerson's millions are targeted to be spent on the following:

- New products—introducing *twice* as many as in the past five years.

- Geographic expansion—*doubling* sales in the Asia/Pacific region over the next five years.

- Joint ventures.

- Acquisitions.

Will this be money well spent? If we were to revisit Emerson in the year 2000, would we find its growth objectives met? Positive answers to these questions depend on much more than judgments about the adequacies of Emerson's four strategies. They are really not all that different than the growth plans many American manufacturers are preparing. What will really matter most to Emerson's success is an issue more complex than just preparing a good game plan. In fact, it's an issue not just for Emerson; it is the same set of factors that will be behind the following:

- Southwest Airlines' ability to sustain its remarkable, profitable growth record.

- Silicon Graphics' ability to be more than this year's flash in the pan.

- Bell Atlantic's ability to find an up-ramp to the information superhighway.

- Microsoft's ability to hold on to and enhance its strong market position.

- *Your* business's ability to _____.

Achieving growth objectives such as these requires more than the right plan, analytical technique, or consultant. It requires a skillful custom blend of these ingredients:

- A *strategic path* that *connects the demands of the marketplace with the inner world of the company.* There's more than one way a business can grow; there's more than one way a company can deploy its talent. In a given situation, some paths are more promising than others.

- An *organization* that *focuses its people's attention on the growth issues* that matter most to the business's success. This sounds simple, but the net result of most of today's organizations is a blurred focus, a sense of distraction on the part of many of those on whom the business depends to be alert to carry out its plans. Most corporate structures are monuments to past successes, not power bases for future growth.

- A careful *match between employee capabilities and the work at hand*. Too many businesses are like the shipwrecked sailor who attempted to cross a rough ocean with a crew that had never left coastal waters before.

These are the critical issues that Emerson, and any other company looking for sustainable growth, must address. They will shape the future of any business.

Fear Can Destroy the Future

A sound approach to growth is the best insurance that a business has for the future. To be sound, though, such a plan needs a strong foundation and must motivate people to move forward. It has to be based on something more than fear. Bob Dylan was probably right when he warned that all who are not busy growing are busy dying, but there are limits to how far fear can effectively motivate.

Cost-cutting has been largely fear driven—fear of lower-cost competitors, fear of impatient stockholders, fear of fickle customers. This kind of motivation may be necessary in the short run. It is a good way to wake up a sleepy company or to induce a crisis mentality in a laggard. But it wears thin after a while; it is dispiriting and burnout inducing. Fear puts us on constant guard, worrying about covering our backs and watching our flanks—postures that make it easy to miss those subtle, future-oriented growth clues that the market constantly offers. Fear does its greatest damage when it blinds you to the strengths that exist inside.

If a growth goal is to endure, it has to come from *inside* the organization. Emerson's growth prospects are brighter because they trickled up from the managers directly responsible for serving the company's individual markets. They weren't imposed on the company from Wall Street or from its strong-willed CEO. Bausch & Lomb's sales jumped when its managers combined a keen understanding of the value of what was already in place with a perspective on the opportunities the market had to offer. Kodak's new chief executive didn't carry along a new miracle technology or product line from Motorola; instead, he brought a discipline, a willingness to appreciate the growth potential already within the Kodak organization. All too frequently, more attention is given to carving pieces out of the business than building on what is already there.

You Can't Rent Your Future

Outsourcing has become a widespread practice in American business. "Contract out what others can do better or cheaper," is its rallying cry. Perhaps the logical extension of this mind-set is the creation of a "virtual corporation," one whose lean complement of employees exists primarily to coordinate the work of subcontractors. This is an enticing vision, one with great appeal to headcount-reduction-driven businesspeople, but it is also a dangerous one. It is a vision that can lead a company to cutting its heart out, if the heart is not carefully identified before the company is deconstructed.

Outsourcing does have its place. It is a useful way to move overhead and routine administrative activities out of the core of a business. It can, at its best, keep managers from blurring their vision about what elements of the company will really fuel its growth. Be wary, though, of overdoing it. **Outsourcing is no substitute for growth.** The question "Should I make something in-house, or would it be better to purchase it on the open market?" is really a question about where the *seeds of a business's future* are to come from. Sadly, it is too often a question answered only with reference to today. In the short run, a particular part or component may be cheaper to buy rather than build. But what else may get lost if it's not made in-house? For one thing, the experience and knowledge that are acquired in parallel with making something may never be gained. Neither may the new technologies that know-how could lead to. Nor will outsourcing make any easier the discovery of new or spin-off products that may emerge as an old one fades in usefulness.

Psychic Benefits

Growth has many financial rewards to offer, but it also provides the opportunity to forge a link between the material world of a business—

products, money, and promotions—and the "softer" needs of the human psyche. Being a part of something bigger than ourselves and building something that can outlast ourselves are important cravings. They offer a chance to grow personally, to forge new relationships, to acquire new talents, and to challenge old assumptions. *Growing a business and growing a person have a lot in common.* They are certainly mutually interdependent. Wayne Calloway of PepsiCo appreciates this connection. He wants PepsiCo to be a company that offers more than the daily grind to its managers and employees. To achieve this goal, the company has to keep people energized and has to become a magnet for new talent and new ideas. Without an orientation to growth and building, what is left but slow-motion death? Good, energetic people leave, and those remaining turn inward and build Byzantine bureaucracies instead of strong market positions.

Look into the career histories of your company's most entrenched corprocrats, its best skilled turf builders. More likely than not, some were once among the business's aggressive, forward-thinking, high-promise talent. What happened? The business might have slowed, limiting the number of positions that could usefully direct their talents toward the marketplace. Alternatively, the business might have achieved a dangerous degree of success—dangerous in that it started to take its strong competitive position for granted. Corporations that fall into this trap—AT&T and General Motors in the 1970s and IBM in the 1980s—tend to turn inward. Rewards flow to those who tend this inner world; good talent spots the shift in incentives and redirects itself accordingly.

Others, maybe less aggressive but just as bright and talented, just hunker down hoping to avoid the next wave of downsizing. Keeping their heads low and their ideas to themselves, they try to cope with change by feigning compliance. This is the kind of behavior that derails many change efforts.

The Catch-22 of Reengineering

Last year, for the first time in 20 years of consulting, I encountered a group of middle managers obviously trying to hide information and otherwise attempting to deceive me. They didn't even bother to do it in a very subtle way. They directly obstructed the consulting team's requests for information, thinking that they could get away with doing so because the consultants would look ridiculous if they had to go to senior management every time a problem about collecting information arose.

Eventually, after getting over my anger and surprise at their breaches of corporate etiquette—they were working for one of the world's largest, most respected publishing houses—I realized there was some amount of logic behind their disruptive behavior. Their department had suffered countless reorganizations, cutbacks hidden in the guise of quality improvement, and many shifts in leadership over the past five years. The reengineering effort of which I was a part was cynically perceived as the vehicle to either eliminate their jobs or get them to do more with less. They were sick and tired of change being shoved down their throats; sabotage had become for them a simple matter of ensuring career survival.

This kind of entrenched resistance cannot be overcome by an inspirational speech and slick-change management program. Opposition like this to corporate improvement efforts is spreading in many companies. It's the catch-22 of reengineering: the more it promises the corporation, the less it seems to offer the individual. And for process improvement efforts to succeed, they need the best thinking and commitment of those actually responsible for them.

Growth offers one of the few ways out of this dilemma. **It is an essential lubricant for many change programs.** Capital Holding Corporation, a financial services business based in Louisville, Kentucky, found that the key to getting the ideas needed to cut staffing by up to 50 percent in some operations was to make a very active effort to retrain and redeploy the affected workers to other units whose growth required adding staff. The people at Capital made sure that the staffing programs of both types of units were closely coordinated, avoiding the demoralizing revolving door common in hurriedly planned restructurings: laying off high-potential employees in one division while spending money to recruit and train new hires in another.

Breaking Free from Old Ways

Let's be fair, though, to downsizing and its trendy cousin, reengineering. These tactics do have a place in the manager's toolkit. They are not always the antithesis of growth; sometimes they are its prerequisite.

Like many unpleasant medicines, they hurt while curing. Sometimes they make up for past errors, while other times they set the stage for the future.

Moving to a business's next level of growth almost always requires pain for the gain. Established ways of transacting business must be put aside. A new perception of the marketplace, and how the company intends to thrive in it, must first be acquired and then reflected in the business's structure. New ways of approaching customers, competitors, and products need to be reintegrated into the core of the business.

Many years ago, I was an advisor to the president of the Burlington Northern Railroad. His main concern at that time was running the railroad efficiently, especially in minimizing the number of new locomotives he had to purchase each year. Like many people in his industry, he was well immersed in railroad lore. Photos of large steam engines, long gone, lined his office. Models of sleek, efficient diesel trains painted in the company's new, bright green logo dominated the tops of his bookshelves. He was clearly a *railroader*. He even offered the use of his private railroad car to conduct my efficiency study.

Friend or Foe?

Like most railroaders of his time, he hated trucks and truckers, a natural reaction given the competitive threat they posed. He hated the fact that they rode on taxpayer-subsidized highways. He hated the fact that, unlike his capital-intensive railroad, trucking was a relatively easy business to enter. And he especially hated that they were stealing his customers.

What he, and many of the company's other executives, chose to ignore was that some truckers were also customers of the railroad—those who took advantage of one of the services that Burlington Northern and other railroads offered and had their trailers hauled over long distances on top of specially designed flat cars, piggyback style. Top management's ambivalence about the trucking industry was mirrored in the lack of aggressiveness in the railroad's marketing of this service. In 1981, Burlington Northern actually ranked at the bottom of the U.S. railroad industry in the performance of this "intermodal" business.

At that time, railroads were about to experience the kind of massive upheaval that jolted the telephone industry in the mid-1980s and the health care industry in the mid-1990s. Congressionally mandated deregulation was about to change all the rules about how successful rail-roads were run.

Converting Competitors into Customers

Rising to meet this challenge was one bright, aggressive, team-oriented middle manager who was buried in the Burlington Northern's back-water marketing department, Bill Greenwood. With his bosses' ap-proval, he took charge of a recently formed intermodal business unit. From that obscure power base, Greenwood took on every assumption that the railroad's executives had about truckers being, at best, a neces-sary evil. Looking outside the ingrown traditional boundaries of the in-dustry, it was clear to Bill that deregulation's new pricing freedom would encourage many of Burlington Northern's customers to move their goods out of railroad box cars and into containers and trailer trucks. Bill, a natural optimist, saw this as a great opportunity for the railroad to grow the intermodal business.

The Growth Team

Not wanting to challenge the entrenched power structure singlehand-edly, Greenwood assembled a team of six like-minded people from across the railroad's functional fiefdoms and from outside the industry. By using a series of carefully crafted carrot-and-stick scenarios, they slowly but surely focused middle and senior managers' attentions on the opportunities of forming alliances with the truckers. They backed these projections up with detailed blueprints for constructing 22 intermodal hubs at points where the Burlington Northern freight tracks intersected the most heavily trafficked interstate highways. They scoured the rail-road, looking for opportunities to cut costs so as to raise funds to build these hubs. After they got the green light to go ahead, they even hired ex-truckers to run them. It took years of political infighting and a healthy dose of what one team member termed "Jesuit management." ("It's always easier to ask for forgiveness than permission—if the new idea works, nobody will ask if it was approved in advance; if it fails, the reason you are fired will have nothing to do with your failure to secure an advance OK.")

The rest is, as they say in the railroad industry, history. The inter-modal concept was fantastically successful. Burlington Northern became the nation's number-one intermodal carrier, and a new billion-dollar business was built in less than ten years. By that time my client had long since retired. Who had his job? Bill Greenwood, of course. And as for me, I should have taken my old client's offer to ride across the Rockies in his private car back when it was extended. These days, Burlington Northern's executives are too busy for that sort of thing. They all fly on commercial jets.

People-Centered Growth

This book is based on a simple premise: When it comes to growing a business, what really counts most is people. **Strategies and organizations only exist to help channel people's efforts. Debates about the future that lead to new insights about the marketplace occur among people. New ideas are created, nurtured, championed, and even squelched by people. The Herculean efforts required to crush a sales target or produce and ship a critical rush order come only from people. Change happens only when people change. Growth happens only when people grow.**

The good news for many American workers is that the contraction era is drawing to a close. It's being replaced with a time of growth and expansion in many industries. For some, this is a period of frenzy and fun, a time to work hard at building a future for themselves and their business. A culture of growth *is* very different from a culture of containment. This is not an unmitigated blessing, however. Growth is an anxiety-inducing process that requires vision, courage, tenacity, and cunning, but it sure beats the alternative.

CHAPTER 2

Growth Isn't
What It Used to Be

Many companies have cleared their decks and battened down the hatches. A period of what economist Joseph Schumpeter calls "creative destruction," the demolition of the old order to set the stage for the new, is coming to an end. Like a small boat sailing in rough seas, these businesses are in need of a good compass, a strong hull, and a powerful engine. Managers and employees have similar needs. They are looking for a sense of new direction, an anchor for stability, and a source of renewed motivation.

The good news is that the past decade's emphasis on efficiency and cost-cutting has provided many businesses with a sound economic base from which to move forward. A strong U.S. economy and a weakened dollar helped open global markets to companies once content with staying at home. Productivity, the revenue generated per employee, is at an all-time high in many corporations, generally because the number of employees is at an all-time low. The job ahead now is to **keep productivity growing by increasing the revenue part of the equation**—and to keep the economy growing by creating new companies with new jobs.

Growth is also vital, if for no other reason than to release the human pressures building in many organizations. There are real limits, both physical and psychological, to the sustainability of the superhuman efforts advanced by many employees in leanly staffed, change-prone businesses.

Don't Be Seduced by Growth

Be wary, though, of growth's seductive charms. Going for growth is riskier than cost-cutting. It can make the boldest reengineering of a business's inner workings seem tame in comparison. The worst consequences of spending too much effort seeking efficiencies are the opportunities missed when managers behave too much like ostriches. Opportunity costs never directly show up on financial statements. Neither do these mistakes haunt executives the way that misspent dollars on a balance sheet do when they have to be written off.

Ford's executives were endlessly pilloried in the press when they tried to excite consumers with a flashy new car called the Edsel. Despite all the promotion the Edsel was given—it was even named after a Ford family member—its sales went nowhere. Several years later, another new Ford design, the Pinto, became the object of nationwide controversy regarding the vehicle's safety. Perhaps these costly new product flops made the automaker overly cautious when considering new ideas. It was barely noticed when a group of promising but frustrated midlevel Ford managers and designers left and went on to Chrysler. They left because Ford showed little interest in their plan for a new type of vehicle: a truck with a car's personality. At Chrysler they fleshed out and tested their hybrid, the auto industry's first minivan. Still a best-seller for Chrysler, few realize that the lion's share of minivan revenue all might have gone to Ford.

Following a growth trajectory can sometimes require commitments so large that they take on a "bet the company" character. These are also "bet your career" kinds of decisions, moves that when worth making should be made with both eyes wide open. Frederick Smith made such a decision when he put all his personal wealth at stake to found Federal Express. So did the several dozen managers and pilots who put their own careers at risk to join him.

Dealing with the high-stakes risks that accompany expansion strategies requires a very careful understanding of the *real nature of business growth*. This isn't something to be just taken for granted. It's not an escalator that gives you a ride as long as you know where to get on. **Many seasoned executives have very outmoded views of how to grow a business.** Simplistic solutions such as investing in R&D, hiring more salespeople, upsizing the ad budget, or increasing capacity are seldom as effective as they once were. **Many more junior managers and employees have never had first-hand experience in organizations that were doing anything but contracting.**

The Old Realities

Growth is frequently misunderstood. Many of the "old truths" about growth just don't hold anymore. It is essential to take apart some of the key components of this conventional wisdom.

How many of the following five myths of growth do you agree with?

- A rising tide lifts all boats—an expanding economy drives the growth of all the businesses in it.

- Small, entrepreneurial companies in fast-growing markets will provide the lion's share of future economic growth.

- Growing a business means making it bigger.

- If a company grows, its competitors must shrink.

- Success begets more success.

Each of these ideas sounds logical. Each has a ring of validity to it. But each is wrong, dead wrong. Believing in them can be harmful to your companys', and your careers', health. To understand why, consider them one by one.

Myth 1: A Rising Tide Lifts All Boats

Being at the right place at the right time is a wonderful path to success. Unfortunately, it's about as chancy to pull off as is picking a winning lottery ticket. This attitude, however, is still commonly held. Its promise of effortless growth by riding a rising economic tide doesn't hold the way it once did. The amazingly rapid growth spurt of the American economy, and many of the businesses within it, in the years between World War II and the Vietnam War was an anomaly. This was a time when pent-up consumer demand from war rationing was released. It was a period of massive new family formation as the baby-boomer generation was conceived. It was a time when American products and companies were in unmitigated demand throughout the world.

In those days, production was king. In many markets, companies found it relatively easy to sell whatever they made. It was a period when you could make a five-year business or career plan and have some degree of confidence it would be achieved. Those days, however, are unlikely to return soon.

New Global Competitors

A reasonable portion of credit for this unrestrained growth has to be given to the limited amount of global competition many American businesses faced during those go-go years. Two strong international economies, Germany's and Japan's, had been bombed to rubble. Great Britain, the previous world economic superpower, was among the victors, but it lost its empire, a key driver of its long reign of commercial dominance. In short, the playing field was wide open.

Those days are past. While the mid-1990s are also a time when long pent-up demand is larger than ever (think about the opportunities offered in places such as China, India, the former Soviet Union, Eastern Europe, Mexico, and the rest of Latin America), the competitive arena is not as empty as it was in the decades after World War II.

Ten years ago only a billion of the world's people lived in countries that were integrated into the international market economy. Now 5 billion would-be consumers are potentially able to "shop the world." But unlike the recent past, American companies face strong competition for these growth markets from Asian and European global giants. Many of these emerging markets also have scores of tough and nimble home-grown entrepreneurs chasing after the same opportunities. And both sources of competition are eagerly eyeing the American market as a source of their own expansion.

It is a messier world out there than it once was. Unfortunately for many senior executives, their last real experience with growth came early in their careers during a time that, because of its uniqueness, might have taught them the wrong lessons. They need to look hard at *the world as it is today* and be wary of nostalgia for an era that's not likely to return. Growth may be just around the corner for many businesses, but it may be like nothing ever experienced before. The "growth escalator" that once existed has broken down, and like the escalators in many New York subway stations, it doesn't show signs of being fixed anytime soon.

The Demise of Mass Market

The world really *has* changed. The idea of a single, global mass market exists only in the rarefied atmosphere of elite business school classrooms. The same is true of the domestic economy, which is predominantly built around consumer spending, and American consumers are less homogeneous than ever. Its once strong, central core, the middle class, has deeply fragmented. It has polarized into clusters of upper-middle class, well-educated knowledge workers and groups of less-skilled, fighting-to-stay-above-the-poverty-line consumers. It is split along generational and lifestyle fault lines. Its linguistic and racial minorities are as separate as they ever have been.

This is why companies that used to aim for what corporate strategist Michael Kami likes to call the "disappearing middle" are in so much trouble. Sears, Roebuck lost business both to discounter Wal-Mart and to tonier, expensive speciality retailers. Airlines, unable to identify a common middle ground of service and value desired by most flyers, are stumbling over each other as they all shift to the low-fare common denominator.

A Limited Role for Government

Not only is the idea of the mass market disappearing but so is that of the safe, protected domestic market. Few U.S. businesses are immune from foreign competition. Few U.S. businesses have the luxury of considering only domestic suppliers. Free trade has become the battle cry of the 1990s. Even counties long reputed to be protectionist holdouts, like India and Japan, are gradually allowing their consumers access to the world's goods.

Rising economic tides used to be generated by government actions. Public spending has long been a stimulus to many American industries, from highways to defense. This is another played-out trend. The U.S.

government either can't or won't play the role of growth stimulator. Due to a combination of budget deficits, inflation fears, and an emerging sense of humility about what government can actually accomplish, the federal role is shifting to one of "trying to do no harm."

Growing a business used to be a lot easier. The tides of the new century's economy promises to lift some, deluge others, and give us all a rough ride. That's the new reality that growth-minded managers must accept and find ways to thrive in.

Myth 2: Growth Requires Entrepreneurs in Growing Markets

It's important to look beyond what will (or will not) drive growth. A more important question is: What kinds of companies and industries are most likely to find it?
Consider this question:

Which have the best chance to achieve high growth?

A. Small, entrepreneurial companies.

B. Medium- and large-sized, established firms.

The correct answer is B.

In spite of all the media hoopla about small business being the driving force of the American economy, the reality is that most small companies *stay small.* And a frighteningly high percentage of entrepreneurial start-ups shut down before reaching their second anniversary. Extensive studies conducted by Bennett Harrison, a Carnegie Mellon economics professor, indicate that most growth in sales, employment, and new products comes from established companies with hundreds, if not thousands, of employees.

Even Silicon Valley, fabled hothouse of innovative, garage-based businesses of the future, is now and always has been dependent on large corporations and institutions to fuel its growth. Its history was driven by Stanford University and Fairfield Semiconductor. Its future will be shaped by Apple, Intel, Hewlett-Packard, and the U.S. government. Only 5 percent of computer companies have over 500 employees. But these firms account for more than 90 percent of all the revenues and jobs in this industry.

Most start-up ventures that really make it, make it big relatively quickly. They don't remain small for long. *Fortune* publishes a list of America's 100 Fastest-Growing Companies each year. It is quite an honor to make the list, but those that do find that it is a slippery place to remain. Of the most recent 100 companies on the list, only six appeared on it more than twice before.

Consider one more question:

What kind of industry can provide the most favorable prospects for a business's growth?

A.   Industries with higher-than-average revenue growth.

B.   Industries with lower-than-average, or even negative, growth rates.

The correct answer, again, is B.

The secret of many star baseball players is to hit the ball where their opponents *aren't.*

Some companies are able to find growth, regardless of how bleak or favorable their industry prospects are. A recent research study examined the growth rates of the leading companies in a dozen industries, ranging from banking and metals to retailing and pharmaceuticals. Some of the industries grew as much as 12 percent per year; others actually had negative growth rates. But in every one, *some* companies found ways to grow their businesses *at least three times as quickly* as their industries were growing. Even the troubled savings and loan industry, which declined an average of 6 percent during each of the years studied, has some banks in it growing at nearly 40 percent per year.

David Birch, a Cambridge, Massachusetts, economic researcher, finds that the best place to look for fast-growth companies is within aged and moribund industries. He has noticed that industry sectors that do exceptionally well are often dominated by large, strong firms, such as Wal-Mart and Home Depot. These commonly called "category killers" are often so dominant that they leave little room for other's growth prospects. On the other hand, large companies in the slower-growing segments of the economy tend to be more conservative, more oriented toward cost-cutting and restructuring around "core competencies." This leaves a lot of maneuvering room for agile, growth-driven competitors. The severe problems of companies like Digital and IBM can represent wonderful opportunities for the Gateway 2000s and Compaqs of the world. Birch found that between 1989 and 1993, there were more fast-growth companies in mature industries, such as paper products, chemicals, plastics, and electrical equipment, than there were in more glamorous, high-tech businesses.

There are many unlikely places to find growth. The fastest-growing company on a recent *Fortune* survey, Grow Biz International, sells *used* merchandise (computers, clothing, musical instruments). Few other entrepreneurs have considered stealing market share from the Salvation Army! But that's the kind of imagination necessary to find growth opportunities in increasingly maturing, increasingly fragmented markets.

The bottom line: Don't give up hope for either career or business if you are in a largish company operating in a dull, slow-growth industry. *Every company* has some potential opportunity for profitable growth. Find the appropriate strategy, select the right people, focus their talents on the most important issues, and the future can be very prosperous.

Myth 3: Growing a Business Means Making It Bigger

In the last half of the twentieth century, growth has gotten a bad name, from both the left and right wings of the economic spectrum. Adherents of the "small is beautiful" philosophy have waged war over many years with those more comfortable with the idea that progress is our most important product. Some environmentalists, social activists, and economists have warned that the real cost of economic growth is far higher than its reward. Pollution, social disintegration, economic inequities, and inflation are all associated with growth. Driving past crime-ridden shantytowns skirting the high-growth metropolises of places such as Mexico City, São Paulo, or Johannesburg can make you quickly concede that rapid, unplanned growth is often accompanied by many unwanted side effects. Bhopal, the Valdez oil spill, and the savings and loan scandals have caused many to question how well business can keep control of its growth initiatives.

At the other side of the political spectrum, the junk-bond–fueled Wall Street raiders of the 1980s worked hard to dismantle many corporate structures whose rate of organizational growth outpaced their rate of return to their shareholders. Claiming that some businesses were worth more dead than alive, these restructurers—often with a sense of great missionary fervor—forced companies to avoid the threat of hostile takeover by pruning back or shutting down major segments of their businesses. Many of these were units that only a few years earlier had been anointed as cornerstones of their company's future.

Both perspectives on growth and its by-products have caused problems and pain for many managers. The environmentalists have made them feel guilty, and the corporate raiders have made them feel afraid—what a formula for anxiety induction! On one hand, some managers are uncomfortable admitting to friends and neighbors that they hold a corporate job; on the other, they are not really sure how long they will have the option to keep it.

The 1970s and 1980s are, fortunately, behind us, and criticism from both camps has softened. Fears of global economic slowdown, or never-ending job cutbacks, weakened their appeal. These are perspectives, though, that cannot be totally dismissed out of hand. Both the liberal and conservative critiques of business as usual seem to converge on one point: What goes around comes around.

Size Slows Growth

Peter Senge's ideas about a "fifth discipline," systems thinking, have encouraged many to think about the inevitability of getting feedback from their actions. Do something, wait a while, and eventually something else happens because of what you did earlier. Or as Senge is fond of saying, "Today's problems come from yesterday's solutions."

The idea applies to businesses as well as individuals. Out-of-control pollution and marginal rates of return may just be nature's ways of saying, "Slow down." There are, in every business situation, natural limits to how much growth is achievable. However, the limits are not the resource constraints usually blamed for slowing growth, for example, "If we only had more capital . . . ," "If we only had more talent . . . ," "If we only had more ideas. . . ." The real limits to growth are constraints that emerge as a result of rapid but unbalanced growth. **Having your business grow in sales without increasing at the same rate the value added to customers will only create opportunities for competitors to move in.** Having salaries increase faster than the productivity of those receiving them will create extra costs that will eventually limit the ability of the business to reinvest in itself.

A small business may grow rapidly because its employees are highly motivated by the prospect of the salary and career advancement they will receive if the venture succeeds. Assume the business develops into a megacompany. This growth is great for the early employees, but how likely are such rapid advancement prospects for the second, third, and fourth waves of employees hired?

Eventually, the line of people awaiting promotions becomes longer than the opportunities that emerge—such pyramids can grow only so big without becoming nightmares to direct and control. Malaise sets in, some of the more aggressive people leave, and the business soon tends to attract newcomers more interested in stability than rapid forward movement. Motivation levels drop, and growth—to no one's real surprise—drops off as well. Market saturation, new technologies, or overseas competitors may be blamed, but the real culprit is that common by-product of most corporate growth: size.

Growing Better, Not Bigger

Fortunately, there is a way out of this dilemma. Be careful not to confuse *growth* with *size*. These are really two very different ideas, related only in that one will eventually limit the other.

Recently, my four-year-old son started to articulate a personal growth objective: to be bigger than daddy. (I've been told this goal is related to a "developmental phase" he's going through.) He is diligently pursuing this course by vast increases in milk and pasta consumption, so he has a reasonable chance of reaching the objective by age 20 or so. But what then? If he remains a competitive sort, he'll probably find a new target to benchmark against. Hopefully he will still stay concerned about growth, but how he defines growth is very likely to change.

Growth for those in their twenties has more to do with getting established, trying out a lot of alternatives, being seen as an equal, discovering how to build lasting relationships, and keeping busy.

Another 20 years after this onset of early adulthood, an entirely different set of measures of "growth" will emerge. Marriage and children (in other words, joint ventures and spin-offs) will signal success. Having a career that satisfies and contributes will be hallmarks of his achievement.

Growth Has Multiple Meanings

You can grow bigger, grow older, and grow wiser. At each stage in a person's development, varying measures of successful growth are most relevant. The goal isn't just to get bigger. Peter Drucker likes to warn: "The idea that growth is by itself a goal is altogether a delusion." He has never felt there was virtue in a company just getting bigger. Drucker believes the right goal is to become *better*. Sound growth is that which comes from doing the right things. He worries that **too many companies have put a too-narrow definition of growth on too high of a pedestal.** And he's right. Good measures of growth are economic measures. They may include volume, but they also deal with life-cycle issues such as product introduction milestones, market share, customer satisfaction, and ongoing cost reduction. Just wanting to be a "billion-dollar company" or to appear on the *Fortune* 500 list is neither sound nor rational. But it is still, sadly, very common.

Avoid the Growth Disease

If you have a conversation with Robert Haas, chairman and chief executive of Levi Strauss & Co., you will hear a very different spin on the idea of growth than leaders of consumer goods companies commonly provide. Ask him what the annual growth target is for Levi Strauss and he will quickly respond: "We don't define our goals in terms of annual growth rates. That is one of the great diseases of American business." Haas is the great-great-grandnephew of the company's founder. He's observed, "We used to have a growth-oriented culture. However, the trouble is, if you pursue growth, you'll get it." You may not *sustain* it, but you will get it. However, Haas warns, "You'll also get some of the undesirable consequences, which are badly considered investments, profitless products, and shabby business practices." These are the side effects of today's growth that will lie in wait to destroy tomorrow's growth.

Robert Haas might have been a useful person for Daniel Gil, CEO of Bausch & Lomb, to talk with. Gil's strong instance on double-digit growth (discussed in the previous chapter) has, according to a *Business Week* investigative reporter, led to a variety of types of unethical behavior. These included accusations of distributors being pressured to take unwanted merchandise, knowingly selling products to "gray markets," and booking shipments as sales before orders were even placed. Eventually overstocked distributors stopped reordering, and sales in many Bausch & Lomb divisions collapsed.

If you push the point further and ask Haas what targets a business should aim toward, he will probably say, "If you provide a good product, provide preeminent customer service, and create an environment in which your people feel rewarded and fulfilled and are energized by the work they do, the growth and profitability will automatically come." That's a tall order. It requires a degree of faith in your ability to do something *today* that will pay off *tomorrow*. But isn't that the whole point of growth? Today's problems may come from yesterday's solutions, but tomorrow's growth will only arise from the seeds planted today.

Some executives mimic Haas's disdain for a narrow definition of growth. Beware of those who are using words like his to rationalize less-than-superior competitive performance. Haas's rhetoric is built on solid results: Levi Strauss, a $6-billion-a-year company, is the world's largest brand-name apparel manufacturer.

Waiting for Future Payoffs

One key ability sets growth-oriented managers apart from those who are merely entrepreneurial. **Growth managers have the ability to deal with events that are separated in time. They know there is often a long wait between the time something happens and the time its consequences are apparent.** Managing growth requires a keen appreciation of the nature of these time lags. This is not always easy. Most of us tend to assume that whatever trend we are currently experiencing will persist indefinitely, especially when we are in a hurry (like most entrepreneurial types).

Have you ever stayed on an upper floor in a high-rise hotel? Rushing through a shower to get ready for an early breakfast meeting, you turn the water on, discover it's too cold, and quickly adjust the temperature upward. Thirty seconds later you nearly leap from the enclosure as scalding hot water streams from the shower head. You know you've overdone it and you need to cool down, so you sharply lower the temperature setting. After a minute, and just before your shampoo starts to form ice crystals, it dawns on you that the temperature control is not an instantaneous device and that your lack of appreciation of the time it takes for water to travel from the basement to the floor you are on is causing you to overreact dangerously.

Making decisions that are intended to grow a business involves similar dynamics: Investments are made, new people are hired, the advertising budget is increased, a promising company is bought, and a new technology is licensed. Few of these moves pay off immediately; few pay off independently. New people and ideas take time to be integrated into the ongoing operation. Just having them on board may make the old business bigger, but that is not enough to be better.

Myth 4: Growth Is a Zero-Sum Game

I win; you lose. That's traditional, macho management personified. If I grow, you must shrink—a cornerstone of much classical economic theory. Traditional economics, though, is becoming increasingly ignored by many growth-oriented corporations. Instead, they are turning to new schools of economic thought, ones that tend to pay more attention to the actual behavior of real people as contrasted with the "black box" view of human behavior favored by the old school. Economists used to be content to let the details of how people function be the concern of psychologists and sociologists. This is a concession that, over time, made many of their ideas irrelevant or dangerous.

This omission is one that a group of contemporary, broader-gauged economists are working hard to correct. Sometimes called "evolutionary economists," they draw on a broad range of ideas from game theory, genetics, and quantum physics. They believe the environment in which most businesses operate has more in common with a biological organism than it does with some machinelike abstraction that is subject to a Keynesian's manipulations. A number of their ideas are starting to win broad acceptance among both economists and leading-edge business people. A recent Nobel economics prize went to several economists who showed that businesses compete and armies do battle in much the same way that people play poker and chess. These ideas offer a perspective on growth in tune with the new competitive environment that many corporations are facing.

Lessons from the New Economics

Some of the principles of this new economics include the following:

- Destroying an opponent is not necessarily the best path to long-term survival and growth—live and let live may well be a better motto.

- Too much selfishness will be self-defeating—the high rewards it provides in the short term will only serve to attract new competitors.

- The key to sustainable growth is knowing how to adapt to circumstances that are constantly changing—long-term winners are the best adaptors, not necessarily the winners of today's race for market share.

- A business's future is probably much more linked to its competitor's future than it may want to admit.

- A company seeking long-term growth should include in its plans a viable role for these competitors.

- Cooperating with suppliers to deliver the greatest value to the final customer will pay off much more than coercing suppliers only to minimize their price.

Doing Well While Doing Good

These are not just theoretical precepts. They are guides to growth already being put into practice by leading companies who realize that Pyrrhic victories are just not worth the trouble.

- In recent years, General Motors has fought tooth and nail with its car parts suppliers to obtain the lowest possible price. Alternatively, Ford and Chrysler have offered a hand of partnership to select groups of suppliers, sharing financial and product information with them that actually strengthens the suppliers' ability to negotiate prices with the two automakers. The pay off: In an industry where innovations increasingly originate with the suppliers, a number of them have admitted they are much more willing to share new ideas first with Ford and Chrysler and not with General Motors.

- Many IBM veterans at its Charlotte, North Carolina, manufacturing facilities are doing a double take when they see IBM assembly lines producing archrival Apple Computer Co.'s products. Opportunistic cooperation (and swallowing some pride) is a much more viable alternative, though, than closing down a facility temporarily short of orders. American Express has been willing to use its computer facilities to process credit card bills for archrivals Visa and MasterCard. That way, at least some of the revenues that American Express loses to these competitors come back to where American Express wanted them to be in the first place.

- Merck's merger with Medco Containment Services, a mail-order seller of rival products, is a move to adapt to, rather than fight, the new cost-conscious health marketplace.

- Though it may never be admitted publicly, AT&T's plans for strategic growth are very dependent on the strength and scrappiness of competitors such as MCI and Sprint. Without able rivals such as these, AT&T may be seen as just another monopolist, to be avoided by customers and controlled by regulators.

- Burlington Northern Railroad's eventual willingness to offer long-distance piggyback service to the truckers it competes with (described in Chapter 1) generated a billion dollars of new business instead of rounds of endless internal finger-pointing as its customers moved shipments from box cars into highway trailers.

The New Rules Also Apply Inside the Company

These kinds of behavior, sometimes dubbed "strategic altruism," apply equally as well inside the company as with external competitors or suppliers. Many managers are finding their own careers advance the most when they avoid directly attacking their internal rivals. Breaking another employee's "rice bowl" might appear tough minded in the short term, but it can lead to many difficulties when applied in the corporate world of repeated interactions and ongoing relationships.

Similarly, the unwritten rules are changing as more companies become team, rather than job, based. **Businesses hoping to grow through team efforts are making sure the greatest rewards are flowing to high performers who expend effort upgrading the skills of their teammates,** not just publicizing their individual accomplishments.

Myth 5: Success Begets More Success

The fifth myth about growth cuts to the heart of another common misperception about business success: Getting it right, preferably the first time, is what counts the most. **The belief that momentum drives growth and that growth comes from a rapid succession of victories is deeply ingrained in the American business psyche.** It is the marketplace equivalent of manifest destiny.

Like the other growth myths, this made some sense in the wide-open marketplaces of the post–World War II era. But its relevance is very questionable today. Think about this in light of the earlier discussion (Myth 3) about the secondary effects, the unwanted by-products of growth:

- Unwise investments.

- Excess staffing.

- A "we-can-do-no-wrong" sense of smugness.

Over time, **a string of wins will accumulate a massive number of these obstacles-in-waiting.** They will combine and conspire to turn record revenues into profitless bloat. When continued success becomes the expected norm, a business puts on a pair of heavy blinders. The only reality that counts is that which exists within ("We must be smart, look at how well we've done"). Signals about subtle shifts in market requirements are missed. Clues about changes in customer preferences count less than company-determined projections. Competitors' new products or shifts in tactics are underestimated ("We've always beaten them before, haven't we?"). In short, **success sets you up for failure, which really isn't all that bad. Sustainable, real growth is driven much more by failures than successes.**

Edwin Land's Motto

In the days when Edwin Land was chief executive of the Polaroid Corporation, upon walking into his office, it was impossible not to notice the only plaque this inventor of instant photography had put up on the wall. It summarized a philosophy that preserved Land's sense of self-worth during the struggles and failures it took him to create a unique product and build a company around it. It said: "A mistake is an event, the full benefit of which has not yet been turned to your advantage."

Examine the wording that Land admired so much. A mistake is an *event*, a one-time occurrence at one point in time. It is something that happened, not a label to be hung around the neck of the person responsible. Note also Land's appreciation of time lags, of cause and effect being separated by some interval. These are hallmarks of a growth-friendly mentality.

Growth Occurs on the Rebound

When Levi Strauss, a Bavarian immigrant, arrived in San Francisco in 1853, he had a very firm business plan in mind. He had traveled on a clipper ship for over 17,000 miles carrying with him all the materials he would need to start a dry-goods business in gold rush-crazed California. He planned to sell tents and canvas covers for the horse-drawn wagons that the miners were using to haul their tools to the gold fields. It was a good idea for a booming market. Sales, however, were not especially strong.

Rather than pack up and return to Germany, Strauss did notice that some customers were using his material to make clothing that could withstand the rigors of digging and panning for gold. One thing led to another, and he soon found himself in the business of producing the world's first jeans. This business boomed to the point that his name, Levi's, was associated with the product he invented, just as later happened to Xerox's and Federal Express's innovations.

Rebounding from missteps has become ingrained in the Levi Strauss culture. For a variety of reasons, the company's attempts in the late 1970s to develop a product line of leisure wear beyond its traditional jeans offering met with only marginal success. This was surprising, considering all the high-powered professional marketing talent that Levi Strauss had assembled at its headquarters to plan and roll out the new garments.

A few years later, the company tried again. However, instead of following all the classical, top-down approaches to consumer marketing, the company experimented and watched closely what interested its customers the most. One of its employees based in Argentina, far from the California home office, put together plans for a product that could fill the gap between the jeans and the dress-pants markets. The idea, christened "Dockers," was actually given its first major trial in jeans-crazy Japan. An immediate success, it was quickly repatriated and became the core of a new billion-dollar business as well as the fastest-growing brand in the history of the apparel industry.

The Key to Sustained Growth

Sustained growth is seldom straightforward. It thrives best in an atmosphere that is tolerant of misjudgments—one that allows for standing back, learning from failures, and being willing to try something new, again. Why is this so? Try thinking about growing a business as if it were a form of real-life personal problem solving. There are two kinds of problems in the world. Some have a single, right answer (How much is two plus two? or How many companies are on the *Fortune* 500 list?). Solving these is usually straightforward, the routine application of some analytic tool. These problems are seldom of grave consequence, and their answers tend to provoke little debate. Other problems, more significant and more related to growth, beg easy solutions. They seldom have one, simple right answer.

Growing a Business Is Like Picking the Right Marriage Partner

Whom should I marry? How should I plan my career? How should I raise my children? The key to answering these questions, as many know from hard experience, is trial and error, learning from mistakes and moving on, not always expecting to get it right the first time.

The special mind-set needed to tackle these harder, growth-related problems is easier to aspire to than carry out. Consider the recent ups and downs the Chrysler Corporation has endured.

Chrysler: A Work-in-Progress

In the late 1970s, Lee Iacocca was credited with dramatically turning around the performance of Chrysler. A combination of his willpower and charisma, temporary federal financial assistance, and fortuitous consumer acceptance of the K-car kept this near-bankrupt automaker from disappearing. But just as Iacocca was earning his place in American business's hall of fame and as his life story was becoming a best-seller, the company reverted to its old ways.

White-collar employment, cut almost in half to 21,000 in 1982, crept back to 27,000 five years later. Businesses unrelated to auto production were added. They even started making corporate jet aircraft. Then in the late 1980s, the bottom fell out of the car market—again. Recession and renewed competition from import car makers caused Chrysler's performance to slide. Many of these new jobs and businesses were cut. For a while, it seemed like the previous decade all over again.

Necessity has always been the mother of invention at Chrysler. Having to cope again with limited quantities of engineering talent, the company abandoned its reliance on large functional staff departments. Instead, lean teams made of many specialists who had never directly worked together before were assigned to each new car development project. Suppliers were asked to loan talent to help keep the teams fully staffed. The concept worked beautifully. Ideas were generated faster than ever before. The absence of functional fiefdoms allowed a lot of the development work to occur simultaneously, rather than sequentially, which is the key to getting a product into the market quickly.

Iacocca has since retired, and Chrysler's roller coaster has taken more of an upward turn. The company now has a broad range of record-selling products: the minivan it pioneered, the petite Neon, and the unique cab-forward design of its larger cars. But the hubris is gone. Just look at the words in a recent shareholder's report. Even though this was an all-time record year for Chrysler, its annual report, up front, alerts its owners to the *three big dangers inherent in blockbuster success:*

- You can forget to stop and figure out what you're doing right to be sure you keep doing it.

- You can forget that you still have to do some things differently if you are going to have more years like it.

- You can forgive yourself for all the things you did wrong because, after all, they don't seem to be holding you back.

Self-awareness, continual change, forgiveness—these are not the usual themes of an annual report full of good news. But they are a strong indication that Chrysler has begun to master the ability to make failure work for it and to keep success from limiting future success. Its president, Robert Lutz, likes to define Chrysler as a work-in-progress: "We're not the company we used to be, but we're not yet the company we want to be." This statement, one Lutz never tires of repeating again and again in his talks with Chrysler employees worldwide, is the hallmark of a true growth company.

Fueling Growth with Failure

How can the wisdom of Polaroid, Levi Strauss, and Chrysler be applied to your situation?

- Start by examining your disappointments, your failures. Look at objectives that were met but that no longer provide the reward they originally promised.

- When goals are not met, do you tend to recycle the same old approach, just trying harder? It is amazingly common, for both companies and individuals within them, to recommit themselves to a failing course.

- Or is your reaction more one of giving up, going through the motions without any expectation of real change or success? This tack is common in businesses that have adopted downsizing as a way of life, in companies really engaging in slow-motion liquidation.

- Or, perhaps you have stopped believing in the myth of success always breeding more success.

Are you able to utilize failure as a clue that possibly your initial targets, and some of the assumptions behind them, need rethinking? Can you suspend some of your present beliefs and quietly listen as your customers, the marketplace, or perhaps other employees provide the information needed for midcourse corrections?

It is awfully hard to hear these clues when you are on course, busily charging ahead. Immediate success can be wonderful, but the keys to continued growth are the missteps you make along the way. Think of these as goods you have already paid for but haven't bothered to go out and pick up. Go get them; they aren't doing you any good just sitting at the store.

The New Rules for Growth

The five myths of growth can be turned around to serve as guideposts for reenergizing a business through growth:

- The only real growth opportunities are those you find yourself.

- Look where others aren't.

- Make your business better, not just bigger.

- Assist your rivals to make the industry bigger.

- Find the seeds of growth in your failures.

A battle is occurring in many companies between the old thought and the new thought about growth. The old rules for growth have become, at the least, increasingly irrelevant. The new ones, because they are anchored in the reality of today's marketplaces, have the greatest promise of propelling your company and your career safely into the next century. The struggle is one for dominating ideas—the perspective that will drive your thinking and ultimately your company's thinking. May this be a battle successfully won in your company, and may your competitors still be playing by the old rules.

The last chapter warned of the dangers of the "contraction mindset." This chapter cautions against following the logic of the past—what got us to this point may not be what is needed to move us forward. The world, and the rules for operating in it, really have changed. Now, with a sense of what's different out there, it is time to select a path for growth.

CHAPTER 3

One Size Never Fits All

"You sure look tired."

"I feel worse."

"How come?"

"I'm being zigzagged to death."

"What?"

"Do you know how many times our business has shifted course over the past five years?"

"Well, we still make microwaves. . . ."

"That's not what I'm talking about. Five years ago we started worrying about cheap ovens coming in from Taiwan, so we launched a big cost-cutting campaign so that we could lower our prices."

"Yeah, I remember that. It was the campaign that eliminated the level of management to which I was hoping to be promoted."

"Then we started getting all those customer complaints about quality."

". . . and we all were sent to 'Quality School'."

"Yep, sort of remedial education for middle management."

"Come on—cut the cynicism."

"Cynicism my foot. Do you know that just after I was empowered to pull the plug on the assembly line when tolerances were missed, headquarters announced that the plant was shifting to time-based management?"

"No more shutdowns?"

"Only speedups were allowed, but it wasn't all that bad. I went out and visited a lot of other companies' plants, and I even got a trip to Japan out of it."

"Sounds like benchmarking."

"It felt more like I was some sort of 'industrial tourist'."

"Did you learn anything?"

"Yep. Just because something works well for one outfit, don't assume it will have an impact here. Every company is different."

"Did you learn that on your travels?"

"No, that's what I found out when I brought somebody else's great idea back here and tried force-fitting it into our operation."

"Have you E-mailed in your sales growth forecasts? I've heard that headquarters is looking to see some pretty big top-line increases."

"Increases? Growth? Who has any time to think about *growth?* We're too busy fixing everything in sight."

"What are you fixing now?"

"Everything. Haven't you seen the video sent home to everybody explaining how we're going to reinvent this company from scratch using something called 'reengineering'?"

"What's that?"

Reengineering: Uses and Abuses

Reengineering is a change program of which few managers can publicly admit ignorance. Called everything from "the second industrial revolution" to "the major job destroyer of the 1990s," these efforts to redesign business processes are underway in virtually every major corporation. Ubiquity, unfortunately, seems to be the source of misapplication. Few of these large-scale improvement programs live up to their promise. Reengineering's leading proponent, Michael Hammer, observes that many well-intentioned efforts have turned into morasses because the executives who commissioned them lacked either sufficient courage or intellect. He may be correct, but his observation suggests that before these programs are bottled and promoted, a warning label should be affixed, specifying the prerequisite smarts and guts required for successful implementation. Then those who feel fainthearted can look elsewhere for a remedy for whatever problem reengineering was to address.

Unfortunately few managers seem to be looking elsewhere. Instead, **reengineering is being used the way "quality" or "strategic planning" were in the past—as a general purpose, cure-whatever-is-ailing solution to a business's problems.** This misapplication, of an otherwise useful but still limited tool, is very common. "To a hammer," pundits like to say, "everything looks like a nail." To a reengineer, every problem requires a blank sheet of paper, a radical transformation of a business's core processes. This force-fitting has led to frequent misapplications of the techniques along lines such as the following:

• **Using a hammer when a screwdriver might have been better:** Reengineering projects take years, not months, to bear fruit, but it has become very common to see reengineering—an inherently long-term, multifaceted program—attempting to deal with problems requiring more immediate, focused solutions (for example, addressing why customers are leaving us in droves, and reducing costs so we can meet next quarter's payroll). One exacerbated manager in a company at a key interchange point on the information superhighway exclaimed, "We've just launched a three-year effort to reengineer customer order scheduling, but our entire business is going to change dramatically over the next 12 months! I really wish our right hand was in a little closer touch with our left."

• **Taking a high-risk approach to solving low-priority problems:** Real reengineering requires major top-executive commitment and broad-based political support for the wrenching change it promises. Why then is so much of this valuable currency wasted on such backwater reengineering efforts, such as the perennial favorite, speeding up bill paying? Why not start with issues that matter more to customers or have more promise of directly touching the business's future, instead of spending megabucks and many months redesigning the trivial?

• **Missing the point:** Reengineering is supposed to tear down a company's "functional silos." It deals with business processes, things that by their nature tend to cross over departmental and functional boundaries. I was recently asked to help a chemical company reengineer its human resources department. When asked why, the client-to-be said, with a slightly embarrassed expression on his face, "Look, we all know nothing is wrong here. Our costs are under budget, and our internal customers love what we're doing for them, but every other department in headquarters has been reengineered. We're going to look stupid if we don't get on the bandwagon."

• **A great excuse to do something else:** If you want to get something done, call it reengineering. That's the great unwritten rule of the 1990s—a game many have played, just doing the right thing for the wrong reason. Often the consequences are minor, just as each counterfeit dollar debases the currency only a little. Sometimes, though, the amounts are not so trivial. The U.S. Department of Agriculture is in the midst of the most far-reaching modernization effort in its history. This multi-billion-dollar effort to improve service delivery to its rural clientele has been a target of severe criticism by the congressional watchdog agency, the General Accounting Office (GAO). The GAO investigators found that, despite considerable rhetoric about reinvention and reengineering, the agriculture department was managing the modernization primarily as a way *to acquire new information technology,* rather than as a way to fundamentally improve business processes. This is not just a mislabeling of funds. The GAO feels that hundreds of millions of taxpayer dollars will be spent to automate the current ways the agency does business rather than contribute to any real reengineering.

Reengineering is being singled out here, perhaps a little unfairly, because it is so much in vogue. Similar criticisms can be made of many quality change, overhead reduction, and cultural change efforts. Think about the other major change programs your company has undertaken:

- Which have produced the hoped-for results?

- How many were also susceptible to these kinds of misuses?

The Case of the Disappearing Advantage

What is it about business improvement initiatives that makes them so easy to misuse and abuse? Is it something inherently wrong with the techniques, or does the problem lie more in their application? Bouncing from fad to fad and from program to program has become a way of life in many American companies, and **just when a majority of the employees seem to be "getting with the program," the game plan shifts, and a new direction is announced.** The result: many cases of near-terminal whiplash and a sense of chronic exhaustion arising from playing perpetual catch-up. These frantic dashes to keep up with the latest wave of management thinking do little to enhance competitiveness. How can they? Just as one company is mastering the technique of the moment, so are its competitors. They all seem to read the same books, watch the same tapes, and hire the same consultants. Often, whatever advantage is gained provides only fleeting distinction.

Even national boundaries are highly porous to new ideas. The internet, faxes, and global management conferences spread new ideas even faster than they can be tested and updated. Translators in Tokyo were busy working on my previous book, *Rethinking the Corporation* (AMACOM, 1993), months before its initial publication in the United States. Free trade—the wave of the future—spreads ideas and techniques, not just goods and services. Some corporations attempt to deal with this situation by boasting of their abilities to thrive by "out implementing" the competition. Over the long haul, though, deriving success from an opponent's stumbles puts a company's future squarely in its competitor's hands. The net result of management by whatever ideas are most in fashion is a *continual leveling of the playing field.* Just when you thought your business was at the cutting edge, it slips to the middle of the pack. This is the corporate version of the Myth of Sisyphus. Sisyphus was an ancient Greek king whom the gods punished by condemning him to spend his eternal life pushing a heavy boulder up a steep hill. Every time he almost reached the hilltop, the boulder would slip from his hands and roll down to the bottom, and his toil would begin anew. Sound familiar?

A Wolf in Sheep's Clothing

Keeping up with the latest management trends takes a lot of time and effort and can also be very distracting. Managerial whiplash, while bothersome, is a relatively minor problem. The real cost is measured in *missed opportunities:*

- Failure to notice and respond to the clues customers constantly provide about unmet needs and benefits they would like from your business in the future.

- Failure to observe closely how competitors are dealing with these issues.

- Failure to listen to the insights of close-to-customer and close-to-technology employees, because the company is too busy getting them on board with the latest top-down improvement initiative.

Everything Leads to Cost-Cutting

Most corporate improvement efforts—regardless of initial high hopes and lofty aims—deteriorate into cost-reduction exercises:

- *Downsizing* is set out to eliminate bureaucracy, speed decision making, and empower employees. Unfortunately, most downsizing efforts solely cut payroll.

- *Outsourcing* is intended to "declutter" strategic focus and return a business to its core competences; however, too often its net result is a search for the cheapest outside contractor.

- *Quality programs* start to find ways to exceed customer expectations but end up justifying themselves with elaborate calculations intended to document the cost of rework and poor service.

- Finally, *reengineering's* bold promise to reinvent the business from scratch, usually through heavy doses of information systems and software, is usually accompanied by an equally bold price tag. Cost savings need to be found to fund all the change that is required.

While cost reduction is not necessarily wrong, it does not necessarily lead to growth. Usually, the best it can do is allow for price cuts that—if not matched by an equally nimble competitor—may deliver short-term market share gains. Unfortunately, this kind of growth is becoming less and less sustainable because customers are demanding more than low prices. Competitors are fueling growth by discovering new technologies, new sources of supply, and substitutes for old products. Western Union was, at one time, the lowest cost provider of telegram services—something that matters very little in an age of telephones and faxes.

The High Cost of Staying Trendy

We all are limited to 24-hour days, the working portion of which is spent either paying attention to the world outside the confines of the business (the world of customers, competitors, and technologies) or keeping attuned to the company's inner reality (the territory marked by job descriptions, performance objectives, and unwritten rules). The more attention given to the inner world, the less available for the outer world. Things are always broken in the inner world; improvements can always be made. The danger arises when the fix-it process becomes all-encompassing. Don't let it become an end unto itself. Avoid being so caught up in the details of restructuring, reengineering, or transforming that little or no attention is given to growing the business.

This is something much easier said than done. Self-improvement is a very American idea and lies deep in the culture. Horatio Alger promoted it, and many managers' cars are cluttered with scores of cassette tapes full of advice and motivational techniques. Jimmy Carter even practiced it while in the White House, studying Spanish in many spare moments. However, the Carter presidency has been judged more on how much the country, not its chief executive, grew during those four years. Steve Jobs, cofounder of Apple Computer, liked to talk about "the journey being the reward." Although it has a trendy, metaphysical ring to it and made a good subtitle on his biography, his business career is more accurately marked by his Macintosh marketing failures, ill-chosen successor, and stumbles in building a new company, NeXT, than by Jobs' faithful adherence to the philosophy of Zen. We can learn from both Carter and Jobs that when the dust finally settles, we are judged on our accomplishments more than on the path we took to reach them. This is not to say abandon all efforts to improve the inner workings of your business, but just realize that they alone are not enough and that some attention needs to be reserved for other things.

Avoid the Mechanistic Mind-Set

Avoiding the distractions of the moment's hottest management buzz words is important, but even more so is the cultivation of a growth-oriented mind-set. How managers *think* about getting something done often determines what they actually *do*. It sounds straightforward and would be if it was not that so much of how we think about things is hidden or taken for granted. The best clues about how a situation is being mentally approached are found in the language used to describe it. How often have you heard expressions such as these:

- We're going to *cut over* to the new organization tomorrow.

- Let's *fix* this problem so we can get back to *business as usual*.

- We need to *shut down* this operation and *pour on* a little more fuel over there.

- I can't afford any *downtime*. Get a consultant with the right *toolkit* over here ASAP.

You don't have to read too far between the lines to find the underlying theme in these common expressions: The company is a *machine*, a bundle of fine-tuned machinery. This is still a very pervasive mind-set in American business, despite the warnings of Tom Peters and Bob Waterman and despite our own common sense.

Get the Metaphor Right

We may all speak prose, but we think in metaphors, a word or phrase that means one thing but is used to describe something else. Metaphors are the tip of the mental iceberg and are efficient communications tools. They are visible signs of the underlying mind-set, or paradigm, that is actually guiding (or hindering) a business's development. Managers are heavy users of metaphors. Some will borrow language from football or baseball to signal that they view business competition along the lines of sports rivalries: Who's on first? or, It's time to pay more attention to basic blocking and tackling. More aggressive executives may favor the metaphor of war: We've just launched a take-no-prisoners marketing blitz.

The business-as-a-machine metaphor was ushered in by Adam Smith over 200 years ago at the birth of the industrial revolution. Its logic was codified by the father of scientific management, Frederick Taylor, and put to practice by Henry Ford in the early twentieth-century assembly lines. Its principles were institutionalized in the form of work rules and seniority rights in the labor contracts of the midcentury. The machine metaphor has proven very durable, has become deeply entrenched in our psyches, and has dominated recent waves of business improvement programs (productivity, quality, and reengineering), but if managers really want to grow their businesses, they must loosen the grasp of the mechanistic mentality.

The era that Adam Smith and Frederick Taylor ushered in is showing signs of coming to a close. Michael Hammer's reengineering may be just what is needed to expose its fatal flaws. **Reengineering is something done to a machine, not to a living, breathing, forward-moving enterprise.** To the extent a company reengineers things it shouldn't be bothering with in the first place, it is fated to slip behind. Machines are things that get designed, operated, fixed, and eventually written-off and replaced. Their components are interchangeable and discardable. Machines crave stability. They run, not grow.

A very bright consultant (but one that is still caught up in this old school of thought) observed that many companies finally possess a well-tuned machine. He feels that they are now wrestling with the issue of where to point it. It is an astute observation but only half right. The problem of "tuning" an organization will be considered later, but first, the organization needs to be pointed in the right direction, a direction that may—depending on the company's situation—run counter to how its well-tuned machine is operating.

Get the Growth Mind-Set

A growth mind-set is more dynamic than mechanistic. It finds expression in metaphors of movement, not stability. In growth-oriented companies, people talk about the following:

- Getting from *here to there.*

- How fast can people *come on board?*

- We've a *long way* to go, so now is the time to *get moving.*

- The business seems *stuck*. Find someone who has *been down this path before* to give us some *directions*.

Heavy use of language like this throughout the organization is a leading indicator that top-line growth is on the way.

The underlying message is one of motion, of being on a journey, not a static mechanical apparatus needing some updated engineering. The essence of managing for growth is acting now to influence some future happening. Today's actions need to be keyed to that future objective, not to the logic of some about-to-be-outdated business process.

Put out your antenna, and listen for the kinds of language used in staff meetings, over the water cooler, or at lunch. What words or metaphors are most common? What clues do they provide about the direction your business is taking? Is it *moving forward* or *fixing up?*

Southwest Airlines vs. People Express

Contrast Southwest Airlines' early experience with growth with that of People Express, its once superficial east coast look-alike. Both offered minimal service amenities and very low fares, but that is where the similarities end. People Express followed an innovative but rigid model of how to structure its operations. Its efforts at minimizing hierarchy, cross-functional job rotation, and employee ownership received widespread acclaim. By the time its formula was enshrined in a Harvard Business School case, it was impossible to adjust to changing conditions, especially those dictated by its rapid transformation to a national carrier with fledgling routes across the Atlantic.

Southwest, founded a few years earlier, was less addicted to a machine-driven vision. It lets its customers' needs and a strong sense of how to improvise set its growth course. It learned early on the dangers of too-rapid growth. Flights began in June 1971 with three aircraft. Business was so good that a fourth was added that fall. Unfortunately, payroll costs rose faster than revenue, and the fourth plane soon had to be sold to maintain a positive cash flow. Rather than let its style be cramped by too few planes—and too few flights to attract regular business commuters—Southwest *innovated its way out of adversity.* One of its employees, perhaps concerned about his own long-term career prospects, invented the "ten-minute turn." This is Southwest's now-famous ability to deplane passengers and baggage, board new passengers and belongings, refuel, and clean the cabin all in ten minutes. This allowed the airline to maintain the same number of flights with one fewer airplane. This was not an idea dreamed up by a chief executive–to–be in a three-color business proposal intended to circulate among venture capitalists; it was not part of the logic tree in a cover-all-the-bases contingency plan; and it was not produced by a multiyear, multiphase reengineering project, but it came from *within* an organization where every employee was deeply involved in doing whatever it took to keep the business on course. Southwest is continuing to discover its growth tactics while it stays in motion.

Today, People Express is a disappeared airline, a money loser forced into a merger; however, Southwest is one of the few airlines in the 1990s that has been consistently profitable, and its unique growth path is now seen as a threat by every major, long-established U.S. airline.

Reflect the New Realities of Growth

The five myths of growth, discussed in Chapter 2, are overlearned lessons from the 1950s and 1960s that don't hold up anymore. When recast, though, each provides some clues about actions to take now to ensure future growth. Success, as Southwest demonstrates, requires the following:

- a unique competitive advantage;

- matched with an unmet market need;

- oriented at making the business better, not just bigger;

- a willingness to view rivals as co-inhabitants of a shared turf; and

- an ability to turn mistakes into a positive advantage.

There is a strong common thread behind each of these new rules for growth: *success goes to those who customize.* Rewards will flow to those best able to match their game plan, their strategy, with the specifics of their competitive situation. There is neither one path to growth appropriate for every company nor does one size fit all. This may sound like Common Sense 101, but considering the rapid spread of management fads, many in business still seem to act as if this is true. The fear of being left behind is strong in Corporate America, but it is one that masters of the new rules of growth, like Southwest, have overcome. So resist fear, stick to your guns, follow your common sense, and identify the particular path to growth *best* for *your* business.

Match the Vehicle with the Voyage

The key to successful customization lies in matching the company's organization with its growth plan. Just as some types of ships are appropriate for calm seas and others for rough seas, some organizational forms are better at creating new marketplaces, while others thrive in segments of established ones.

Defining the most common competitive arenas and what it takes, organizationally, to prevail in each is the purpose of the rest of this book. It addresses a problem common to many businesses: **trying to use an organization successful for yesterday's growth journey to carry it on tomorrow's.** You wouldn't try to cross the Atlantic in a yacht built for an America's Cup competition, nor would the special features of a speedy hydrofoil be of much use if your mission were that of a lumbering tug boat.

Five Voyages: Five Ways to Be Successful

There are five ways a business can grow successfully.

It can follow the conventional wisdom of seeking out marketplace requirements, developing products that address customer needs, carefully producing them, aggressively promoting and selling them, and providing flawless customer service and support thereafter. These straightforward, tough-minded businesses excel at grabbing market share. They know well the rules of competition, and they know how to use them to their advantage. They know how to play the game, and they play to win. They take a given situation and make it grow. These are the Coca-Colas, Marriotts, and Procter & Gambles. Let's call them *Game Players*.

However, there are other ways to be successful. Herb Kelleher at Southwest Airlines demonstrated that you don't always have to follow the rules. Some businesses thrive by breaking the rules and by changing the basis of competition. They may be aware of the rules, but they are just better at getting ahead by ignoring them or upsetting them in a way that plays to their particular strengths. These business rebels cultivate their inventiveness. They enjoy being pioneers—they must, because they really don't know any other way to behave. This mold suited MCI in the early 1980s as well as Federal Express, in its start-up days, a decade earlier. These are industry *Rule Breakers.*

Success often breeds greater success. Some market share acquirers eventually manage to out-compete all rivals, and a few pioneers make such better mousetraps that customers wait in long lines to buy them. These businesses eventually find themselves in the enviable position of defining the industry standards. They dominate their markets. These are the Wal-Marts of the 1990s and the IBMs of the 1970s. They don't just play by the rules, they make them.

Although many companies may compete—and find growth opportunities—in an industry, there is room for only a few such standard setters, or *Rule Makers.* Some businesses compete very successfully as *Specialists,* serving only a particular type of customer or making a very customized product. In their often narrowly defined domains, they frequently are market leaders, though they seldom attempt to dominate an entire industry (consider AMP, star of the connectors segment of the electronics industry, or Midwest Express, king of the Milwaukee airport).

Others lack this sharp focus. They make up for it, though, with speed, cunning, and flexibility. They are *Improvisers* and have a special knack for shifting their strategies to meet the needs of the moment. They survive, and sometimes thrive, by rolling with the punches—a great skill to have if you were a stockbroker in the 1980s or working in parts of the publishing industry today.

Sustain Growth by Changing Course

These are not static categories. In its relatively brief history, Apple Computer has evolved from an upstart Rule Breaker into a multi-billion-dollar Game Player and is now showing signs of thriving through improvisation and flexibility. General Motors, once the worldwide Rule Maker of the automobile industry, has succumbed to attacks from Game Players like Toyota, Specialists like Chrysler and Mazda, and rebel Rule Breakers like Honda. Now, GM is trying to reinvent itself through an innovative rule-breaking offshoot of its own: Saturn.

One type of company is not inherently better than any other. One-time industry dominators as varied as IBM, Sears, and the Pennsylvania Railroad have found the fall from market dominance a steep one. Glamorous innovators like Atari and People Express are no more, and their stronger peers such as Club Med and Federal Express find once-unique market positions crowded with imitators. Specialization, clinging to a market niche, is no guarantee of survival, either. Commodore Computer's unique focus wasn't strong enough to resist the digital marketplace's ongoing tidal changes. Even Microsoft, today's consummate Rule Maker, will someday find that its moment in the sun has past.

There Is No One Best Way to Grow

Each growth type has a distinct personality, corporate character, or core competence. Changing the basis of competition (the hallmark of a Rule Breaker) requires knowing how to make innovation pay off—a different set of skills from those behind achieving and holding onto a dominant market position (a Rule Maker's forte). Game Players are skillful marketeers and salespeople, while focused Specialists are highly savvy about their technologies and how to use them to benefit their customer segment. Improvisers manage to stay alive in turbulent industries where pure survival is, itself, a major accomplishment.

Each type of company has a particular ethos associated with it. The kind of organization best suited to one might cause another's failure. Some are able to thrive in certain stages of an industry's development and in certain competitive positions yet decline in others. Each has unique strengths, as well as special blind spots and excesses. **There is no one best way to organize and manage a business. But, for a given situation, some ways are much better than others,** and **as the marketplace and competition change, a company's structure and management practices must also evolve.**

Not every business neatly fits into one of these situations. Some companies, such as the ones mentioned above, are close to "pure plays." Many, though, are hybrids of two, and sometimes three, of these types. For example, Xerox has worked hard (and still is working hard) to combine the Game Player (its traditional copier business) and the Rule Breaker (the stream of innovative product ideas that flow from its famed

Palo Alto Research Center). Exxon, at the height of the oil price boom, struggled and ultimately failed to create a corporation built around the combined attributes of Rule Makers, Specialists, and Rule Breakers.

Stereotypes or Building Blocks?

To get real value from these characterizations of growth strategies, it is necessary to do a good job at diagnosis. This is what distinguishes the best management consultants from the "cookie-cutter-of-the-moment" vendors. You can do the same thing. All good diagnosticians, whether they are physicians, psychiatrists, or business consultants, share a common starting point. They all begin with a *conceptual framework* that helps sort out their observations. In their analytic work, they keep eyes open for patterns, common themes, events, or behaviors that seem to be occurring in tandem. They match these with similar "packages" they have seen in other situations and relate all this back to some of the "standard" models of things that are supposed to happen that their professional training provided. In the medical field, these packages are called syndromes. Sociologists call them ideal types. Historians term them patterns or cycles. Whatever they are called, they are useful shortcuts to sizing up a situation and planning what needs to happen next. The point of all this labeling is not to stereotype a situation but to raise productive questions about it. Hypotheses, not answers, are generated.

This is the same mentality managers intent on growing a business need to adopt. Good customizers—as contrasted with fast imitators of the fad of the moment—are good diagnosticians. They start where they are, not where they want to be. They begin by asking questions about their company and about their industry, not by trying to force-fit themselves to whatever management solution is being touted as the moment's hottest. They

- Look hard at what they've got.

- Relate what is found back to some useful framework (the subject of the next five chapters).

- Plan their unique approach to growth based on the clues the framework provides.

They don't necessarily try to turn their business (or themselves) into one of these five pure types of competitors. These categories are starting points for planning, not final goals.

A Journey, Not a Machine

A company on a growth trajectory is not a machine requiring repair. It's a vehicle that needs to go somewhere. Examine now, one by one, five of the most important sources of growth and consider when and for whom each is best.

Those called Rule Breakers make a good starting point. These are the creative risk takers. Rule Breakers are the most exciting of the five growth types. They are also the most problematic. Rule Breakers provide the most trouble for their competitors and are also the most dangerous to themselves.

The Five Paths

*Match the Game Plan with
the Business and Its People*

CHAPTER 4

Breaking the Rules

Destabilize an Industry
to Create New Markets

E very industry and marketplace have their accepted rules. These may include the following:

- Assumptions about what customers want, when they want it, or how much they're willing to pay.

- Trendy best practices or tried-and-true standard operating procedures.

- Old technologies or state-of-the-art methods and processes.

Collectively, they make up what are called the "industry standards." The bigger, older, and more prosperous an industry is, the more entrenched these rules of the game become. What rules are just begging to be broken in your business?

For most businesses, the key to a strong competitive position—and the financial results that come from it—is the ability to conform to these rules, to play the game, and to know what Peter Drucker calls "the theory of the business." At some point they may even become so taken-for-granted that they disappear from conscious awareness, which is when things become interesting and when the industry is most vulnerable. When conditions change—market growth slows, competitors become deeply entrenched, customers seem less concerned with value and only look at price, and the technology plateaus—the rules can always be broken, walked around, abandoned, made obsolete, or just ignored. A business that breaks the rules—and in the process, conveys special benefits to its customers—is in a great position to grow, but it takes a unique company to bring this about.

Breaking the Rules

- Apple Computer, in the early 1980s, defied the conventional wisdom that computers have to be big and difficult to run. It created the pioneering Apple I and II and Macintosh computers—the first *personal* computing machines.

- Almost a century earlier, Ford Motor Company produced the first automobile that didn't require great wealth to purchase.

- At about the same time, Kodak put a severe crimp in the portrait painting industry with its introduction of the first consumer-friendly camera.

- Polaroid later developed a camera that eliminated the stop at the photo processor for a finished picture.

- Philips found a way to capture images electronically on a videotape, making the need for photographic film or paper unnecessary.

- Federal Express found that the shortest distance between any two points in the United States was to route every overnight package it delivered through Memphis, Tennessee.

- Nuccor found a way to recycle discarded metal into first-class steel.

Creating New Expectations

In ways big and small, each of these businesses drove its growth by deliberately ignoring the industry standards of its time. They did not set out to meet *existing* customer expectations but grew by creating *new* ones, which were as robust as they were novel. They had the inherent strength necessary to *displace* the customer's *previous expectations* about how things were supposed to be. Although this is a tall challenge and one with many perils, it is a recipe for growth. Rule Breakers are America's prototypical business heroes; they are the Davids who topple Goliaths. However, the path that they follow is far from the easiest way to grow a business, and it is a path that many have found difficult to stay on or to retrace after an initial success.

Companies on the rule-breaking path to growth stand apart from other businesses. They have certain unmistakable characteristics, a unique persona. From these they derive great strength, but from these they also acquire a number of built-in weaknesses. They are the companies most likely to get to the future first but are seldom the businesses that will reap its greatest rewards. In some situations they thrive, while in others they are prone to stumbling. Sustained growth, for most Rule Breakers, requires an ability to transform themselves into something else.

Hallmarks of a Rule Breaker

A Rule Breaker always starts with an idea from someone whose vision is just a little bit different from the conventional. Many corporate labs and new product committees are littered with good ideas, but these alone are insufficient. Rule breaking also requires someone with the drive to challenge the accepted order by converting that idea into a new service or product. When these two orientations are fused, a Rule Breaker is created, and the marketplace frequently is never the same again.

The Prophet and the Barbarian

Larry Miller, an astute consultant from Atlanta, likes to refer to these modes of operation as those of the prophet and the barbarian. Prophets, he says, are more interested in ideas than results. They may excel at vision and at creating new ways to meet customer needs, but without the action-oriented impatience of the barbarian, their visions tend to stay unsullied by the marketplace. A good barbarian will grab the prophet's vision and run with it for all it's worth. Ray Kroc did just that with the speed-oriented hamburger drive-in restaurants that Richard and Maurice McDonald opened in southern California in the 1950s. A generation later, "barbarian" Steve Jobs teamed with "prophet" Stephen Wozniak, a combination that beget Apple Computer.

The real trick to rule-breaking growth is keeping these orientations in rough balance while continually building momentum in the marketplace. Rule breaking requires an organization whose employees appreciate the value each orientation provides and a leadership with enough statesmenlike abilities to tilt toward one or the other, depending on the needs of the moment.

The Power of Ideas Combined

Rule breaking has the greatest chance of success when it moves the business forward on several fronts, simultaneously. A single new idea is seldom sufficient, as the following Rule Breakers illustrate:

- Apple's original Macintosh was a revolutionary product, innovative in both its hardware and software, but equally innovative was the highly automated facility in Fremont, California, that was invented especially to produce it.

- The original Xerox machine, the venerable Model 914, was a product that ushered an era of "copying for the masses," but it was the innovative approach Xerox took to leasing and pricing copies, not machines, that really put the product in the hands of its enthusiastic customers.

- Charles Schwab was one of the pioneers of the discount stock brokerage industry, but it was his heavy investment in customer-serving information technology that propelled the business ahead of other price-cutters.

- General Motors' Saturn and Nissan's Infiniti cars both received rave reviews from their purchasers, but what brought many potential customers initially into the showrooms was the total redesign these companies did of the salesperson's role and the car-buying process.

Rule Breakers that achieve megasuccess are those that combine new ideas from several domains. That's often the difference between having an interesting new *invention* to sell and being sufficiently *innovative* to pioneer a new industry. Rule Breakers become innovative by building the kind of organization that allows these idea combinations to happen as naturally as possible.

Leaders Who Create New Realities

This kind of organization-creating requires architects and builders. Rule Breakers are created by leaders who leave deep footprints. Their founders engender a bet-the-company, high-risk, high-gain sense of commitment throughout the business. Leaders of Rule Breakers know that feedback and recognition from the marketplace is often slow in coming, especially when the mission is to change the nature of the industry. So they provide inside-the-company substitutes, instead.

In the early days of Federal Express, Fred Smith, its founder, had little cash available for employee bonuses. Instead, he gave his top performers coffee mugs with the words "Federal Express" printed on them. He promised that as the company prospered, the mugs would be replaced by stock options. It did, and they were. The awarding of these mugs—cheap, throwaway tokens in many companies—had incredible motivational value in Federal Express. Why?

Because its early employees trusted Fred Smith and internalized a piece of his vision about the kind of business they were all working together to create. Smith's role in all this was to behave in a trustworthy manner, articulate a clear vision able to attract and excite others, and focus his and his employees' efforts on single-mindedly achieving the vision. It was a simple formula but incredibly hard to pull off. There are many easier and less risky ways to make money, as will be discussed in later chapters.

An All-or-Nothing Commitment

Working in a Rule Breaker is a bit like being part of a small infantry unit, cut off from reinforcements, and under attack. The old military adage that "there are no atheists in a foxhole" applies to employees in these companies also. Only in this case, the shared faith revolves around trust in their leader and the importance of their common mission.

Few managers choose to start or go to work in Rule Breakers when they feel they have a choice. It takes an all-or-nothing commitment to restructure an entire industry, to create a new one from scratch, or to force an aging one kicking and screaming into the new century. It's not something you would willingly do if you could find something better. Some people, though, can't find something better. Perhaps their situation offers few options. Rule breaking might just be in their blood—an integral part of their nature, their psyche, and their genes.

The risks and uncertainties that surround Rule Breakers could easily lead to paralyzing anxiety throughout the business, but it usually doesn't. Instead, the mood within many Rule Breakers is the kind of vigilant calm experienced by those in the eye of a storm. Successful Rule Breakers quell anxiety by absorbing it. These people are often called charismatic, though this is a different kind of charisma than that evoked by stirring speech making or an impressive physical presence.

Although people from many backgrounds with many personalities have led Rule Breakers, one thing they all have in common is an incredibly strong attachment to a new way of doing business. They are not all in Silicon Valley; they can be found in some industries where they would least be expected.

Waking Up a Stodgy Utility

Consider James Rogers, president of Cinergy Corporation, a holding company that owns two midwest energy utilities. Although it is unlikely that many would break the rules in a tradition-bound, heavily regulated, conservative power business, Rogers is hard at work doing just that. The long-sheltered world of electric utilities, circumscribed by captive customers and prices set by regulation, not the marketplace, is about to shatter. Following the path of AT&T's breakup into long-distance and local telephone companies, the power business is likely to replace local monopolies with widespread competition.

Many companies now "integrated" with divisions that generate, transmit, and locally distribute electricity will find that these are really three separate businesses, each with its own set of customers and competitive dynamics. Just as consumers are now free to choose among a variety of long-distance telephone providers, they might someday choose from several power sources and a variety of companies offering to carry the power to their homes. Ecology-minded consumers may choose to buy only electricity generated by wind power, while others may prefer nuclear power.

Guts and Vision

Rogers thinks that "someday" should come sooner, rather than later. The keys to transforming this industry are guts and new approaches to regulation. Rogers is providing more than his share of personal courage; he voluntarily opened up his transmission wires to any utility interested in selling wholesale power over it. In return his company became the first to receive significant leeway from existing pricing regulations. His vision is to sell his low-cost midwest-generated power to east coast customers tired of high rates from their local power companies.

Rather than resisting change, the norm in this hide-bound industry, Cinergy's efforts are being directed at reshaping the basics of how it does business with its customers. Rogers sees himself as a breaker of rules, but what he is doing is actually, at its core, very conservative. He and most of the industry know that change is inevitable; the only issue is when. But Rogers feels that his company will have little credibility with tomorrow's customers—the ones who will need to be marketed to and convinced to choose Cinergy—if it fights tooth and nail to keep the competitive era at bay.

Don't Look in the Usual Places

Rule Breakers seldom emerge in expected places. Economist Burton Klein, an apostle of the new realities of growth discussed earlier, has looked hard for the real source of business innovations. He found no instance of a major advance ever successfully coming from within the industry most affected by it. None. Never. No railroads have become successful airlines; no buggy whip manufacturers have transformed into auto part suppliers; and makers of mainframe computers have a hard time (at best) staying at the leading edge of the personal computer market. Is a company whose revenues are driven by selling machines that copy documents likely to lead the charge to the paperless office?

Another observation is that Rule Breakers are almost invariably *stand-alone* enterprises. The persona of those who start them seldom function well in anything else. They are seldom the products of "royal marriages," such as joint ventures or consortia or strategic alliances. These popular forms of corporate partnership have their place, but **the compromise and accommodation central to their functioning make it hard for them to serve as vehicles to challenge the wisdom of their parents.** Partnerships may be very trendy, but remember the earlier warnings about things that are trendy.

Lead, Don't Ask, the Customer

Ideas that drive Rule Breakers seldom come from expected places. Rule Breakers are poor prospects for sellers of market research. Actually, many start out by not listening to customers at all. When asked to explain the secret behind Sony's rule-breaking growth, its former chief executive, Akio Morita, said that he always planned to lead the public with novel products and that he did not bother asking consumers what they wanted from Sony because he had a strong conviction that they really didn't know what was possible to make, but he knew.

Hal Sperlich is the former Ford manager who had to relocate his career to Chrysler to get support to develop his idea of the minivan. His colleagues at Ford were skeptical about investing in a new product whose market segment didn't exist at the time. Sperlich even confessed that throughout the ten years it required to create the minivan, not one customer wrote in asking for one to be invented. But he kept on developing his idea regardless, even though it required a risky career move.

Avoid Market Research

Rule Breakers find their inspiration inside, not from systematic surveys of unmet market needs. This makes sense—most customers, when asked, seem to want minimal disruption. Incremental improvements find more favor with them than having a front-row seat at an industry revolution.

Rule Breakers know, at least intuitively, that polling customers has significant dangers. For one, it misses the opinions of those who don't buy from you (most every company with an impressive customer list can generate an even more impressive list: those that don't buy from it). A more serious danger is that it may easily miss detecting needs that customers don't know they have. Edwin Land, Polaroid's founder, said his function was to sense a deep human need and then apply curiosity and knowledge of basic science to find a clever way to fulfill it. He enjoyed making only those products that other companies couldn't.

A Mission, Not a Job

Land's zeal provided tremendous encouragement and motivation to Polaroid's employees. They felt they had a mission, not a job. In a Rule Breaker's early years, the sense of mission is frequently so strong that minimal attention is needed to fine-tune an organization structure. When most employees' attention is 100 percent focused on a common goal, a fluid organization with a flexible division of labor is both possible and necessary. **Rule Breakers seldom need to take time away from work to attend team-building programs; an exciting, shared mission serves that purpose even better.**

However, rule-breaking missions have shelf lives. They are hard to keep alive over many generations of managers and require periodic revivals. Kodak, another photo-industry giant, strayed and stumbled from its industry-creating role. In some ways, it was a victim of its great success. Eventually, diversifications far from its photography roots, competitors much better skilled at marketing, and a fluid organization turned bureaucratic all led to diminished profits and the ouster of a chief executive.

George Fisher, the ex-Motorola chief brought in to restore Kodak's competitive position, likes to quote Machiavelli at employee meetings. Reading from *The Prince,* he reminds them that "nothing is more difficult to take in hand, more perilous to conduct, or more uncertain in its success, than to take the lead in the introduction of a new order of things." Then, as the challenge implicit in these weighty words starts sinking in, Fisher quickly adds: ". . . or more invigorating." Fisher is spearheading many changes at Kodak that are likely to reenergize its growth, but he is not likely to lead it to the rule-breaking path again. A certain type of corporate personality is required to execute Machiavelli's vision. It is a temperament that emerges at a company's founding and is seldom something into which a business transforms.

The Rule Breaker's Persona

Harry Levinson is one of the leaders in applying the insights of psychology to understanding how corporations really function. When "diagnosing" a business, he asks managers to think about their company as if it were an individual, a real person. Then he asks them to look closely at the "individual's" typical behaviors, likes and dislikes, strong points, and deficiencies as a way to better understand the company and why it behaves the way it does. This is a good way to get a fresh perspective on a company, to try to describe its collective psyche. Imagine your organization as if it were an individual. What kind of a person would it be?

An Unreasonable Man

What would be the persona of a typical Rule Breaker? George Bernard Shaw has probably summed it up best:

> Reasonable men adapt themselves to their environment; unreasonable men try to adapt their environment to themselves. Thus all progress is the result of the efforts of unreasonable men.

Although Rule Breakers such as Anita Roddick of Body Shop might fairly quibble with Shaw's masculine bias, the quality of unreasonableness is at the core of the Rule Breaker. They are rebellious, sometimes stereotyped as individuals that have a hard time accepting authority. If forced to choose, they would invariably prefer delinquency to conformity, and if successful Rule Breakers are delinquents at heart, at least they are socially useful ones. Their distrust and suspicions of authority figures motivates them to devise situations where they are in charge, exerting their own control and independence. Out of such behavior, new industries have been formed and countless jobs created.

Fusing the Person with the Business

Rule Breakers are driven people. They make use of an imagination that sees what others don't and make connections between ideas that most never notice. Anita Roddick sells cosmetics by plausibly linking her business with environmentalism and third-world development. Rule Breakers are stubborn and tenacious. Their identification with what they do is total. Rule Breakers resemble Ferdinand Porsche who enjoyed saying that all he did was to build his personal idea of a dream car. He refused to rely on sales forecasts or return-on-investment formulas. He was always certain he could find buyers who shared his dream.

Rule Breakers may be like a firstborn or an only child, strong and self-reliant. They might have lost a parent at an early age but had the remaining caregiver more than compensate for the loss. Rule Breakers may have spent years serving their career—equivalent of Ghandi's or Mandela's prison time or Moses' years in the desert—but it only served to deepen their attachment to a vision, not to break their spirit. Rule Breakers are attractive people and others seem to need them more than they need others. Their protégés are often extremely loyal, often so much so that they blind themselves to the Rule Breaker's faults.

Fighting Failure

Despite a veneer of strength and confidence, for many Rule Breakers life is a constant struggle against failure. They do many things because they feel they must, not because it is what they want. Premonitions of failure, however, keep few Rule Breakers from trying something new. They do this because they are remarkably resilient when setbacks occur. One of their core competencies is a tremendous ability to pick up the broken pieces and start again when disappointed. The conventional wisdom about risk taking is often reversed for Rule Breakers. Not to take a risk is often a riskier choice than remaining safe but uncomfortable.

Some of their failures are major public spectacles. Like John DeLorean's ill-fated attempts at becoming a rule-breaking automaker, they are at times embodiments of Edna St. Vincent Millay's famous image of a candle burning at both ends, not fated to last the night but capable of producing a spectacular light.

Self-destructive tendencies are all too common among Rule Breakers. Many have contributed to their own demise, often ironically at times in their development when things appear to be moving in a favorable direction. Bitter disagreements among the founders, or between the founders and those they convinced to join them as financial partners, have crippled pioneering companies such as Advent, Diners Club, Word Star, and VisiCalc.

Strengths of the Rule Breaker

It is possible to steer clear of these dangerous tendencies—especially if those working in a Rule Breaker do their homework and *carefully study the histories of similar companies that have come before.* Then the path is clear for what Rule Breakers excel at doing: creating change and uncertainty in a marketplace. Their greatest impact is often a permanent one (at least until another Rule Breaker comes along). At their best, they are able to change the rules of competition in a way that plays to their inherent strengths. This is essential because most Rule Breakers are small, young, and underfunded. To survive, they have to be adept at innovating their way out of resource limitations. This ability leads them often to being the first to profitably employ new know-how.

It also leads some to innovative forms of financing. Part of Federal Express' lore includes a story about its founder, Fred Smith, meeting an early payroll through luck at Las Vegas' gambling tables. He is also reputed to have sold his much-loved personal airplane to buy fuel to keep his package-carrying planes in the air. This kind of spirit is contagious. During the business's long start-up period, a delivery truck driver pawned his watch to buy gasoline for his delivery truck when he discovered the corporate credit cards he was given had been canceled.

Rule Breakers are, of course, the unquestioned champions of new product development. Without them economics would truly be the "dismal science" and economic growth a thing of the past. These are impressive strengths. If you work in a Rule Breaker, do all you can to build upon its strengths.

Weaknesses of the Rule Breaker

Behind all this pioneering excitement and committed activity lurks a dark side. Having a strong vision is great, but *too much vision can be blinding.* When a business is being propelled by a sharp, narrowly focused mission, it is hard to make midcourse corrections. It's easy to create an "insanely great product" that no customer seems interested in. This is an occupational hazard of Rule Breakers, something that just has to be accepted. It's something very hard to hedge against and still remain capable of creating a new industry. Compromise and consensus are not part of the Rule Breaker's vocabulary.

Redefining Reality

Redefining reality *is* hard work. Keeping one's eye on the ball and staying focused in the face of many naysayers requires a measure of tunnel vision. (Fred Smith's Yale professor gave him a "C" on the term paper he wrote proposing the idea of an overnight delivery service.) It may require ignoring aspects of the business environment, missing key shifts in market preferences, and exaggerating some product features. Apple Computer's first Macintoshes were so quietly user-friendly because they lacked the noisy fans common to other early personal computers.

However, *changing reality* is not the same as *distorting reality*. Macintoshes, like other small computers, did get hot, and third-party manufacturers quickly produced awkward add-on fans. Eventually, Apple faced up to the laws of thermodynamics; the fanless Macintosh is now an object for computer museum display.

Avoiding Strategic Myopia

Good Rule Breakers are frequently so caught up in their inner reality—the place where all these great visions are generated—that they have weak insight into the form that the new market they've helped create will take. Apple Computer's history is replete with decisions that ignored the importance of power and price to its customers. Some industry watchers even accuse Apple of being so product driven that it missed the opportunity to rival arch-foe Microsoft as a "computerless computer company"—one that added value through innovative software, not commodity-like machines.

Federal Express has experienced similar difficulties. Its success with an innovative hub-and-spoke system of air courier flights shaped its approach to designing a nationwide facsimile network—dubbed Zap Mail. This was an innovation that never took off. The emergence of ubiquitous low-cost fax machines eliminated the need for Federal Express couriers to pick up documents and bring them to a central point for transmission. Bottom line: a multi-million-dollar write-off.

Create, Don't Withdraw, from Reality

Some Rule Breakers turn into escapists. Unlike the more successful ones where the uneasy alliance between the "prophet" and the "barbarian" eventually favors the instincts of the activist, some businesses almost completely withdraw from reality. Danny Miller is a Canadian business school professor who has studied the fates of many pioneering companies. He has found that too much vision can have consequences worse than distracting diversifications.

Companies such as Polaroid, Rolls-Royce, Sun Microsystems, and Wang Laboratories all followed initial profitable innovations with a stream of "ahead-of-their-time" products. These emerged from loose organization structures, excessive decentralization, and employee empowerment that was granted without reference to needs of their evolving marketplaces. These four Rule Breakers continued to do all the right things to pioneer new markets, but they now had established customers and imitative competitors. The competitors needed watching, and their customers needed care and feeding. Instead, these companies retreated to their skunk works and adopted the faith of the ostrich (all will be well if I can just get away from all these distractions). As a result, they all suffered serious business setbacks.

Some escapists fall victim to the Manhattan Project Syndrome: if you throw enough people and money at a problem, you are bound to come up with something. This might have helped the United States bring World War II to a conclusion, but the advantage it provided was fleeting as proliferation of the atomic bomb led to the Cold War decades. Rule Breakers who can afford Manhattan Project–style product development often have forgotten that what got them to the competitive position they have (innovation) may not be the right strategy to keep them there.

Love Your Customers, Not Your Products

John Scully, one-time chief executive of Apple Computer, criticized his predecessor for building only products that fit the founder's vision, often ignoring the needs of the customers. In spite of his insight, Scully remained a prisoner of Apple's rule-breaking culture. He spent millions developing a product *he* fell in love with, Newton, the hand-held pen-driven personal communicator.

Like Apple, many Rule Breakers have trouble sustaining growth. Their weak or repressed antennae miss signals from the marketplace. Their aversion to internal controls minimizes their chance of discovering that they are off course until it is too late to do anything about it.

Keep Your Eye on the Ball

Rule Breakers are known for their constant, take-no-prisoners battles against routine, orderly ways of doing things. They resist administration of any kind—something fine in the earliest stages of their corporate development, but these enemies become necessary evils as the idea becomes a business on a growth trajectory. Although the conventional wisdom is that lack of attention to organization and administration kills off many Rule Breakers, this is seldom the case. Few file for bankruptcy because they forgot to file their income tax forms or failed to have an up-to-date personnel manual. **The real danger is that the up-and-coming Rule Breaker diverts so much attention and energy resisting encroaching bureaucracy that not enough is left to develop new ideas.**

Are all Rule Breakers doomed to this fate? Is self-destruction inevitable? Or is there a way to keep the vision of the prophet alive while the barbarian part of the business matures? Let's examine a neighbor of Apple Computer whose offices are close geographically but whose approach to managing growth is several light years away.

Silicon Graphics: A Maturing Rule Breaker

The box office hit movie *Forrest Gump* broke all the rules. Its star, Tom Hanks, interacted with images of long-dead figures such as John F. Kennedy and John Lennon—all made possible by the computer imaging products of Silicon Graphics, Inc. *Gump* brought historical figures back to life. In another movie, *The Crow*, the leading actor died before filming was completed. This was not a problem for Silicon Graphics' world of digital virtual reality, which allowed filmmakers to digitally insert his image into the last scenes. This is a cyberspace twist on the old injunction that the show must go on.

Silicon Graphics (SGI) makes an enabling technology—something that helps others produce spectacular results. SGI makes the tools, and its customers make the applications. Its core talent is the ability to put the instructions that guide a computer in making fancy, colorful graphics *into* the computer chips themselves, not in the external software. This is the meaning behind the company's name, and SGI is another example of a business that found a way to do something better by cutting out a middle step.

Vision + Fun = Success

SGI has a clear vision about what a computer screen needs to become and feels that the display is a window into a virtual world. This world is made of color graphics, in 3-D of course, that move and talk. SGI puts all the capabilities of a VCR into the personal computer and then makes it a machine the user can interact with, not just something to sit passively in front of. This is hot stuff and a lot of fun also.

This spirit of fun and irreverence pervades the company and its products. SGI is committed to the idea that growth doesn't have to be boring. It doesn't confine its high jinks to employee-only Silicon Valley Friday afternoon partying. It shares them with customers by giving its machines names such as Indy, Indigo, and Power Onyx. Eschewing the traditional beige or platinum colors for its machines, it paints them electric purple, teal, and crimson. The company philosophy of having serious fun is reflected in the pebbly finish of one machine (as befits a company specializing in 3-D) and another with the look of two stacked pizza boxes, each one slightly ajar.

Visual computing, SGI's speciality, is much more than fun and games. Because the human brain processes information in three dimensions, people are much more likely to find new insights in reams of data when they've been converted to pictures. So in addition to creating the dinosaurs of *Jurassic Park*, SGI's computer graphics equipment simulates car crashes for Ford, helps Boeing design new jet aircraft, and helps molecular biologists visualize the inner workings of the immune system.

In an industry characterized by disappearing profits, product half-lives measured in months, fickle customers, and commodity-like pricing, SGI has sales of almost $2 billion and rapidly growing earnings.

No Escapists Here

How has it managed to avoid the escapist tendencies that have stunted many Rule Breakers' growth plans? How has it kept a strong vision from distorting its sense of reality? The company's well-honed sense of humor sure doesn't hurt. It is a great antidote to taking one's self too seriously. So is its approach to product creation.

Most companies eat their young, i.e., kill off promising new ideas before they come anywhere near the marketplace. SGI takes a different approach. It risks stunting the growth of its "adolescent" products with each succeeding generation of new products. Its Indigo workstation was still gaining market share when SGI introduced the Indy system—a product with more features and a lower price than the Indigo. SGI would rather obsolete itself than fall victim to a competitor unrestrained by an installed base.

Look for the Lighthouses

This continuous renewal cycle is fed by constantly cultivating customers who want to do things that can't be done with the SGI current product lineup. The "best" of these are even willing to spend what it takes to achieve the impossible. SGI likes to call these "lighthouse customers." Its first lighthouses were the military and intelligence services. Now, the post–Cold War U.S. defense budget is shrinking, and SGI has shifted its attention to the more flexible checkbooks of Disney and Hollywood.

Organizing around Boutiques

At its outset, a key job of SGI top management was to come up with new product ideas. Now, the primary focus is organizational. Its role is to ensure that the organizational structure is one that continually keeps its brightest technologists in close contact with its leading customers. Small, boutiquelike units are constantly created around key customer segments; old ones are subdivided or disbanded. Managers are more than urged to work closely with customers—those that don't, quickly find that their twice-a-year performance reviews include some unpleasant feedback.

Hollywood represents only a small fraction of SGI's business, but a high percentage of many engineers' days are spent with customers at

Disney's and George Lucas's studios. These lighthouse customers are full of complaints—they are constantly pushing Silicon Graphics equipment to its limits; they are SGI's best source of organizational learning. Their suggestions for improvements quickly become the built-in features of SGI's next generation of products.

Running Fashionably Late

SGI combines keeping up with leading-edge customers with an approach to product development that can best be described as being "fashionably late." Many companies work hard to speed their product development cycle so they can get ideas from market research to engineering and then into the marketplace fast—SGI goes them one better. It also pays great attention to development cycles and the latest approaches to time-based competition, but it does so to be able to wait until the last possible minute until it has to begin serious product development. This maximizes the amount of time its engineers spend hearing directly from customers what features they want next and minimizes product development accompanied by second-guessing common in most companies.

Separating the Founder's Ego from His Creation

Another source of renewal at SGI was the 1994 departure of one of its founders and former CEO, James Clark. He was its "prophet," a former Stanford professor who started SGI only after many other computer manufacturers showed little interest in his dream of bringing 3-D graphics to a desktop computer. Clark, as most prophets do, had strongly felt ideas about his company and its future direction. Rather than allow his disagreements with other executives about SGI's approach to the mass consumer market slow the company's momentum, he left SGI and started another company. Attempting to become the "Henry Ford" of the internet, his new company, Netscape, is setting out to build a fast, simple-to-use, upramp to the information superhighway.

Many Rule Breakers have missed achieving their potential because their founders lacked Clark's insight. It takes a special ability to separate a creator's ego from his creation, but at some point in every business's growth, this becomes essential.

Keeping a Bold Sense of Direction

Clark's successor, ex-Hewlett-Packard veteran Edward McCracken, is a quiet electrical engineer from the Midwest. But his soft-spoken demeanor belies a bold sense of direction: "Our goal is to put an affordable supercomputer on the desktop of every scientist, engineer, and creative professional from New York to Kyoto, from Oslo to Sao Paulo. We intend to define the future of interactive graphics and visual computing. . . ." Silicon Graphics is an impressive company. How long it will remain so, though, is still an open question, as it is for every business.

Where Rule Breakers Thrive

Future success depends on both the strength and adaptability of the firm and the kinds of conditions it must adjust to. Some business conditions perfect for one type of company can sink another. Before moving on to examine other growth paths, consider the environment most conducive for rule breaking.

Forces Driving Rule Breaking

Rule breaking requires more than sheer brilliance at problem solving. The goal is not just to solve a problem, but rather *to create a whole new industry* in the wake of the solution. The business turf in which rules cry out to be broken is often found in times of great discontinuity, at the intersection of forces such as the following:

- entrenched monopoly or ogopolist competition,
- ossified regulations,
- a just-over-the-horizon technological revolution,
- consumers that take for granted the value they receive from the existing products or services that industry provides,
- companies that take their customers for granted,
- blips in demographic or social trends, or
- another form of impending disaster.

Which of these driving forces are present in your industry? What possibilities do they offer for some creative rule breaking?

Watch for Imminent Sea Changes

Rule Breakers thrive when a "sea change" is imminent. Consider the plight of the endangered businesses species, the "middleman." In industry after industry computers are bringing customers and suppliers together, without the need for intermediaries and the long, costly supply chains they breed. In businesses as different as health care and automobile windshield repair, consumers are being steered as well as served by information systems that guide them to "preferred providers." These suppliers pay for the privilege of doing business through the "network," and those that don't, fear being cut off from their old customer base.

The quick access to information promised by computer networks will reshape forever many marketplaces. Change like this is capable of turning entire industries who are used to "pushing" products onto customers into ones regulated by the "pull" of customer demand. Some companies in these industries will adjust accordingly; others will disappear. And many opportunities will emerge for the new, rule-breaking, electronic intermediaries.

King of Embryonic Industries

Rule Breakers thrive in embryonic industries (after all, they played a major part in creating the industry). At their inception, though, they will most likely hold a weak competitive position in a mature or aging business—at least until they stir things up. Then Rule Breakers find themselves in a situation with potential as far as the eye can see. Growth may be exponential, partly because of all this potential and partly because the Rule Breakers' sales started at zero. Few or no competitors may exist—which is good, because the real competition is the status quo. A Rule Breaker has done a good job of entering an industry when its tracks are covered carefully, making it hard for imitators to follow. The Rule Breaker's financials will be simple: assets will most likely be few, and the return on them will be negative. Cash will flow out much faster than it comes in. Sales may rapidly grow, but profits are likely to be slow in appearing. Market share at this stage of an industry's development is a meaningless concept. Customers barely understand the new product, or their need for it, so purchasing patterns are completely up in the air.

Advantages of Moving First

If the Rule Breaker's business idea "takes off," a whole host of benefits may follow. These are often termed "first mover" advantages, the rewards associated with being among the first firms to establish themselves in a new marketplace. They include the following:

- Establishing *customer loyalty*—a successful Rule Breaker's product or service quickly becomes the standard against which subsequent offerings are judged. The market is theirs to lose.

- Maintaining *technology leadership*—while competitors are struggling to learn how the Rule Breaker did it, the clever pioneer is busy perfecting the next generation of technology.

- Setting *industry standards* and seizing the most favorable position in the market. A revolutionary product can embed within it the standards the new industry that grows up around it will have to follow. The first player in a new market faces virgin territory. It can choose the image and position for itself that will play to its strongest advantages.

- Depending on the industry, pioneers may gain important *patent protection*—an opportunity to *clog the channels of distribution* to keep competitors away and a crack at forcing customers to invest so heavily in a new product or service that they will be very *cautious about switching* suppliers.

Where Rule Breakers Stumble

These advantages can be impressive. But they are not available in every industry and every marketplace. There are some competitive arenas where Rule Breakers are at a clear disadvantage. Silicon Graphics' McCracken feels that the key to competitive advantage is not reacting to chaos, but it's producing the chaos (said like a true Rule Breaker). The next section discusses what happens when the chaos slows down, as it eventually does—or companies with double- or triple-digit growth rates, like Silicon Graphics, would come to consume the country's entire GNP!

When Chaos Slows Down

Because the odds are stacked against them, many more Rule Breakers stumble than succeed. Too many things have to happen just so, and at just the right time, for a Rule Breaker to take off. It takes excellent timing to enter a market just as demand starts exploding. **Constantly staying on the cutting edge can become a tiring and expensive position to maintain.**

While being guided by a single, strong inner vision may seem like an admirable way to earn a living, it puts a lot of pressure on everyone to be sharing the *right* vision. Visions can be elusive and slippery, they can get old, they can be replaced, and they can also succeed, but their success is in an environment that demands that all attention go to defending the success.

Rule Breakers face other dangers. By their nature, Rule Breakers operate in an in-your-face manner, which can become old quickly. Customers may tire of always being told what they need. Sleeping-dinosaur–type competitors may prematurely awaken, counterattack, and overpower the often-weak Rule Breaker.

The Perils of Success

Rule Breakers need the protection provided by very embryonic (or, ironically, by quietly aging) markets. Most require a long gestation period—the time when they are free from the burdens of counting sales dollars. Fast-moving growth markets seldom offer this luxury; Rule Breakers too quickly become road kill. It is too late, in high-growth/high-volume businesses, for the special talents of the Rule Breaker to prevail. Industries that have reached the mature point can be equally inhospitable. They are often dominated by a small number of successful competitors, companies who watch each other and any potential entrant like a hawk.

The financial pressures on a company operating in late growth or early mature markets can be unbearable. These companies are expected to have either rapidly increasing earnings or sizable positive cash flow. Return on assets should peak as the unit cost of producing whatever is being made drops rapidly. Financial expectations like these do not allow much room for industry-defying experimentation and risk taking. Bottom line: size up the situation carefully before taking the plunge, break the rules only if no other choice is available, don't let the latest business fad lead you down a path where you don't belong, and be sure to customize any popular business advice you find attractive.

Fine-Tuning Hamel and Prahalad

Business school professors Gary Hamel and C. K. Prahalad have attracted many followers with their ideas about strategic intent and core competences. Their thinking is fresh and creative. In some ways, though, their suggestions can be as dangerous as they are popular. Implicit in much of their advice is a strong call to arms: go out and challenge the orthodoxies of industry incumbents! Be rebels! Be subversives! They implore managers to gain foresight and to be equipped to debate with colleagues key industry trends for at least eight hours nonstop. Although Hamel and Prahalad feel that this is the way to be in control of a corporation's destiny, they are only half right.

The Necessity of Choice

Some management teams *are* more "foresightful" than others. It's *one* way to grow. What they miss, though, is an appreciation of *the necessity of choice,* the critical importance of customizing a growth strategy to the particular situation and capabilities—at a particular point in time. Not every manager is cut out to be a rebel. Not every industry is ripe for destabilization. Some orthodoxies offer, and will continue to offer, a variety of ways to grow profitably. Let's explore them next.

Hamel and Prahalad enjoy urging managers to "get to the future first," but getting there *second* has it rewards, too. For many companies, especially those we call Game Players, the benefits can be sweeter than those tasted by rule-breaking pioneers.

Rule Breaker   **What Is It Like Working for a Rule Breaker?**

Here, and after each of the next four chapters, are brief descriptions of what it is like to work inside each type of growth company. Written in the first person, these are composites drawn from oral and written statements made by people employed in companies following each path. These are pro-totypes of one company presented from two points of view. The first is from someone in love with this company, and the second is the perspective of a person who would probably be happier and do better elsewhere.

Read between the lines in these "face-offs" to discover the "real" inner reality. Each of these is a caricature. Fill them in from your own experience. Keep in mind that no single company is right for everyone, but one of the five is probably best for you.

This is the BEST place in the world to work.

Listen to the words a young design engineer uses to portray his impressions of work life at a high-tech Rule Breaker. His idealism seems matched only by his energy level. He is clearly someone in the right job at the right point in his life.

■ ■ ■

I can't imagine being happier anywhere else. I never thought I'd come to love working 70-hour weeks. I still feel pleasantly surprised that I'm actually getting *paid* for doing what I most want to do.

Sure, the hours are crazy, and the money isn't what it could be (at least not until my options vest and I cash out), but I feel I'm really making a difference here.

The leaders of this industry have been asleep at the switch for too long. Our company—and our new technologies—are going to give them a wake-up call they'll never forget, and *I'm* a part of it all.

It feels like this industry is about to go through the equivalent of the American Revolution and that I've just joined the Sons of Liberty.

I've got a mission here, not just a job.

I love the way our founder has been able to pull back from day-to-day operations. I know many start-ups that failed because their creator

could never let go, but not this one. He's delegated
profusely. He's also brought in a couple of seasoned
executives from companies of the kind we aspire to become. They are
hard at work on our rough edges.

Rule Breaker

Meanwhile our founder is living up to the accolades showered in
last month's *Fortune* cover story. I've never known anyone able to
combine insight with energy the way he does.

I've never missed one of his impromptu "state-of-the-company"
speeches—usually delivered at our end-of-the-week parties. They are
a great way to let off steam and also to make the rounds and find out
what's really going on.

It's also nice having a real live role model working only a few paces
down the hall—I can bounce ideas off of him anytime.

This company has made bureaucracy Public Enemy Number One.
Everything Tom Peters writes is required reading (whenever we get
around to having any time free for recreational reading). There are no
policy manuals, probably because nobody has time to write them, read
them, or keep them updated.

We walk our talk here. We keep our structure loose and flexible,
and we don't imprison people in job descriptions. The organization
chart looks more like a spider web than a pyramid. We never print it
on paper— it changes so frequently that I've only seen it drawn on
white boards.

We attract the kind of people who thrive in this kind of open
environment. Those who can't, never get beyond the front door. I
mean that literally. If applicants come in looking for the employment
office, the receptionist tells them we don't have one. They walk out,
puzzled. Recruits destined to fit in find a job here through word of
mouth. They know someone who knows someone here. It's a network
organization, and you've got to network your way in.

Our products and our customers are state of the art. Our
customers love us, and they love what we make for them. They can't
wait for more.

We don't have a shipping department. Our customers' trucks line
up at our loading dock, awaiting their allocation.

Rule Breaker   By looking at our ads and listening to our sales spiel, it is obvious that we practice in-your-face marketing. We have to—the competition is bigger and swimming in cash. Our boldness is the only hope for survival.

Is this place stressful? You better believe it. We put adrenaline, not sugar, in our coffee. A few of us have burned out, but we're all in this with our eyes open. You know the old saying, "if you can't stand the heat, get out of the kitchen."

We don't allow employee-coddling, back-rub-providing masseuses in the break room. Apple Computer tried that—look what happened to them.

We take what we are trying to do very seriously, but we never let that stand in the way of work being a lot of fun. I've already mentioned the Friday afternoons. To add to that, every year we rent a nearby rock club and fill its amphitheater with employees and families for the annual lip-synch contest. Each division forms a group to parody its favorite hit song. We even fake the instruments, American karaoke style.

I've heard that Bill Gates used to do something like this at the Seattle Kingdome. I bet ours is a lot more fun.

In some ways this firm has become my surrogate family. My best friends work here. We work together, we party together, and corny as it may sound, we do feel like we are creating the future together.

Hey, have I showed you what's cooking in the advanced project lab? It's in the building next door. Come on over and take a look. . . .

This is the WORST place in the world to work.

Now let's listen to someone else in the same company. He is a little older than the design engineer we have just heard from, and he works in one of the Rule Breaker's headquarters administrative units. These departments are a backwater in this company, which is probably reflected in some of this manager's cynicism about his career. Notice his take on some of the same observations made by his colleague in engineering.

■ ■ ■

I've mentally drafted and redrafted my resignation   **Rule Breaker**
letter a dozen times. As soon as the economy picks up,
I'm out of here.

This job has become my worst nightmare. I thought I was coming
to work at an elite high-tech superstar, *the one* everybody was expecting
to shake up this industry by its roots. Instead, the only thing getting
shaken up is me.

I've never seen such a totally disorganized place. It makes Times
Square on New Year's Eve look like a Sunday school picnic. I think the
guy who wrote the book on *Chaos* got his start here. Everything is up
in the air all the time. No job descriptions, no titles (except for the top
execs), no budgets, no personnel handbook, no personnel policies
(which, I guess, explains the missing handbook), and damn few
benefits!

Asking when we're getting a retirement plan is supposed to be
cause for instant dismissal. It probably doesn't matter anyway. At the
pace we are all working, few are likely to survive until retirement.

We are wide-open to complaints of employment discrimination.
The only way you get interviewed for a job is to know someone already
here. That leaves out a lot of good potential talent, and it makes us
dangerously ingrown.

There are no offices—I've got to attempt being productive at a
desk in the middle of some trendy, open-plan bull pen. So many stray
conversations are in the air that I'm constantly losing my train of
thought—no wonder everybody's working 70-hour weeks.

Did I mention that there are no organization charts? To be honest,
they aren't missed. Charts wouldn't have much credibility anyway, and
besides, everyone knows who is in charge. You don't need a
weatherman. . . .

This place is run by a clique of old-timers—old only in the
sense they've been around since the founding. I doubt anyone of
them is over 35, and none of them has the maturity of judgment
exhibited by a typical teenager (but they are the ones who control
access to the founder, the ones whose favor you must curry if you
want something to happen). What they do have is absolute power.

Rule Breaker   The old man (now pushing 40) who founded this
place has his head in some cloud. Everybody but me
seems to think he's some sort of visionary, though. I think . . . well,
never mind what I think. I still have heavy mortgage payments to
make.

The clique also has one big pile of stock options. Class A
options—worth a zillion times more than the Class C shares with
which they are trying to handcuff me.

Things wouldn't be so bad if the old-timers acted more like a
team, with some common interests. Instead, each behaves like a baron,
overseeing his feudal fiefdom. Budgets aren't allocated; they're fought
over—or stolen.

This is Infighting City. Back-stabbing is practiced as a recreational
sport. It's just not my style—I survive by keeping a low profile and
biding my time.

Talk about having a bunch of juvenile delinquents for role models!
A couple of them, though, came from companies much larger than
ours: one from IBM, the other an ex-P&G executive. They both seem
lost here. They keeping moaning about no leverage, but what they
really miss is their old armies of secretaries and staff assistants. I think
they're quietly conspiring to bring more overhead on-line. Yesterday a
salesman from Gulfsteam signed in at the front desk. Last week
someone was here from Lear.

Me, I fly coach. When the company was in a budget crunch a few
months back, I was even asked to fund tickets for a sales call from my
frequent flyer mileage account. Talk about sacrifice.

I can't completely blame the clique for everything that's wrong
here. Our real problem is success. We've had a few strong early hits
in the marketplace, and they've gone to our heads.

We've acquired a dangerous walk-on-water mentality, a feeling that
we can do anything. We're arrogant, thinking that if we didn't come up
with it here, it's not worth coming up with. If we're not more careful,
these attitudes are going to snowball. They'll get reflected in our
product line, and we'll fall in love with something the market is just
going to spit back in our face.

If I hear one more story about our glorious begin-   **Rule Breaker**
nings in a garage, I'm going to shoot the storyteller
and then commit an act of arson on the garage. (. . . Somebody even
said it should be turned into a museum!)

We are starting to take ourselves too seriously, romanticizing our
past, and distorting our reality. We have this image that we're all driven
by some great sense of mission. Good PR. Maybe it was once true, but
it's not reality today.

What drives this business today is fear. Fear. *Fear.* Fear of failure.
We're afraid of falling behind; afraid of our customer base being
devoured by some giant, steamroller-driven competitor, and afraid
of some hot start-up outgunning us with a new technology.

How do we deal with all this? By doing what we always did, just
more of it and faster. We are as impulsive as ever, and we seldom
distinguish the long term from the tactical.

We thrive on taking risks, being bold. That might have been fine
in the garage days—when our greatest risk was going nowhere, but
we've established a beach head in the market. We've got to move
forward in a unified direction. We've got something to loose, and
we need to protect it.

I guess my biggest gripe is really a personal one. The long hours
and travel keep me almost continuously away from my family. And the
ongoing pressure and uncertainty make me a near-burnout basket case
when I'm with them. It's really not fair. Maybe I signed on to change
the world by working here, but my wife and kids didn't.

I know the *Journal* likes to portray the business as a bunch of bold
risk takers. It's a nice image, but I just wish it wasn't *my* career that all
the risk taking seemed about.

■ ■ ■

*What is a Rule Breaker really like? Judging from these two accounts
of the same company, beauty truly does lie in the eye of the beholder. For
some a glamorous veneer is just that, while for others it is what they need
to fuel their ambitions. Reality is, of course, somewhere between these two
extremes.*

Playing the Game

Excel by Satisfying Existing Needs in Growing Markets

We all know the drill: First, study the customer with a high-powered microscope. Use market research, questionnaires, telephone interviews, and focus groups to get under their skin. Find out what makes them tick, what they want, and what they don't want. Then, take what is learned and reflect it in products or services planned to exceed all customer expectations. Make certain the products do not merely fulfill needs but add something extra, something that might even bring expressions of delight to the faces of jaded consumers. Produce the goods with processes that conform to total quality management (TQM), ISO 9000, and all other relevant best practices in factories laden with MRP, lean production, and flexible teams. Finally, put the results of these labors into the hands of customers through the efforts of a high-powered sales force, spurred on by charismatic marketing leadership and the best motivational cassettes available—and rewarded by a scientifically planned blend of bonus cash and incentive trips.

These practices combine into a formula for growth that has propelled the fortunes of many Fortune 500 companies. While *Rule Breakers create desires* in the marketplace, these companies, which we will call *Game Players, excel in satisfying them.* A Rule Breaker's genius lies in uncovering hidden needs or discovering new ones. Once these are out on the table and the features and benefits—the basis of competition—are apparent, a different type of company is required.

Hallmarks of the Game Player

Although economic growth spurts are frequently driven by innovative Rule Breakers, the foundation upon which the high-growth percentages build was usually laid by past Game Players. At any point in time, an economy is primarily the aggregate of transactions aimed at *satisfying existing needs*, which is the realm of the Game Player.

While Rule Breakers are often very attached to new ideas and the products that embody them, Game Players are more attached to what they can do with or get from these ideas. Rule Breakers compete to survive; Game Players are in business to win. Some Game Players seem to thrive on competition for its own sake. This may be a subtle distinction, but it is one that requires a very different corporate form to successfully bring it about.

Market-Driven, Not Vision-Driven

Game Players are truly market-driven businesses. They are quintessential marketeers. The art of product positioning is second nature to them. Game Players understand the value that good design adds to a product's appearance and utility. They have deep appreciation of advertising's ability to add value. Game Players have mastered the mysteries of branding and know how to create products through brand extension.

Game Players are companies that *act as though* their life or death depends on a few points of market share, although their reality is just the opposite. Most of the risks they take are small; however, losing one sale is unlikely to derail a career, and one new product flop will seldom destroy the company. Two good examples are Coca-Cola, who survived New Coke, and Procter & Gamble, who never made much money in the orange juice business. Because Game Players get feedback quickly from the marketplace, missteps are usually caught and corrected before serious damage is done.

Their corporate cultures fit the *work hard/play hard* mold. They have to be fast-paced, action-oriented places to work, because the environments in which they thrive are dynamic, growth markets. The worst thing that can happen in these situations is to stand still, and while resting on your laurels is a natural human tendency, it is one that Game Players combat daily.

Never Stand Still

Game Players live for quarterly results and celebrate each week's successes. They use many measures of performance and check the score cards regularly. F. Ross Johnson led Game Player RJR Nabisco for several exciting years. He was known for an approach to motivation that combined strong doses of both money and fear. He offered his management team some of the highest compensation packages in the food industry. In return, he expected high performance and an unwavering loyalty.

Group identity is important to Game Players. Team work and team spirit are vital in companies whose performance derives from many relatively small wins—no one player is all-important, but the business's growth is highly dependent on the cumulative impact of these minivictories. Sales volume is the key, and ongoing contests, clubs, and incentive trips are significant drivers of the frenzied activity that produces it. This frenzy, at least in the short haul, produces high morale. Employees are spirited and confident. Even in periods of adversity, the cup is usually always seen as being half full.

The Home of Multifunctionality

Organizationally, Game Players tolerate specialists, but broad-gauged employees and managers are most valued. Game Players work hard to achieve a balance between producing something and selling it, and between thinking and doing. At their best, they resolve conflicting internal functional demands in a way that delivers the most benefit to the customer. Early adopters of the matrix form of organization, Game Players frequently construct global organizational matrices that attempt to manage the multiple trade-offs necessary among the competing demands of customers and countries and of products and markets.

The focus of attention in these companies is not so much on earth-shaking new product development but on taking something good and running with it. This frequently leads to the creation of decentralized divisions and, as the market starts to mature, an ongoing mapping of the emerging customer segments in the marketplace onto their organization structures. Alfred Sloan used this approach to build General Motors. He had a specific car brand available for each socioeconomic strata of car buyer. With some updating, Sloan's method is still practiced by Honda, Nissan, and Toyota, and it also works for Procter & Gamble and Pepsi.

Competing by Being Different

Game Players compete with each other through *differentiation*. Some choose to pack their products with every bell and whistle imaginable; some offer customers broad and deep selections of goods; some, like Marriott and Nordstrom, focus their efforts on keeping their level of service a quantum higher than their competitors provide; and still others are the clear low-price leaders. The best Game Players make a clear decision about what their special competitive advantage is and build their organizations in a way that maximizes the resources supporting that advantage.

Reorganizations may be frequent, but most have a similar purpose: to surround the customer with employees of the Game Player attuned to meeting their most pressing needs of the moment. Some Game Players have become skilled at hedging their growth bets by operating in very diverse segments of a market or even in multiple industries. This approach, favored by conglomerators such as ITT, Litton, and Textron in the 1960s and 1970s, has fallen into disfavor. Regardless, a few businesses—led by General Electric—have made this management skill into a distinctive competence. GE operates, with significant business success, in areas as diverse as aircraft engines, light bulbs, railroad locomotives, and plastics. GE's experience also illustrates the limits of managing such diversity, as it has stumbled in markets further from its manufacturing base, such as broadcasting and financial services.

There's More Money in Imitation Than Innovation

Baruch College marketing professor Steven Schnaars has a unique perspective on Game Players. His academic research confirms a key lesson taught in the school of managerial hard knocks: Imitation is frequently a better way to make money than innovation. Schnaars feels that the benefits of innovation and being the first to enter an unproven market are vastly overrated, but the mystique surrounding entrepreneurial Rule Breakers is so strong that it has clouded balanced judgments about what works best when.

Schnaars buttresses his argument by citing research that shows that 84 percent of new consumer products (and about 70 percent of new industrial goods) are destined to fail. He also studied case examples of new product development across 28 industries. In two-thirds of these, a large company came along in the wake of an industry pioneer and was able to seize control of the market. Perhaps the American folklore about the heroic pioneer has made it difficult to publicly admit that those settlers who followed also made a contribution, and many did much better than those who came first.

Watch and Wait

Pizza Hut stood back while Dominos perfected the formula for a nationwide pizza delivery franchise network and then imitated that service. Pizza Hut's shift to home delivery happened when its management team realized that keeping up with its customers' preferences required a change in mind-set, not just a lowering of the fat content in its pepperoni. No longer was Pizza Hut a pizza restaurant, realized its managers. It needed to become a pizza distribution company.

Few remember the first seller of the handheld calculator (the Bowmar Instrument Corporation of Fort Wayne, Indiana). Most of us associate the product with companies such as Texas Instruments, Hewlett Packard, and almost every Japanese consumer electronics maker. Bowmar filed for bankruptcy protection a mere four years after it entered the market, but the "latecomers" all thrived.

The British airplane maker, DeHavilland, was the first to take the World War II–developed technology of jet propulsion and apply it to commercial aircraft. But a series of well-publicized crashes of its Comet airliners opened the market to Boeing and its late-developed 707 (and led to the mantra of many early commercial jet pilots, "If it ain't Boeing, I ain't going.").

The foregoing examples show that for many astute Game Players, being second is less of a matter of fate and slowness and more of a studied practice. They are the watchful waiters of the business world.

Professional Copycats

The first diet and decaffeinated colas were not products of Coke or Pepsi. These, and other soft drink innovations, were pioneered by less well known companies, such as Cott Beverage and Royal Crown Cola—a pattern that has been repeated with today's clear "New Age" beverages. A Coca-Cola executive once admitted that the company deliberately avoids taking the "high ground" in new product introductions. Instead, they let others move first, stand back and watch, and then apply Coke's well-honed marketing genius to figure out a way to take over the newly established beverage category.

When the imitating is completed, attention at Coke shifts to the real competition—Pepsi. This rival also follows the Game Player philosophy. A Pepsi executive once expressed the view that "stealing ideas" was one of the most honorable ways of making money. Leaving ethical considerations aside for a moment, this approach permits both soft drink juggernauts to compete on the battlefields they know well: national advertising, bottler promotions, and trade discounts.

Imitation is just as common among the stores that sell their soft drinks. Supermarket competitors watch each other like hawks. One chain offers home delivery, while another quickly follows suit and does its rival one better by accepting credit cards. Soon the crosstown competitor also honors plastic forms of payment, while quietly planning a double-coupon promotion to steal more market share. . . . Legendary Game Player (and sometimes Rule Maker) Sam Walton admitted in his autobiography that almost everything he has done was copied from somewhere else.

Fight to Make the Industry Bigger

This kind of tit-for-tat competitive behavior can bring quick benefits to the customers in Game Player–dominated industries. It also serves well the companies practicing it. Chapter 2's discussion of the new rules for growth noted that competition is seldom a zero-sum game. The old ethic of "I win, you lose" holds up in fewer and fewer markets. **Game Players, like Coke and Pepsi, thrive when their competitive actions serve to expand their markets, not to destroy each other.** They know, but seldom publicly express, that a worthy battle is one between equals, not between one who is domineering and one who is cowering. Game Players nourish themselves and grow through well-matched combat. Where would Avis be without Hertz, American Airlines without United, or the metroliner without the air-shuttle?

Create, Don't Complain:
The Louisiana-Pacific Approach to Growth

Louisiana-Pacific's approach to growth is another example of how the new rules are being practiced. This forest products company has dealt with the challenge to its future posed by increasing federal government restrictions on logging old-growth timber in a very creative way. Rather than whine about environmentalists and spotted owls, as some in its industry have done, this company let these regulations spur its creativity. With its traditional wood supply source threatened, Louisiana-Pacific's managers gave thought to finding profitable ways to use smaller trees, what the industry likes to call "waste species": aspens and the like. These can be shaved into wafers that when glued together under great pressure turn into a product very similar to more expensive plywood. This "waferwood" can also be combined with other types of "engineered lumber" to substitute for increasingly scarce wood used to support floors and roofs.

Buoyed by this success with waferboard, and their new core competence (the ability to make silk purses from sow's ears), Louisiana-Pacific's product designers discovered a way to convert discarded newspapers into a stronger, more soundproof wallboard. This development puts them in a position to steal large chunks of market share from the makers of traditional wall products, like sheetrock, or to be more accurate, it puts them in this position until the competition does them one better.

Inspired Imitation

Does Louisiana-Pacific's hotbed of creativity classify it as a Rule Breaker that just strayed from Silicon Valley into the forest? Not at all. This company prides itself on not spending a nickel on R&D! Admits a former chief executive, Harry Merlo, when asked for the source of its innovations, "We just copied." He visited a number of Canadian lumber producers who were already turning shaving from small trees into useful products. He copied creatively from them, figuring out ways to make the product at lower cost or with more features to appeal to the customer.

Merlo has an organization secret behind his inspired copying: He stays far away from the corporate culture of the downtown headquarters tall office buildings that is common in his industry. He minimizes the size of headquarters staff and keeps all of his key managers in the lumber milling plant whenever they are not traveling to get new ideas. He loves the mill and prefers to hire only operations-oriented staff who delight in being around wood-cutting machines. The result: a team of managers who know how to take an idea and run with it, that is, real Game Players.

Game Players consider benchmarking as a way of life. This long-practiced technique of ongoing monitoring of industry's best practices was elevated to an art form by Xerox, now a classic Game Player. (Remember, Xerox acquired rights to the Xerox technology; it didn't invent it. Likewise Microsoft's first product hit, DOS, was bought, not created.) If Rule Breakers are poor marks for consultants selling industry surveys and market research, Game Players welcome these services with open arms. They know how to make their investment in this kind of research pay for itself many times over.

Many Degrees of Freedom

Few Game Players are plagued with the "not-invented-here" curse. Instead, they are often able to productively seek counsel without becoming excessively dependent on any one advice giver. Game Players are in such a position of independence because they have *more tactical flexibility* than any other type of business grower. These options include the following:

- Bringing a "new" product into a market they already "own" (making use of their existing distribution system, advertising clout, and customer credibility to give a "free ride" to their latest hope for growth).

- Lowering their cost to produce a product, allowing them to lower its price and thus gain market share.

- Globalizing a product, taking something that has done well in one geographic region and adapting it to sell well in others.

- Holding back a good product until the market is most receptive to it. This strategy takes cunning, careful timing, and self-control—and an ability to closely monitor market trends.

- Offering near-blatent imitations of someone else's successful product, ensuring that the knock-offs offer better value to the customer (either a smaller price tag or more bells and whistles). This is how Compaq Computer first challenged IBM.

- Forgetting the special features all together, and just turning someone else's success (IBM's personal computers, for example) into a near-generic commodity (the many Asian PC clones).

- Using leap-ahead technologically. Louisiana-Pacific's innovations were confined to the millworks—they knew better than others how to design versatile, cost-effective wood-processing machines. They boast of making use of every part of the tree but its shadow. Back in Silicon Valley, pioneering companies that produced WordStar and VisiCalc found themselves left in the dust as Lotus, WordPerfect, and Microsoft seized the market with products attuned to the latest technology standards.

Although many tactics tempt skillful Game Players, what kind of corporate psyche can best take advantage of them?

Persona of the Game Player

Imagine that a company could be critiqued as if it were a person. What would be the persona of a successful Game Player? It would be a blend of the disciplined warrior and a talented athlete—a marine who once competed in the Olympics. The athlete would excel at games that require the player to beat an opponent, not the course: tennis, not golf; soccer, not the long-distance marathon. Game Players live to compete. While losing a battle here and there might sting, real pain for a Game Player would be when told that he or she could never compete again.

Friendly extroverts.   Game Player–like people tend to judge themselves and their successes in relation to others. They want to belong, to be liked, and to please. If the Rule Breaker can be compared to the oldest child in a single-parent household, then Game Players are middle kids in families where "father knows best." They tend to be extroverted and come alive in their relationships, and their decisions are made by talking things over with others.

Getting with the program.   Game Players are strong and tough, but they're not rebels. They identify easily with authority figures. Rules are things that make Game Players' lives easier, not obstacles to go around. Wanting to avoid ambiguity, they are clear about expectations, the goal, the game plan, and the rewards. Then they follow the plan; they get with the program and are relatively easy to incentivize.

Easy innovators.   Because Game Players like new techniques, they are receptive to the ideas and innovations of others. Game Players don't have to make something to enjoy it. They are early adopters of new technology, and they upgrade their software frequently.

Trend followers.   They also try hard to walk their talk. When they can't, at least the talk is current. They are global thinkers, and words like empowerment, delegation, and participation roll easily from the lips of Game Players.

Team players.   At times they may be called militaristic, but this is only partially true. Game Players embrace the team spirit, the camaraderie of a platoon in the field, but they have little patience with the bureaucratic "mickey mouse" that too frequently defines peacetime armies. Game Players make excellent teammates. The best have really grasped the idea that the victory belongs to the group; to win as an individual means to be part of a winning team. Game Players are seldom hung up over pride of authorship. Loyalty is important. At times they may be indifferent or even hostile to their chief executive; the real ties that bind Game Players to the company are the personal ones they have with their close colleagues.

Flexible.   Game players show a lot of flexibility. They are sometimes accused of bending too much with the wind, leaving their colleagues asking, "Just where do you really stand?"

Strengths of the Game Player

Organizations of Game Players have many distinct advantages. Game Players take an I^2 approach to growth (in other words, they are great imitators and great improvers). They excel at winning the battle for market share in the trenches of marketing warfare, gaining one inch (or 0.1 percent market share) at a time.

Operating in Perpetual Overdrive

Game Players win these battles with more than a sales force in perpetual overdrive. Just consider the bra market, for example. When the Sara Lee Corporation introduced its trendy Wonderbra into trial markets, rival apparel maker, VF Corporation, stayed on the sidelines until it was certain the innovative design was a hit. Then VF moved like lightning. Its state-of-the-art distribution system put VF's version of Wonderbra into stores across America almost half a year ahead of Sara Lee's "original." VF has its own special version of the computerized automatic reordering systems that the supermarket industry is moving toward. Its computers talk directly to Wal-Mart's and Penney's. Orders are taken without the use of paper or the time-lag–inducing intervention of salesforces and purchasing departments. VF also makes Lee and Wrangler jeans, and playing the game this way has allowed it to sell more of these than Levi-Strauss, the inventor of denim pants.

For all the tough, macho talk heard around Game Players, many actually take the least risky path to growth. VF has turned the apparel business from an art into a science. By allowing others to take the lead, VF has been able to avoid the missteps endemic in the fickle business of fashion. Sidestepping the financial gyrations that plague the industry, VF has managed to grow both sales and profits at almost 20 percent a year. Has your company ever moved as fast as VF to score an end run around a competitor?

Lines in the Sand

Game Players are good at drawing lines in the sand. They set ambitious performance targets and more often than not find a way to meet them. At MCI brash, young managers like to boast of leveraging the weight of their opponent against itself. AT&T may be six times the size of MCI, but it has been repeatedly forced to react to MCI's marketing initiatives.

MCI's dedication to the game-playing ethic enabled it to "think outside the box," to imitate the competitive strategies of other Game Players rather than be trapped by the prevailing mentality of the old telephone industry. MCI borrowed from consumer products companies the tactics of branding and brand extension to add sizzle to what had over years become a commodity: long-distance calls. The result was a stream of marketing coups, such as Friends & Family, Friends Around the World, and "1-800-COLLECT," all designed to attract AT&T's customers and put the former long-distance monopolist in an ongoing reactive mode.

Clear Line of Sight to Each Customer

Game Players have a real genius at keeping their organization in sync with the desires of their customers. At one point, Xerox kept all its headquarters executives aligned with the ebb and flow of customer needs by designating each, in turn, as officer of the day. That individual would be expected to answer all customer complaint calls that came to corporate headquarters that day, but the impressions gained hearing, first hand, customer needs and problems had longer impact than that one day every month or so of phone duty. Most Xerox senior managers kept what they heard in mind during the time they spent on their ongoing responsibilities.

To ensure that the executive had a chance to understand at least one customer's needs in greater depth, many of Xerox's major accounts were also "double-teamed." In addition to the account management provided by someone from the marketing department, another executive—with regular responsibilities in another functional area such as manufacturing or personnel—would meet regularly with the customer and jointly plot selling strategies. How clear of a line of sight do you have to your customers? How much direct customer contact do your senior executives have?

Weaknesses of the Game Player

At their best, Game Players seem to be doing everything right, but they are prone to a number of weaknesses, problems that if left unchecked will severely limit their abilities to keep growing with their markets. The full-speed-ahead, damn-the-torpedos attitude of some Game Players is bold and heroic. Their managers all share a theory about how best to compete; most of their attention goes to managing the business within the confines of this theory.

Tunnel Vision

However, a very sharp focus on what works well today can lead to tunnel vision, and it can keep the corporate "radar scopes" attuned to only events affecting the short and medium term. **Game Players that miss the long-term dynamics of their markets—demographic shifts, technological discontinuities, globalization, and the like—may find themselves with an increasing share of a shrinking market.** Eventually, something has to give, usually the Game Player's profit margins.

Some Game Players discount the value of long-range planning. They feel the need to move so quickly when a new product reaches the market that there is little point to developing detailed plans that will only be discarded later on. At Compaq Computer, a Game Player that rebounded from a series of planning missteps, a complex computer simulation model is now used to plan the exact timing, features, and pricing of each new product introduction. The model is an industrial strength equivalent of the popular game program SimCity. It is a vital necessity in a market that Compaq manager Kevin Bohren describes as one where once every new product could expect six months of uniqueness. Now, he laments, *a long weekend in the sun* is the best for which a new PC can hope.

The Winging It Mentality

Game Players are prone to being seduced by growth. Ever-increasing sales statistics can create dangerously misleading expectations. The numbers are frequently misinterpreted as implying, "All we have to do is keep working hard, and growth will go on forever." Many "for-the-time-being" growth companies are hotbeds of frenetic activity, leading to a "let's wing it" approach to dealing with problems, applying bandages when stronger medicine may be necessary.

When sales targets and production volume become the key driver of a business, it is easy to lose sight of quality and cost. The selling activity, especially, can become a dangerous end into itself. All the company's creative efforts may be directed to inducing customers to buy, through special deals, rebates, and prizes. These usually mirror an impressive array of sales incentives and rewards used internally to encourage the sales force to sell. In the short range, overemphasis on these artificial stimulants can lead to customers buying what they don't need more than what they do need or both, often at the wrong time. Eventually a backlash is created, and customers look elsewhere.

Louisiana-Pacific's rapid growth stumbled in the wake of lawsuits from customers who charged that some of its innovative wood products were being sold for purposes beyond what they were capable. When used as outdoor siding, some of these products had difficulty resisting humidity. Homeowners complained that the boards rotted and cracked, occasionally even sprouting mushrooms. Concerns such as these, and fears that Harry Merlo was playing the growth game too hard, eventually led Louisiana-Pacific's board of directors to request his resignation.

Teaching Customers the Wrong Lessons

In some industries the customers have reacted in logical but harmful ways to these cascades of buying incentives. In food retailing, for example, the practice of "forward buying" has emerged to respond to the food manufacturer's periodic price discounts and special merchandise deals. Many retailers only buy certain products when they are on sale, buying in quantities much larger than they can sell during the period of the price promotion. The extra stock is either stored in expensive warehouse facilities, for sales to consumers at a later date, or sold to a "shadow" industry of "diverters" that has emerged. Diverters are Specialists who buy surplus products from a retailer, store them, and later put them back on the market after the manufacturer's special sale or promotion has ended.

The net results of all this game playing are uneven production runs for manufacturers, profits for middlemen, and higher prices for consumers. This is the system that some rule-breaking, information systems–armed food retailers are working hard to reform. Equivalent forms of market perversion occur in other growth industries, the well-known "gray markets" for blue jeans and personal computers, for example.

Dangerous Distractions

Some companies try to hedge against the profitability swings common in Game Player markets by conglomeratization, *diversifying* to create a corporation with a number of marginally related businesses—the idea being that when one market turns down, others will be buoyant, and the company as a whole will do well. This may be a nice theory, but it is one that is difficult to pull off. Eventually all the diversity this approach creates requires the imposition of layers on layers of financial controls. Financial measures of performance, while important, are by necessity abstractions. Overreliance on them reduces the number of corporate decision makers with direct customer contact and an intuitive feel for the marketplace, or factory floor.

Another dangerous hedge for many Game Players is *backward integration*—using profits generated by a growing business to purchase a key supplier. This is an attractive-sounding management dogma: Take advantage of a secure source of raw materials and profit by being your own supplier. Unfortunately, the need to focus on managing the economics of the newly acquired supplier can easily take the company's eyes off the needs of its real customers. Attention is directed at selling what the supplier likes to make (to keep these newly bought plants busy earning money to justify investment in them), not on keeping current on what the external customer wants. Companies as dissimilar as General Motors and A&P have suffered the consequences of this kind of rearview mirror management.

Losing the Edge

The above-mentioned distractions can turn Game Players into what Danny Miller, a Canadian business school professor, calls drifters. These are companies that give such great priority to appeal based on image that the package they sell becomes more important than what is inside. Their concern for *maximizing sizzle* overwhelms attention to the substance that customers actually value.

Mediocre products proliferate in Game Players with this affliction. Plans to "blanket the market" or create a full line of products are driven—just under the surface—by a need to maximize internal career opportunities. Brand distinctions become meaningless and confusing. Eventually, strategic focus is lost and managers—now hopelessly out of real touch with their customers—resort to running the business solely "by the numbers."

When a business loses its focus, heated conflicts—always present within Game Players—revolve more around internal squabbles and less about conflicting views of market trends. *Dividing the pie becomes more important than growing it.* Winning a department political contest offers more rewards than besting a marketplace competitor. An accurate organization chart of such a troubled Game Player will group employees into baronies and fiefdoms, not business units and divisions. How strong are the turf divisions within your company?

Drift has plagued once-stellar Game Players such as General Motors and Sears. In a 30-year period, GM's number of car models increased sevenfold, but many of the models were so alike that customers fled to more market-attuned Game Players like Toyota and Ford. Sears meandered from an integrated retail store and catalog business into an array of brokerage, insurance, specialty retail, home repair, and even management consulting enterprises. Both companies are now in the long process of recovery—and offer excellent examples of sins to avoid.

Keep an Eye on Tomorrow's Customer

The best Game Players hang on to the energizing attributes of competitiveness, but they keep that behavior focused outside the organization. Effective Game Players minimize incentives for turf building and align manager's pay with market share acquisition, not only sales increases. A willingness to keep attention on the market and the competition, shared among all the company's managers, is the only way to avoid destructive factionalism.

Some Game Players maintain the discipline to avoid drift but fall into the trap of complacency. At this point, many begin to lose their competitive edge when they willingly settle for less than their fair share of a market. Attention shifts from today's battles to yesterday's victories. Expectations of future growth are diminished—regardless of how much potential awaits them in the marketplace. Complacent Game Players are driven more by enrichment than expansion. Eventually they become cannon fodder for a more aggressive Game Player or a victim of a rule-breaking upstart competitor.

Misusing Outside Advice

Drift, misguided diversification, complacency, and tunnel vision are all signs of a company whose key managers have lost sight of their internal compass. These are occupational hazards of companies whose genius involves flexibility and cunning. The company's management advisers may have a clue something is wrong when the problems brought to them are more about "what should we do" rather than "how should we do it." Both are valid concerns, but the consulting assignments keyed to solve the former can lead to a dangerous dependence on outside counsel.

Destructive trends like these are hard to detect from inside the company. At times a vigilant board of directors will notice signs of these problems before extensive damage is done, but often the burden falls on outsiders who are often in the best position to observe the problems and help develop remedies. However, this requires a measure of ethical discipline on the part of the advisers, because an adrift Game Player can provide extensive repeat business for a consultant unwilling to encourage the client to face reality.

Crossing the Line

Another type of ethical concern frequently emerges in markets where Game Players compete. Whenever a business strategy is built—at least in part—on imitation, moral and legal issues are present. At some point, benchmarking and reverse engineering turn into industrial espionage. Patent and trade secret infringement litigation have also led into legal quagmires. Many Rule Breakers have felt harmed by the imitations of aggressive, latecoming Game Players. Many find ways to successfully fight off the imitator: Polaroid defeated Kodak's attempts to move into instant photography, Soho Natural Soda kept beverage giant Anheuser-Busch from the speciality seltzer market, and tiny Black Mountain Arts won a number of court battles against Hallmark's look-alike greeting cards.

The remedy is that successful Game Playing requires an ethical as well as a strategic compass. According to Baruch College's Professor Schnaars, the key is to avoid copying *too closely*, especially when an industry giant is using its muscle to crush a weaker competitor. Remember the New Rules of Competition: Victory seldom requires vanquishing an opponent. Imitation succeeds best when accompanied by a measure of original innovation. Licensing, joint ventures, and outright acquisition are tools well used by the best Game Players.

Where Game Players Thrive

From a financial perspective, Game Players tend to be profitable businesses, and the best tend to grow their margins year, after year, after year. Which, compared with the financial profile of many Rule Breakers, are significant accomplishments. Both assets and working capital needs rise when sales increase, but this is money that can usually be easily raised. When the cost to produce each product diminishes as more are sold—as it should in a well-managed Game Player—profit growth is almost automatic, and funds are easily available to expand the business. Rapid growth causes some of these companies to periodically run low on cash, but skillful financial management keeps this from endangering the business.

Savor the Rough and Tumble

Game Players thrive in go-go, rapid growth markets. The rougher and more turbulent the environment, the better. Game Player markets tend to be growing faster than the economy as a whole but not at the triple or greater pace common in industries populated with Rule Breakers.

Game Players' natural markets have the potential to sustain this pace of growth for a number of years, but it is relatively easy for competitors to enter, and market share stability is often more of a hope than a reality. The stronger the competition, the more pleased are many Game Players. For example, consider Publix Super Markets, a largely employee-owned business that will be one of the last Game Players to ever succumb to complacency. This Florida-based chain recently noticed population growth rates slowing in its home market. Running out of locations to allow it to maintain a pace of opening a new store a week, management looked northward.

The southeastern states of Georgia and South Carolina are growing by attracting new industries and migrants. They are also served by some of the nation's most aggressively managed food retailers: Food Lion, Kroger, and Wal-Mart. No problem, felt Publix's executive team. Their strong confidence in a well-honed game plan of treating employees exceptionally well to encourage their returning the favor in their treatment of customers was unshakeable. Publix managers believe that if they competently execute this approach, then market share gains will follow. So certain is Publix of its ability to capture a hefty share of the southeast that it imitates the blitz approach of General Norman Schwarzkopf: investing nearly a billion dollars to open over 100 new stores—all in less than two years.

Sustaining Growth

As long as a market is big and volatile enough for a newcomer to jump in and do well, it is a good place for a Game Player. A market can turn treacherous, though, when things start to quiet down. That's when possibilities become more limited and when growing by eating a competitor's lunch becomes less nourishing than it once did.

As markets mature, Game Players frequently restructure their efforts to give them sharper focus. Ralston Purina's chief executive, William Stiritz, keeps a wooden sculpture of a just barely balanced tightrope walker in his Checkerboard Square office. It serves as a reminder of the need to continually shift weight around when trying to move forward in difficult circumstances. Stiritz spun off his Ralston cereals and Beech-Nut baby food businesses, leaving him freer to concentrate the company's marketing talents on Purina pet foods and Eveready batteries.

The secret to sustaining a Game Players' growth is rapid adaptation of its outward form to changes in the market, while never deviating from the core philosophy upon which the business was built.

Image Can Be Very Important

Joseph Galli, a manager at Black & Decker, acted on this principle when he took charge of the company's power tool division. Its highest margin products, the drills sold to professional carpenters, had been battered in the marketplace for many years by a Japanese competitor. Image was a big part of the problem. The Black & Decker name had become associated with tools for do-it-yourselfers and sold in mass marketers' stores, such as K-Mart. Regardless of product quality, it was the last thing a building professional wanted to be seen carrying to the job site.

What was Game Player Galli's solution? It was a new color (yellow), a new brand name (DeWalt), and a massive marketing program. A fictitious "DeWalt Industrial Power Tool Co." was created, complete with its own 800 number, service vehicles, and marketing staff. Finally, the new product line was sold only through stores and distributors that professional builders respected.

These innovations have resulted in a major market share gain, but they were not created out of whole cloth. Yellow is a color that signifies caution and safety in industrial settings; DeWalt was the name of a nearly defunct brand that Black & Decker acquired many years ago. Regardless of coloration and nameplate, the tools were as identical to the existing Black & Decker professional line as a Mercury Sable is to a Ford Taurus. However, most important to a Game Player in a maturing market, all the profits ultimately go to the same place.

Marriott's Formula for Growth

Marriott, one of the world's largest hotel operators, has mastered a similar approach. Marriott has the "watchful waiting" approach down to an exact science, letting others take the lead (and the risk) with new lodging concepts. Then, when an idea has won market acceptance, Marriott moves in with the strength of a ten-ton gorilla. Through a combination of imitation and acquisition, Marriott has properties that reflect the broad range of market segments that have emerged in the hospitality business: Fairfield Inns for the budget traveler, Courtyard for the business person, Residence Inns for the multiweek stayers, and Marriott's for the full-service customer. Soon after all-suite hotels became popular, Marriott rolled out its version.

Marriott's core philosophy revolves around the provision of a consistent high level of service, over a broad range of price points and market segments. This is driven by a rare form of organization. It is one that balances a headquarters staffed with analytic types skillful at identifying emerging markets and a field-operating organization with a disciplined approach to service that is unrivaled. Marriott is a Game Player exceptionally well equipped to roll with the punches.

What's next? When your business grows to the profitable point where all overnight stays are at guest-pampering Ritz-Carlton's, don't be too surprised to find the concierge receiving a paycheck from Marriott and Bill Marriott's portrait hanging next to Cesar Ritz's. Good Game Players are never too proud to associate with others' successes.

What Is It Like Working for a Game Player?

This is the BEST place in the world to work.

You know you are working in the right place when you're a night owl but you still find yourself rushing to get out of bed each weekday morning. Listen to this salesman, a person whose personality seems to be a good match for the profile of the typical Game Player.

■ ■ ■

I love this place.

In college I played basketball. I'm a little old for fast breaks now, but the action on my job is closer to life on the court than I ever thought business could be.

Are we competitive? Is the pope catholic? Competition flows through our veins.

Just last week the national accounts manager arrived early one morning. It was a rainy, muddy kind of day. He replaced every door mat in the front lobby with ones he had custom-made. They all had our number-one competitor's logo printed on them. I tell you, it sure felt good to wipe my dirty shoes all over that emblem.

The incentives programs here are first-rate! They cover the gamut, everything from a reserved parking space right outside the front door (with your name on the sign next to it) for the month's highest sales to free cars and trips.

I live to make trip. My wife lives for us to make trip. Even our kids want me to make trip. Everyone who makes sales quota goes. Last year it was Palm Springs, this year it is Disneyworld, and rumor has it that if we go like gangbusters next year, the company's springing for Maui.

Why not? We're the best.

Talk about a motivation-rich environment: weekly contests, monthly contests, beat the other division contests, beat ourselves

| Game Player | contests. There are teamwork posters in the john,

screen savers with Lombardi quotes (new ones each week), broadcast voicemails daily from the division manager, and even letters and videotapes sent home and a library of motivational tapes for the car.

You just gotta love it. The pace here keeps me "up" all the time. I've never had trouble getting out of bed since I took this job.

I especially like the clear goals we have. I always know what I'm supposed to do—and how well I'm doing.

I also like the emphasis on developing broad-minded employees. Everyone spends some time on rotation through all the functional departments. I may work in sales, but I've got some idea how the people in accounting think. I've also done my time in the factory, and I know just who to call if a customer has a problem with a delivery date or broken part.

I guess I've always been an optimistic type. Every glass I see is always at least half full.

Our CEO has said we will be at least first or second in every market we serve—or we'll get out. That's the kind of challenge I enjoy. That's the kind of homebase I want for my career.

This is the WORST place in the world to work.

For everyone who sees a glass half full, there's someone willing to call it half empty. That's the position the following manufacturing manager seems to be taking about his job at the same Game Player the previous sales rep works at.

■ ■ ■

I've got no idea why I'm here. I feel like I stumbled into fantasy land and haven't found the right exit door.

Sometimes this company seems like a day care-facility for ex-jocks. I never expected to see such juvenile behavior in a Fortune 500 company. Just last week the national accounts manager arrived early

one morning. It was a rainy, muddy kind of day. He   **Game Player**
replaced every door mat in the front lobby with ones
he had custom-made. They all had our number-one competitor's logo
printed on them. Could you imagine a more ridiculous prank?

If the manager was really concerned about taking orders away from
Brand X, he would spend more time in our plant and figure out why
quality has slipped so much.

And then there're the motivational speeches. Maybe Anthony
Robbins has something useful to offer Bill Clinton, but I think I've
been "Robbined" and "Zig Zeiglerized" one time too many. After a
while, all this self-improvement stuff starts to sound the same—and it
all seems directed at putting the burden of the company's problems on
the troops, not on the generals where it belongs.

I don't believe all the frenzied activity here: weekly contests,
monthly reports, quarterly contests, and on and on. There's never time
to step back, get some perspective, and recharge.

Corporate culture says to treat every day as if it were a brand new
day—no management by rearview mirror. My view is that this is a
mind-set that condemns us to repeat the mistakes of our past.

There's no subtlety here. Everything is either black or white. We
all talk about doing "out-of-the-box" thinking, but the reality is we
reject any ideas that don't support what we're already doing.

I'm just not the type to throw caution to the wind. Last year I read
Peter Schwartz's great book about scenario planning: the *Art of the
Long View*. My colleagues gave the book a lot of lip service, but when I
tried to put forward some alternative views of our future, nobody really
wanted to listen. Considering anything but the rosiest scenario is a
heresy here.

We're also losing our focus, our sense of professionalism.
Everybody is assigned to some sort of cross-functional rotation—
musical chairs, I call it. If this keeps up, every department will be full
of tourists, and we'll become a company of amateurs.

There's no such thing as quiet time to think. I've never seen so many
otherwise mature adults roaming the halls, looking for signs of approval.

Game Player   I might as well take my office door off its hinges, nobody seems to notice when it's closed anyway.

This company may be a paragon of excellence today, but I just don't expect it to stay on top over the long haul. Of course, by then I'll be long gone.

Making the Rules

*Dominate the Market by
Controlling Its Standards*

Some companies are just *too* good. Maybe it was a matter of luck, being in the right place at the right time. Perhaps they were Rule Breakers whose innovativeness captivated their customers—and frightened off all competitors, or they were Game Players so effective at doing all the right things, just the right way, that they came to "own" their industry. Let's call these businesses Rule Makers. They set the standards for their markets. At times it seems an entire industry revolves around them. Rule Makers are at the center of an intricate business network rich in mutual dependencies. When they prosper, others—even some head-to-head competitors—thrive, but when they stumble, others collapse. These interrelationships are simultaneously resented and appreciated by their competitors. Rule Makers' savviest rivals may grumble, but they are also aware that Rule Makers define the turf on which mutual profitability and growth depend. Because of their control, Rule Makers are watched like hawks.

Walt Disney, McKinsey in management consulting, Merck in pharmaceuticals, and Microsoft in software, are all Rule Makers. Wal-Mart occupies this position today in mass market retailing. Intel's microprocessor chips run eight out of every ten PCs sold throughout the world, allowing this Silicon Valley giant to call many of the shots in this critical industry.

Although the view from the top of the marketplace is glorious to behold, staying at the pinnacle of a slippery slope is a challenge for even the best. For example, IBM and Pan American World Airways were once Rule Makers. In the first half of this century, the top Rule Makers included then-elite companies, such as A&P Supermarkets, Pennsylvania Railroad (known as "the standard railroad of the world"), United States Steel, and Western Union. The luxury travel industry was dominated by the names Cunard, Pullman, and Wagon-Lits. The U.S. telecommunications business was defined by three words: The Bell System. The largest package mover—the Railway Express Agency—did not own a single airplane. All these companies—both contemporary and those now relics of business history—have many common characteristics, and as with Rule Breakers and Game Players, they share a special set of strengths and weaknesses, as well as a unique persona. Rule Makers commonly have a *very strong and sometimes dominant competitive position* in the markets they serve.

Hallmarks of a Rule Maker

Although some Rule Makers, like Microsoft, emerge at an industry's birth and grow with the market, most find it too difficult to get their hands around the chaotic uncertainty accompanying most embryonic situations. They usually wait until technologies and buying preferences settle down, then—like some Game Players—they make their move. IBM was not the first computer maker. It watched and bode its time while Sperry Rand's UNIVAC machine pioneered a new market. K-Mart set up a national chain of discount stores before Wal-Mart, and Disney was not the first movie maker or amusement park operator.

A Rule Maker's Life Cycle

Rule Makers can emerge at any point in an industry's life cycle, but they are usually most profitable in the late growth or early mature stages. This phase is when wise investments usually provide a generous payoff, cash flows most easily, and customer requirements are clearly visible. Eventually marketplaces mature or even start to show early signs of aging, customer needs begin to fragment, the pace of innovation slows, and the Rule Maker with the one-size-fits-all product line finds its customer base shrinking.

Rule Makers have had a variety of responses to this inevitable decline. Some exit their position of dominance with a bang; others exit with a whimper. Pan American Airways, Pennsylvania Railroad, and Western Union experienced bankruptcies. A&P Supermarkets and Cunard remained in their industries but became focused niche players rather than dominating juggernauts. A handful, such as AT&T and U.S. Steel, adapted to the new order and found other paths to growth.

To really understand the dynamics of the second half of a Rule Maker's life cycle, set aside this book for a few hours and look over the ideas Edward Gibbon wrote in 1776 in his famous *The History of the Decline and Fall of the Roman Empire.* This is a great story of how pressures from without combine with decay from within to crumble a once mighty empire. *The Decline and Fall* is required reading for all aspiring Rule Makers.

Staying on Top

Ruler Makers have a strong, common strategic orientation: stay on top. They organize most of their resources and talents in ways that protect the strong competitive position in which they find themselves. Rule Makers are like a squad of soldiers in combat who have managed to seize the higher ground. While some may have aspirations to repeat their triumph on an even more challenging hilltop, most quickly realize their primary mission is to protect this hard-won gain from other challengers. Seasoned combat veterans also appreciate that, ironically, the higher the summit they've seized, the harder it will be to descend and move on to a new mountain top. When atop one peak, they have to travel farther than their rivals in the valley below to reach another. The pleasant view from where they sit may also contribute to wanting to dig in where they are. Regardless, this high ground still requires defense.

A Strategy Based on Control

Rule Makers excel at near-total market control. They keenly appreciate the essentials of protecting a strong position, and their favorable economics gives them a variety of options; their visibility mandates they not abuse their position of strength. Rule Makers' strategies tend to involve some form of *control*. Most give near-obsessive attention to controlling both their *outer* and their *inner* worlds. Rule Makers work hard to control the business environment in several ways.

Standard Setters

Rule Makers set standards for their industry—often, but not always, a result of having triumphed in a war for market share. They may provide a "price umbrella" under which their competitors operate and thrive, as long as they do not drastically lower their price. Rule Makers may operate in ways that lead their customers and even their competitors to become dependent on them.

An industry with standards is not necessarily a bad place. Standards provide a baseline from which many types of competitors can emerge. It is hard to be a Game Player when the rules of play have yet to be established, because standards can be a precondition for growth. Specialists thrive in markets with a degree of stability.

It is hard, though, to be a Game Player in a Rule Maker–driven industry and not feel at least a tinge of jealous resentment at what seems to be a disproportionate share of the rewards going to the setter of the ground rules. In some situations, the boundary between just rewards and unfair competition is a very fine line. This boundary requires continual policing and self-regulation, lest its demarcation become the job of the courts and regulators.

Always Alert

Like Game Players, Rule Makers are heavy users of market research and benchmarking. Like Rule Breakers, they devote hefty percentages of their sales to R&D. Unlike other businesses, Rule Makers aggressively hone these practices as an essential part of their overall strategy of market control.

Although seldom publicly admitted to, a Rule Maker's greatest fear is that of being overtaken. For them, fundamental research is done not so much to destabilize the basis of competition (why destabilize something that you make money dominating?) but to keep ahead of anyone else who may try to break the rules. Their R&D strategies, despite their megabudgets, are fundamentally driven more by defensive, not offensive, aims. Likewise, the goal behind their extensive use of market research is not so much staying attuned to current customer requirements—a topic their sales force is usually well wired into—but *anticipating new customer needs*. This provides them with the lead time necessary to create new products and services before more short-term oriented, game-playing competitors have an opportunity to wean away customers.

Playing the Game Several Moves in Advance

Like master chess players, Rule Makers are skilled in thinking about the future and plan their actions several moves in advance. They develop contingency plans and alternative scenarios to help anticipate and prepare for eventualities outside their immediate control. Rule Makers, more than the other types of growth companies, are adept at following the advice of the popular business professors Gary Hamel and C. K. Prahalad. Hamel and Prahalad implore companies to set stretch goals based on an exhaustive analysis of trends and technologies. Their favorite strategic objective is "global preemption," a decade-long cultivation of core competences that—if done well—results in unquestioned worldwide market leadership. A worthy goal? Absolutely—*as long as* your company has the lead time, resources, and patience of a Rule Maker to stay focused on the future.

Where Does All the Money Come From?
The Flywheel Effect

How do Rule Makers pay for all this defense and foresight? They pay for it with high profit margins, of course. Rule Makers tend to be profit as well as product leaders. The most prosperous of them take good advantage of **the flywheel effect—that is, once a wheel is moving rapidly, it takes more energy to slow it down than to speed it up.**

The best kind of market to be in—if you like profit maximization along with growth—is one that ignores the law of diminishing returns. In some industries, the more you produce, the less money you make, which may seem counter intuitive and depressing, but it is true. Just ask any American farmer; look at what happens to gasoline prices when a major new oil field is discovered. (This is why the best path to growth for commodity-oriented companies is not that of the Rule Maker.)

Some industries, sometimes called "network" markets, operate under very different rules, where increases in supply stimulate even greater increases in demand. Telephone services and computer software are network markets. The value of these services or products increases as more people use them—what's the point in having a picture phone if few of the people you communicate with also have them, or why have a cutting-edge word processor whose files can't be read by anyone else? When the number of users of products like these gets beyond a certain critical mass, a snowball effect ensues, and more and more products are bought. In the software market, most of the costs are related to developing the program and establishing its reputation. If those tasks are done well, a nearly free ride results: additional copies of software cost very little to produce. Success leads to greater success, larger market share, and higher margins.

Microsoft, the Power of Market Control

Foresight and vision distinguish a merely high-performing Game Player from an obscenely profitable Rule Maker. If Microsoft's aspirations were limited to Game Playing, its business would still be limited to making the latest version of the operating system (once called DOS) for IBM personal computers. This was the product that started Microsoft's flywheel. What kept the flywheel accelerating was Microsoft's unwillingness to completely link its fortunes to a Rule Maker (IBM), one well admired but, by then, in the downward slope of its life cycle. Microsoft teamed with another IBM supplier and aspiring Rule Maker, Intel, to encourage the emergence of the PC *clone* industry. These clones—including Compaq and Dell in Texas and a host of Asian-based imitators—now dominate the personal computer industry, and they all use Microsoft's operating system software.

The Bear-Hug Approach to Controlling Market Growth

As the clone industry grew, Microsoft emerged as a key Rule Maker, one that learned an extremely valuable lesson: how to expand a market while still keeping in control. It also perfected the "bear-hug" approach to keeping rivals in check. The closest rival to Microsoft's popular Windows software is Apple Computer's Macintoshes. When Windows was introduced,

Apple even sued Microsoft for copying too closely the look and feel of its own software. Apple, a one-time Rule Breaker, is in an uneasy strategic position regarding Microsoft. It must deal gingerly with its rival because it is caught in the web of mutual dependencies that Rule Makers are skilled at weaving. Although Apple makes a type of software, an operating system, that competes with Microsoft's Windows, this type alone is not sufficient to make a computer useful. To draft letters or produce spreadsheets, a second category—dubbed "applications" software—is required, and much to Apple's chagrin, more than half the word-processing software used on its Macintoshes is made by Microsoft. Almost 90 percent of the spreadsheets created on Macs were made with Microsoft's Excel product.

Even IBM, one-time dominator of everything related to computers, has felt Microsoft's bear hug. These companies once paired to develop a new computer-operating software, called OS/2, but Microsoft backed out of this venture when it became clear that cutting edge product development is best done alone. Other competitors were also left dangling, companies that invested heavily in new software for OS/2, creating another opportunity for Microsoft to leap ahead in their segment of the industry. The lesson learned is that competing with your *customers'* suppliers is a tricky business, but it is one in which Rule Makers excel. They are also clever at something even more difficult: controlling the future.

Periodic Self-Obsolescence

The shrewdest moves Rule Makers make are those that obsolete themselves on an ongoing basis. Microsoft started as a supplier of the operating system software for IBM personal computers. After this system (DOS) became an industry standard, they invented its replacement, Windows, which mimicked some graphic features of the second-most popular system software, Macintosh's. Ultimately, to keep up with computer users' needs for easy networking, Microsoft supplanted Windows with Windows 95, and so on.

Microsoft did not invent the original DOS product. It was obtained by acquisition early in the company's history—a great way to leapfrog Rule Breakers who at times are too in love with their creations to exploit them fully. Some software industry observers have noted that Microsoft has cleverly managed to allow the rest of the industry to unwittingly serve as its R&D lab.

Control-Driven Diversification

When business presentation software became a hot category, Microsoft acquired the pioneering product Powerpoint rather than becoming vulnerable by allowing a gap in its product line. As personal financial planning took off, Microsoft first tried to develop and market its own software, with lackluster results. When the importance of this product in the marketplace became clear, not just as a stand-alone offering but as a gateway to providing banking and other financial services over computer networks, Microsoft exhibited quick willingness to abandon its homegrown software and attempted to purchase Quicken, the industry leader. These examples show that prejudice against products "not invented here" is seldom exhibited in Rule Makers during their periods of greatest growth.

While Microsoft's acquisitions were worthy stand-alone products, each was also a key component of this Rule Maker's grand strategy: directing the development of future markets in ways most favorable to itself.

Finding Future Choke Points

Like some of the star Rule Breakers, Microsoft has an ample supply of "the vision thing." **Visions that grow businesses are rooted in reality. At their core is a belief about what customers will want and an illusion-free appreciation of what the business is good at delivering.** Microsoft is a rule-making software company. Because Microsoft's vision is based on a keen understanding of the forces driving its industry's future, it knows that the marketplace has a near-insatiable appetite for its products. The progress of some industries is driven by demographics (the housing business, for example), while others are more dependent on regulatory change (telephone and electric power companies). The information business is still a creature of its technologies, and controlling its course requires insight into the dynamics of the scientific principles driving it.

For an information technology company, vision crafting means appreciating something called Moore's Law. When the math surrounding it is stripped away, it tells a simple story: Computing and communications technologies related to computing keep getting cheaper. The performance of semiconductors doubles every year and half. Their price, however, stays the same. Nice set of factoids, but for Bill Gates to make money from Moore's Law, he has to play out its implications. Here's where the smarts and foresight come in. In his strategic planning sessions, Gates and his lieutenants use scenarios based on ideas such as the following: Suppose computing (or communicating) was completely free. What uses would people make of it? How should Microsoft position itself to benefit the most from these uses?

Unlike Rule Breakers, too often very emotional participants in a love affair with their products or technologies, Rule Makers like Microsoft are able to use their foresight more coldly. *They are more interested in control than change.* They monitor trends to identify the critical "choke points" in emerging businesses and then position their products and services around them.

Intel: Microsoft's Strategic Cousin

The "Moore" of Moore's Law fame is a cofounder of a strategic cousin to Microsoft, Intel, the world's largest semiconductor maker. Some observers say Intel has the most difficult growth problem in its industry: it is too successful. Its market share is so far ahead of any rival that it cannot grow faster than the market. It *is* the market.

Intel's R&D budget is larger than the total sales of many of its rivals. It allows the company to launch the next wave of computer chips just as Intel's imitators are preparing to introduce copies of its current bestseller. Intel has an approach to market control through product migration that has an uncanny resemblance to Microsoft's: when a competitor's new product shows signs of taking off in the marketplace, Intel incorporates similar features within its own products. Microsoft has repeatedly added modules to its operating systems similar to stand-alone products of other software makers. Intel's newest chips will handle functions such as audio, video, and communications that now require auxiliary components. This is another variant on the "let your competitors do your R&D and initial market development"—a cornerstone of many Rule Makers' strategies.

Disney: The Power of Controlled Magic

Lest these examples of Intel and Microsoft give the misleading impression that Rule Makers occur only in the rarefied domain of high technology, consider the world of Mickey Mouse. The Walt Disney Company, creator and controller of some of the world's most venerated entertainment characters, is a Rule Maker extraordinaire. With a market value greater than that of many major industrial companies, Disney is the entertainment industry's megagiant. Its businesses, all in some way helping cross-sell the wares of each other, include four theme parks (on three continents), several movie companies, a TV station and cable channel, book and record companies, a hotel chain, a National Hockey League team (named after a Disney movie, of course), nearly 300 retail stores (selling only Disney brand-name products), and the most-watched television network in America (ABC).

Disney's Magical Money Machine

Disney's main product may well be magic, experienced in theme parks and on the screen and—perhaps most dramatically—in its financial statements. What else could explain this company's alchemistic-like ability to turn $50 million into almost 2 billion dollars?

Disney spent $50 million to produce a recent animated feature film. From this investment more than $700 million in box office receipts were obtained worldwide. Also, over $1 billion in additional revenues were generated from sales of retail merchandise based on the movie characters. Then, as movie attendance began to peak, the film was withdrawn from the theaters, a short anticipation-building period was allowed to pass, and then a home video was released. Twenty million copies of the video were sold on its first day in the stores! That, in a nutshell, is the economics of Disney's *The Lion King,* probably the most profitable movie ever made.

More Real than Reality

Disney's products, especially its theme parks, have been described as being more real than reality. Few streets in turn-of-the-century small-town America were as neatly laid out and kept as clean as Main Street U.S.A. No mouse looks as warm, friendly, and unthreatening as Mickey. No Middle Eastern souk is as chaos free as Aladdin's. When John Hench, one of Disney's veteran theme park designers, hears the occasional complaint about the park looking too contrived, too cute, or just plain too phony, he objects strongly. He tires of being told that Disney helps people turn their backs on reality by disappearing into a fantasy land. He protests that Disney's "reality" is as good as, if not better than, that experienced in the outside world. Disney is about leading the way, not deceiving, he maintains.

Creating a new reality, or cleaning up the old, is not easy. Ask Disney's CEO, Michael Eisner, if he likes his job, and he will probably say many positive things about it; however, "fun" won't be among the words he uses. Instead, he will likely moan about how hard it is to create fantasy and moan about how many times Disneyland's Indiana Jones ride had to be reprogrammed to get the effect just right.

Eisner presides over a company that marries the Game Player's strong attention to its outside market with a Rule Breaker's intense internal vision. Rule Makers are more than an amalgam of these other forms of growth companies. They add a new dimension: control.

The Core Competence of Control

Individuals have many differing views about Disney's creations, but most agree they are a product of a company whose core skill is *control*. Disney carefully controls how and when its products reach the market. Disney added a strong dose of control to the random jumble of traditional, litter-strewn, amusement parks. Hench said that even the shape of Mickey's head, three interlocked circles, was designed to exude friendly blandness. Sharp, irregular shapes are reserved by Disney cartoonists for more sinister creatures.

Disney even mimics the practice, usually limited to sovereign nation states, of issuing its own currency. When overseas travelers arrive at Disneyworld in Orlando, Florida, they need only convert their native currency into Disney dollars, which are good for food, lodging, admission charges, and souvenirs at all Disney facilities. (If Disney was a Game Player, just one among many competitors, the "currency" would probably be called something less lofty, like gift certificates.)

Disney's emphasis on control extends deeply into its internal world. Just as the company maintains its link to society-at-large by editing, not distorting, reality, it deliberately edits its organizational landscape. One critic observed that the company does to its employees what it did to Mickey's image: rough edges are smoothed, impulsiveness is converted to compliance, and anger is converted to friendliness.

Buy In, or Else

Surviving at a Rule Breaker requires "buying in" to the vision. Working for a Game Player implies some willingness to "get with the program," to be a part of the team, and to provide at least superficial compliance with the corporate culture. A successful career in a Rule Maker involves a much greater type of commitment.

To get hired at a Rule Maker, such as Disney, it is necessary to suppress part of your personal identity. No facial hair, heavy makeup, or gaudy jewelry is allowed. Thriving at a Rule Maker takes even more: a willingness to fuse a significant part of your identity with the company's. Its mission becomes your mission, its goals your goals, and its ways your ways. Superficially this is similar to what happens inside those hothouses of employee commitment, Rule Breakers, but something here is different.

What Makes Rule Makers So Different from Other Companies?

High performers in Rule Makers are members of what has the look and feel of an elite corporate cult. Their employers have worked deliberately to institutionalize the corporate philosophy the same way a church propagates a system of beliefs. Working in a Rule Maker is like joining the Jesuits, rather than remaining an ordinary parish priest. It is closer to the Marines, less like the slogging foot soldiers of the Army.

A Place to Start a Career

The commitment, for those willing to buy in, is often expected to be career long. Rule Makers, like Catholic priests, are expected to spend their entire career there. New recruits arrive at an early stage of their work lives (before they have had a chance to be corrupted by too many other employers). Half of Microsoft's new hires come directly from college—down from 80 percent in its early years. Even in downsizing-prone times, Rule Makers have higher percentages of long-service employees than do Game Players or Rule Breakers.

Learning a New Language

The specialness of this new identity is reinforced in many ways. Language can be creatively used to emphasize the differences between the elite company and those that are merely playing the game. For example, Disney doesn't have customers; it has *guests*. The status of its employees is evaluated by calling them *members of the cast*, each performing a *part*, not holding a job. Wearing a uniform can be demeaning, putting on a *costume* sounds more like fun. It's a lot easier to complete a *performance* than endure an eight-hour shift. Job descriptions are dull and confining, but few mind memorizing their lines and movements in a *script*. By shifting the vocabulary of the theater and screen to the work life of the amusement park, a different—higher value—experience is created for Disney's customers (oops, "guests"). And a high degree of control is exercised over the individual employees whose encounters with customers can either reinforce or destroy the Disney magic. Neither surly "carnies" nor tattooed, cigarette-smoking, foul-tempered ride operators are allowed.

This language, and the special worldview it evokes, is taught in tightly scripted training programs at Disney University. Admission is offered only to those who pass a battery of screening interviews. After orientation training, new hires are assigned peer mentors—also carefully selected for their role-modeling potential. Contrast this with the typical hit or miss and sink or swim approaches most businesses—especially Game Players—take to selection, training, and socialization.

Managing Cohesion

With regard to this bear-hug approach to employee socialization, Disney operates in the same mode as Microsoft or as IBM in its high-growth days. Microsoft has its boot camp for new managers—a three-week immersion in "the Microsoft Way." There the metaphors are more software oriented and less "entertainment-biz" related (people and projects get "templated" into master plans punctuated with milestones), but the result is similar. IBM developed a similar IBM speak decades ago and even supplemented it with a network of company-managed country clubs to promote IBMers mingling after hours with other IBMers. Recently, Microsoft followed suit. Every employee is given an automatic health club membership—in the same club, of course.

Why is all this attention to creating and maintaining a uniquely co-hesive organization so important to Rule Makers? To understand this, it is helpful to appreciate how this kind of growth company is really differ-ent from the others that we have described. A key difference has to do with the role its products play in the scheme of things.

Products Exist to Perpetuate the Rule Maker

Rule Breakers are primarily vehicles for their products. Rule Breakers are commonly extended shadows of their innovative products and the compelling vision behind them. Think about Ferdinand Porsche's cars, Edwin Land's cameras, or Steve Jobs's Macintoshes. Rule Breakers die when their products lose their luster (for example, Studabaker's automo-biles and Atari's computers). The relation between a Rule Maker and its products is fundamentally different, though.

For Rule Makers, the product exists more as a vehicle for the company and its perpetuation, not the other way around. Disney does not exist to create new animated movies—the movies exist to perpet-uate Disney. Rule Makers seldom fall in love with their products. In Rule Makers, the whole is always more than the sum of the parts—it includes both today's product line and the ability to remain ingrained in the fabric of the market by developing tomorrow's big hits. Microsoft's *capability* to build and market an ongoing stream of products that control a portion of the marketplace is more important than any individual product. Critics of the software industry have faulted Microsoft for producing inelegant prod-ucts, behind schedule, that are often inferior to its competition. They may be right, but they are also, from a strategic perspective, missing the point.

It better serves Microsoft's interests to invest in developing an elec-tronic product registration card (that also reports back to Microsoft all the types of software it finds on its customers' computers) than to put the same effort into adding more features to a word processor or spread sheet Microsoft sells. Having this information about the configuration of its customers' machines—obtained while speeding up the product regis-tration process for the customer—provides valuable intelligence about what customers are using what products and which might be ripest to consider an upgrade to an offering of Microsoft. In this case, Microsoft's product is also a Trojan horse, generating additional information about customers' future needs as well as immediate revenues.

Obsessive Attention to Organizational Architecture

Rule Makers give as much attention to building their unique organization (the source of their future products) as they do to the products themselves. Certainly, Game Players—and to a lesser extent, Rule Breakers—are concerned with their organizations, but none plan them with the obsessive degree of attention to detail as do Rule Makers. For them, **the secret of controlling the market is to control themselves.**

When a person exaggerates a behavior—such as an extreme need to control the surrounding environment—it is often more useful to ask *why* the person needs to behave that way, rather than just branding the person as a "control freak" or as "obsessive." The same principle holds for organizations, as well. What is it about Rule Makers that makes them so control oriented?

The Rule Maker's Persona

To answer the foregoing question, let's imagine, as we have done with Rule Breakers and Game Players, what the persona might be of a Rule Maker. If such a company were an individual, what kind of a person would it be? Perhaps a tall, strong, confident, and bright person with a plan. True, but more accurately a *very* tall, *very* strong, *very* confident, and *very* bright person with a very *well thought-out* plan. Superlatives seem to naturally flow in descriptions of Rule Makers.

Superlatives Provide the Clue

The mention of too many superlatives is a good clue, to psychologists, that the *opposite of what is being emphasized is also a matter of very serious concern* to the individual. Most of us try to keep some measure of balance in our lives. We balance work with play and time spent with colleagues with time spent with family. Our psyches work the same way. When especially bothered by something, the mind can work overtime dwelling on thoughts to counteract what is really bothering us. If this keeps up, **we become known by our reactions to the things that continually disturb our inner tranquility.**

Although the personality of a Rule Maker exudes *control*, the flip side of control is frequently *fear*. Likewise, bright people who need to continually demonstrate how extremely bright they are may well have an inner worry that they are actually not so smart after all, and overly aggressive bullies may really fear, unconsciously, that they are weak. These fears or concerns, ironically, may have no basis in reality; for example, the self-proclaimed genius might well be very smart, and the tough bully may actually be very strong, but neither of these people are comfortable enough with their abilities to take them for granted. Instead, they exaggerate them.

Mild Paranoia

So it is with Rule Makers. Behind their apparent strength, self-confidence, and creative ability to control situations to their best advantage is an underlying, opposite attribute. **Many Rule Makers look over their shoulder quite a bit.** They seem a little more fearful than they need be. Some might even be described as slightly paranoid. This aspect of a Rule Maker's persona is worthy of examination. It may provide some clues about why so many stumble and what can be done to avoid what otherwise seems to be an inevitable decline.

Suspicious Executives

Two Canadian business school professors, Manfred Kets de Vries and Danny Miller, have used the tool of psychology to better understand why executives regarded as especially "suspicious" act as they do. They examined leaders such as Henry Ford II, Harold Geneen, J. Edgar Hoover, and the Hunt Brothers of Texas. They found considerable similarity in how they and other strong but "slightly fearful" executives behaved. For example, each

- gave considerable attention to warding off attacks and personal threats—both real and imaginary,

- was hypersensitive about minor mistakes and disorderliness,

- insisted on unwavering loyalty,

- became personally overinvolved in controlling their businesses through great attention to rules and details,

- had unsatiable appetites for more and more information, and

- was known for his or her vindictiveness and overreaction.

Always on the Alert

These traits can apply to organizations as well as individuals. Companies of this sort, like some who thrive on the rule-making path to growth, are always vigilant and always ready for a fight. They are like a muscle so taut that it springs when only lightly touched. They do not like the unexpected; they are not at home in rough and tumble, go-with-the-flow markets (places that Game Players and Improvisers thrive). Rule Makers are very intense places to work, where all activity is expected to serve some business purpose.

The Price of Eternal Vigilance

Vigilance and focus can be admirable qualities, but they come at a price. Hyperattention to threats in the marketplace can lead to piecemeal reactions to the advances of competitors. Competing products may be imitated, not because they are worthy of copying but to avoid a gap in the product line. Decisions can take a long time to make (and products a long time to ship), while key decision makers await more information or new analyses. Also, as fear of outside threats turns inward, internal suspiciousness can limit risk taking. Finally, if fear of reliance on one key product becomes too strong, the Rule Maker may stretch itself too thinly by overdiversification.

Strong vigilance can help defend a strong competitive position. Unfortunately, it tends to *inhibit*, not facilitate, growth, leading the business away from its customers and the marketplace. Fearful, suspicious companies run the danger of self-delusion.

Internal Filters

Some Rule Makers, driven by self-confidence bordering on arrogance, can too easily become rigid in their thinking. Superficially they may appear very impressive, big-picture thinkers, but excessive concern about turf-protection can cause them to be very preoccupied. They may take in a lot of information about what is happening in the marketplace, but they are prone to interpret it according to their *internal standards* (remember all that socialization). These Rule Makers can be so preoccupied that their perception is highly astute, but their judgment about what they are seeing is completely in error.

Rule Makers are prone to several such "cognitive" errors. They can tend to find what they are looking for when examining market research data—in part because they ignore facts that disconfirm their biases. These Rule Makers miss taking things at face value, because they are too busy searching for some hidden meaning. They can lose a sense of proportion, too easily taking things out of context.

Missing More than Fun

Perhaps the most dangerous characteristic of many Rule Makers is their inability to lighten up, to give in. In some business situations, moving two steps forward requires going one step backward. This kind of pragmatism eludes most Rule Makers. Unlike Game Players who can submit easily to the will of their customers without feeling humiliated in the process or Rule Breakers who succumb to their playful side on a regular basis, Rule Makers are often so caught up in controlling the market by controlling themselves that they can miss a lot of fun—and a lot of market opportunities. Businesses that violate the New Rules for Growth by needing everything may find themselves ending up with nothing.

Successful Rule Makers though, just like successful people, have found a way to make their habits, their personality characteristics, pay off. Intel's CEO, Andy Grove, is famous for his belief that—no matter how successful—only the paranoid survive. Bill Gates, of Microsoft, is reputed to be driven by fear of the time (which ultimately will come) that sales will slow down. Gates is likely to take such a downturn personally, not philosophically. He is more prone to attribute the decline to a mistake someone made years earlier that was just not caught quickly enough. These chief executives may admit to some corporate paranoia, but neither seems crippled by it—at least, not yet.

Few Rule Makers are harmed by their rigidities during times of rapid growth. Their competitive position seems impregnable, too many things are going right. Incipient problems are too easy to miss or deny, but during this period, seeds are frequently planted that can accelerate later decline.

Threats to Future Growth

Let's speculate about how this might happen to one prominent Rule Maker, Microsoft. Consider the steps Bill Gates takes to avoid making that fatal, downturn-inducing mistake.

Covering All the Bases

A key aspect of the "Microsoft Way" requires all managers to keep all their bases covered, to stay on top of their work at all times, and to consider every angle before making a recommendation. A meeting with the chief executive was described by one middle manager as a visit to a haunted house. Everything, she observes, depends on *how able you are to defend your point of view.* You win at Microsoft by presenting things in a "Gates-proof" manner: you act completely unflappable, have all the facts at your fingertips, and make arguments that the chief executive is unable to poke holes through.

Although it sounds tough and brutal, it is really a brittle way to manage. It does not allow much room for creative hunches—those blind leaps of faith many new businesses were built upon (but then again, this is a Rule Maker, not a Rule Breaker). More dangerously, **having to get it right the first time, all the time, is a near impossibility. A management system that expects that is one that will eventually condition the people in it to say what they think the boss thinks is the right answer, not what their information or judgment incline them toward.** It is a management style that does not leave much room for learning (remember the New Rules for Growth: growth often occurs on the rebound; look for the seeds of growth in past failures; few past failures can translate to limited possibilities for future growth.)

Out-thinking the Boss

When the game becomes "out-think the boss," some bright employees will always rise to the challenge. Verbal jousting may be one of Bill

Gates's favorite sports, but Microsoft's continued dominance will be more dependent on accurate, unvarnished information reaching its top decision makers. *The more energy Gates's subordinates give to "bullet proofing" their recommendations, the less time they have to devote to keeping those ideas in sync with the marketplace.* That is when the blind spot is created, when competitors or new technologies are misjudged, when Microsoft's inner world might start to limit its performance in the outside market, and when its growth rate slows.

Not Facing Up to Failure

Some Rule Makers have a reputation for being a little touchy and a bit arrogant. When his customers complained about a potential for error proneness in Intel's Pentium chip, Grove's first reaction was to deny the possibility that its product was defective. Only when publicity about the problem fueled the sales of Intel's competitors did the company admit the flaw and offer replacements to all concerned.

Becoming the "Next" Microsoft

Rule Makers are frequently the role models of American industry. Books are written extolling their virtues, they are cited as critical to national economic competitiveness, and the names of their chief executives are common knowledge. When at their peak, their management practices become every business's benchmarks. In the 1950s, it seemed every business wanted to be the next General Motors. Its virtues and management practices were documented in a book that brought Peter Drucker great fame. Later, the aspirational targets shifted, and IBM had a long period in the limelight until supplanted by Microsoft.

All of this "hero worship" can be very puzzling. So many managers go to such great lengths to learn the "secrets" behind the Rule Maker–of-the-moment's great success, but they probably **could learn much more by examining the causes of the Rule Maker's almost-inevitable decline.** While Rule Makers offer many useful ideas, they offer equally as many cautions. Their strong competitive positions are unique. What works for a company with near domination of its market may be inappropriate for an aspiring Rule Maker or a company that would do better on a different growth path.

The Triple Threat

Some of the most important lessons Rule Makers provide are those best visible in their period of decline. Like the dinosaurs of prehistory, the Rule Makers constantly face a triple threat:

1. Abrupt shifts in the surrounding environment.

2. More adaptive predators.

3. Self-inflicted wounds.

These three often combine to undermine or even destroy many once-dominant competitive positions.

Dominance Lost

- External pressures, such as the emergence of jet airplanes and the interstate highway system, combined with a century-old history of adversarial labor relations and a rigid management hierarchy to end the dominance of the Pennsylvania Railroad. This once-proud transportation giant prolonged its inevitable demise for several years by merging with a rival only to declare bankruptcy several years later.

- Kodak, a company that was synonymous with the photography industry, lost its ability to control its marketplace after suffering two serious legal defeats many years ago. In 1921, it was kept out of the growing private-label market for photographic film. All Kodak products were required to bear the Kodak name. Later, in the 1950s, Kodak was prohibited by the courts from tying the sale of film to the processing of film. Eventually Kodak was able to convince a federal judge to overturn these rulings, but not until the company's competitive position had seriously eroded.

- Throughout this period of decline, Kodak clung to its Japanese-like system of ingrown management. It hired most employees directly out of school and expected them to remain until retirement. It managed to keep them busy by doing internally many things for which other companies relied on suppliers and business partners: chemical feed stocks, electric power, and even the yellow cardboard boxes for its film. Not wanting to trust the local municipality, Kodak also created its own fire department to protect its main plant in Rochester, New York.

Letting the Organization Drive the Strategy

- The emergence of CD-ROM technology nearly destroyed the 200-year-old reign of Encyclopedia Britannica, long the world's most elite reference source. Its competitors, Compton's, Grolier's, World Book, and Funk & Wagnalls (converted by Microsoft into Encarta) rushed to embrace this new, interactive multimedia technology. Britannica was not unaware of this new technology. Its managers were among the first to experiment with it, but company executives were very slow to embrace it. Britannica's problem was its old organization, not new technology.

- The company had become a prisoner of the organization that provided its past successes, its large, commissioned sales force. These salespeople quickly realized that putting the contents of Britannica (whose volumes weigh over 100 pounds and require four and a half feet of bookshelf) onto an album-sized compact disc would result in a product priced much lower than the traditional hardcopy encyclopedia. This would cut deeply into their sales commissions. It might even eliminate marketing jobs as CD-ROMs are easier to sell in computer stores and by mail than by more-costly door-to-door, one-on-one customer calls. Encyclopedias are sold, compact discs are bought.

- Britannica was following the well-worn path traveled by many one-time Rule Makers. Western Union, a one-time communications giant in the age of the telegraph, had no use for the patents a young inventor, Alexander Graham Bell, tried to sell for the telephone. He was forced to go elsewhere. IBM's slow start embracing the new microprocessor technology happened not from technology blindness but by the fear of demotivating its powerful mainframe computer sales force. **Rule Makers are very adept at accommodating evolutionary change, but their keen ability to map the marketplace into their organization becomes a dangerous millstone when the environment makes an abrupt shift.**

The Dangers of Smugness

- Britannica was also a victim of its (once well deserved) great self-confidence. This strength became a source of weakness when it turned to smugness, to an unwillingness to take once-lesser competitors seriously. Other one-time Rule Makers, as varied as Harvard Business School and the U.S. Postal Service, took false comfort in upward performance measures (top-of-the-chart starting salaries for HBS graduates and ever-increasing volumes of mail at the Postal Service). These indicators, interpreted through a "we can do no wrong" mind-set, gave maneuvering room for more nimble competitors (Stanford and Northwestern Universities and Federal Express and fax machines) to steal both reputation and market share.

Making Rules without Rule Makers

- Possibly **the most serious threat to Rule Makers is the decline in the power of rule making itself.** It does not always require a single, dominant company to maintain an industry's standards, especially in many of the hottest technology markets. Virtually all computer modems are now labeled "Hayes-compatible." At one time, Hayes Microcomputer Products Inc. dominated the modem market. Now the company is bankrupt, a victim of production problems, slowness in responding to lower-priced rivals, and a corporate culture that valued extreme secrecy. The standard approach that Hayes developed for computer-to-computer communications is alive and thriving in its competitor's products.

- In other situations, companies that compete fiercely with each other—like IBM, Sun Microsystems, and Hewlett-Packard in the market for computer workstations—also realize the value of using the same underlying software (Unix). They distinguish themselves by the special features they add, while staying uniform enough so their customers are not required to start from scratch each time they buy a new computer terminal. The net result was *faster market growth for all* by practicing one of the New Rules for Growth: assist your rivals in making the overall market bigger.

"Coopetition" (cooperative-competition) as Ray Noorda of Novell likes to call it, can be stronger than all-out competition when the market is just starting to grow fast, and it is something that doesn't necessarily require a dominant Rule Maker to make happen.

The Fear of Changing a Winning Formula

Underlying most Rule Makers' self-inflicted wounds is an *unwillingness to change a winning formula in face of facts that call to question its underlying assumptions.* Sometimes the formula has become too ingrained in the organization to be weeded out, and at other times, the Rule Breaker's management practices make it too difficult to notice and act on the facts. Today's successes are worth celebration, but they are also the seeds of tomorrow's failures. This occurs in all businesses but especially in Rule Makers. The "mental blinders" they seem to almost naturally acquire lead to tunnel vision and eventual stunted growth.

Sustaining a Rule Maker's Growth

Is decline inevitable? Are there actions Rule Makers can take to avoid this fate? What can be done to reduce the threats from both the outside and the internal organization? How can Rule Makers prolong their period of growth? These are valid questions pertaining to a Rule Maker's growth and should be considered carefully.

Share the Wealth

Rule Makers can sustain their favorable economics by cultivating a willingness to share the wealth. Don't try to win every battle and crush every opponent. When a market is growing rapidly, the rising tide tends to lift all boats. Rule Makers may be envied, but there is still plenty of business to go around. Later, as the market slows, this envy converts to resentment and hostility, often not limited to competitors but sometimes expressed by customers who feel locked-in. These are the competitors most likely to seek relief in the courts, not the marketplace. These are the customers most susceptible to an up-and-coming Rule Breaker or a reenergized Game Player. It would be wise not to give others a compelling reason to destabilize a situation that no longer works for them.

Go Where Others Are Not

AST Research Inc. is only the fifth-ranking maker of IBM personal computer clones in the United States, but in China, AST is number one. Getting there early and building a strong network of personal relations are key to doing business in China, the world's leading growth market of the late 1990s.

Management consulting Rule Maker McKinsey is following a similar strategy to keep its global professional partnership growing. Well over half its revenue and even more of its profits are earning outside the United States. Its managing director is Indian-born, and its growth plan targets the emerging consulting markets of Russia, China, India, and Eastern Europe.

These companies constantly keep in mind that increasing revenues in a segment of the market that has stopped growing eventually leads to a dead end.

Cultivate Humility

The key to longevity for many Rule Makers is the ability to fight tendencies to be excessively tough and macho. Not only do these attract unfavorable attention but they also can distort how managers see changes in the market. Personal computers were once written off as mere toys by sellers of "heavy iron." "Real" steel companies once disparaged Nucor and other early minimills, calling them wimps because they made their product from scrap metals rather than in mile-long blast furnaces and rolling mills.

Cultivating an image of greatness can become another form of a millstone. **Eventually everybody in a successful Rule Maker seems to believe everything they do is great because of who they are rather than what they do.** Keep the internal applause and self-congratulation to a minimum; a Rule Maker's best cheerleaders are its customers. If you ask the chief executive of Levi Strauss, Robert Haas, how that business has sustained market leadership for 140 years, he will remind you that "this is a company that historically has had a discomfort with the status quo. We're a very restless and self-critical company. So we're constantly focusing on the things we could do better."

Become Truly Dangerous: Take Regular Risks

Rule Makers are not expected to take great risks, but that does not mean they will not benefit by doing so. The Coca-Cola Company has reenergized its growth by blending the paths of the Rule Maker with that of the Game Player. The world's largest soft drink company stumbled a decade ago with New Coke, but afterward **it focused on learning lessons, not on assigning blame.** The marketing executive who introduced the ill-fated brand, Sergio Zyman, has even been rehired and is leading a worldwide marketing blitz driven by the lessons he learned from his massive failure a decade ago. In an industry where changing just the shape of the container the product is sold in can almost double sales, Zyman's advertising emphasizes Coke's 80-year-old contour bottle every chance it can. This contour, a long-forgotten corporate asset, is now the world's best-known package.

Bite the Bullet

Hallmark is still the world's largest player in the greeting card industry, but aggressive competitors and changing customer tastes are forcing it to turn its back on what drove its past success, its network of 9,000 independent Hallmark Shops. Increasingly, cards are sold by supermarkets, discounters, and drug stores, not in speciality stores. Maintaining its control over half the greeting card market is forcing Hallmark to reverse decades of corporate culture and sell its cards outside of these shops. Although many of its store owners are up in arms at the decision, it is one that can fuel their growth, also. The more aggressive and growth-minded Hallmark Shop owners are starting to sell competing card brands.

Hallmark is mindful of Rule Maker Britannica's stumbles. Hallmark's chairman, Donald Hall, intends to sustain its success. "If the competition's catching up with you," he maintains, "its not that they're getting better, it's because you're not staying ahead. We just have to do what it takes to stay ahead."

Value Competence over Loyalty

Two Harvard Business School professors have advanced a Draconian solution to the seemingly inevitable organizational calcification that sets in as Rule Makers mature. Benson Shapiro and Richard Tedlow recommend that senior managers *rate subordinates on both loyalty and competence.* Then, they suggest, those more loyal than competent should be fired because they are the truly dangerous ones. The more competent employees are most likely to leave when problems develop in the business, leaving a higher proportion of loyal but less competent subordinates who will work hard to demonstrate allegiance by shielding their bosses from the truth. This kind of protectiveness inevitably leads to decline.

Loosen Up on the Socialization

In the late 1970s, when IBM was still the world's most admired computer maker, I had an opportunity to interview several of its executives at the company's Armonk headquarters. The topic was the result of an internal study they had just completed about IBM's future business environment. I was especially interested in their research about IBM's workforce and the attitudes employees had about being part of the company. Because I was there on a benchmarking assignment for another Fortune 100 company, one of IBM's best customers, they were very willing to share a great deal of detail about this confidential project. One of its conclusions—one the IBM staff executives seemed proudest about—alarmed me when I heard it. Considering IBM's problems since, it explains a key internal driver of that Rule Maker's subsequent market slippage.

IBM wanted to gauge how strong its corporate culture was and how effective its extensive orientation, training, and employee communications programs were given its polyglot workforce of almost 100 nationalities. The results of the study indicated that these culture-building tools were highly effective, maybe even *too* effective. IBM's research found that *their employees were much more willing to believe what they were told through IBM's "official channels" than they were through outside sources, newspapers, government officials, or friends who worked for other companies.*

The IBM executives I interviewed thought this was a great triumph. They had created a corporate culture with more influence over IBM's employees than did the net impact of all the individual national and regional cultures from which these employees had come. IBM employees trusted their managers more than anyone else for information about markets, technologies, and even broader societal trends. That kind of trust and loyalty may be admirable, but it put an unrealistically high burden on these managers to be right all the time. This is impossible, but what is very likely in companies with such a high degree of employee alignment is that a minor misperception or faulty estimate is much more likely to be reinforced and amplified than it is to be challenged and corrected.

Rule Makers wanting to stay on that path will do well to **monitor the strength of their corporate cultures.** They should recognize what IBM seemed to miss; that **it is possible to have too strong, as well as too weak, a buy-in to the company's core values.** In other words, loosen up a bit on the socialization! Cultivating diversity in opinions is as vital as cultivating diversity in demographics.

Find Honest Mirrors

Sometimes, but not often, businesspeople can learn valuable lessons from successful politicians. The political figure with the most worldwide credibility today is Nelson Mandela. Soon after becoming President of South Africa, after spending decades in his country's prisons, he spoke at a journalists' luncheon. He noted that history is full of stories about passionate freedom fighters who eventually became part of government and quickly lost sight of the reasons they were elected. Mandela observed that "power can make a person forget their mandate." His solution, for the public sector: a free and vigorous press, one that continually challenges those who govern to carry out their mandate. This is an idea also applicable to the business community, though journalists may not necessarily be the best vehicle for this kind of learning. By the time a problem reaches the cover of *Business Week* or *Fortune*, it is usually too late for easy corrective actions.

Where are the potential "journalists" in rule-making corporations? If the business is to maintain its position over the long haul, they need to be those in middle management. They are closer to outside information about customer needs, market trends, and emerging technologies than many of the senior executives to whom they report. **First- and second-level managers also have less at stake in rationalizing past strategic decisions.**

What is needed are Rule Maker managers with the courage to tell, when necessary, the emperor that he is not wearing any clothes. Senior managers in intentionally ingrown companies need lots of help facing the truth about customers and competitors. Resisting the temptation to tell higher-ups what they want to hear is important in all businesses, but it is a matter of long-term survival in Rule Makers. Doing this requires managers with the ability to maintain some "psychological" distance from their employer. This is the ability *to be in, but not of,* the Rule Maker. It is the skill of not checking in your personal "antenna" just because you have logged on to the corporate E-mail system. Discover and maintain independent channels of information, sources that go beyond those officially monitored, and then build networks within the Rule Maker to spread what is learned.

Information sharing must be a two-way street. Senior officers need to carefully audit how they spend their time, keeping interactions with peers and bosses to no more than a quarter of their day. They should *spend half the remaining time with people outside the company (customers, suppliers, industry gurus, and technology oracles) and the other half with those inside, several levels below, closer to the firing line.* These executives also need the self-confidence to seed all levels of the hierarchy with re-spected, listened-to, devil's advocates. These are habits that executives of evergreen Rule Makers, like Levi Strauss, put into use daily. "I want to maintain a close enough feel for the business so that, when I'm receiving reports, I can validate or challenge them *from my own experience,*" says CEO Robert Haas.

Get Significant Competition

Invest in growing in the most hotly contested segments of the market, not only those your competitors have conceded. The longer a business dominates its market, *the more it forgets* about how to respond to market changes. If a company has never had serious competition, as Kodak lacked for nearly a century, it will find itself dangerously out of practice when competitors emerge. Remember: the most favorable place for a Rule Breaker to grow is in the wake of a fat and happy Rule Maker. If a Rule Maker has always controlled its industry's pace of change, it has never learned what to do when it finds itself on the receiving end of mar-ket upheavals.

Manage People Flow

Continually **seed the Rule Maker's organization with people who don't belong.** Break the fatal pattern of organizational self-containment so common in Rule Makers. Avoid the IBM/Kodak approach to career advancement:

- The chief executive who presided over much of IBM's decline, John Aikers, joined right after college and a stint as a Navy carrier pilot. IBM was the only company for which he had ever worked. He worked up its ranks, with promotions almost annually, from sales trainee to marketing rep to branch manager to director of data processing to vice president to the very top jobs. When his old college hockey coach asked him how he made such an impressive climb, Aikers attributed it all to his ability to be very nice to everyone he met on the way up. He was also promoted so frequently that he was seldom in a position long enough to be held accountable for an organizational unit's long-term performance.

- Kodak's fall from market dominance occurred during the time its key leaders were Colby Chandler and Kay Whitmore. Both joined, as did IBM's Aikers, the business they were to lead directly upon graduation. Each had almost 30 years experience at Kodak before becoming chief executive; each had the technical background common to all of Kodak's leaders since George Eastman founded the company. This combination of an inward career orientation—in an inward-looking company—coupled with educational backgrounds more attuned to achieving astute technical perfection than market timing, can almost certainly guarantee difficulty in maintaining a strong market position.

Now, both IBM and Kodak are, slowly, rediscovering growth, and both are also headed by chief executives, Lewis Gerstner and George Fisher, respectively, their boards recruited from outside their industries. If a Rule Maker is to remain atop changing markets, it needs to never forget to manage its people flow as well as cash flow: keep the gene pool fresh!

Remember the New York Yankees

Remember the once almost-unbeatable New York Yankees? David Halberstram chronicled the fall of these one-time Rule Makers in his book *October 1964*. This was the baseball season in which the Yankees went from near dominance of the sport to just another team that occasionally did well. What happened? They cut costs in areas they should not have, and according to Halberstram, they were especially slow in recruiting the African American and Hispanic players who were to reenergize the sport in the succeeding decades.

Common Patterns in Growth Companies

Now that three of the five paths to growth have been covered, some patterns are emerging. Each type of company has its special set of strong and weak points. Each thrives in some industries, languishes in others. Whereas uncharted territory requires one type of vehicle to cross it, a well-worn path requires another. No one form of organization is necessarily better or worse than any other. It is more useful to distinguish companies by how closely or not they are adapted to the logic of their particular situation.

The core message is very simple: to the victor belongs many of the the spoils, but not forever. The rewards of rule making can be very sweet. Just keep in mind that they, too, will pass at some point.

Does this imply that decline is inevitable and that growth only leads to no-growth? Sometimes, but not always. Consider two other types of growth companies, sometimes maligned, often overlooked. Both offer fine possibilities for ongoing increases in sales and profits. They can provide welcome respite for a Rule Maker whose time is past. In some markets they are clearly the best choice for growth. They are the Specialists and the Improvisers.

Rule Maker | What Is It Like Working for a Rule Maker?

This is the BEST place in the world to work.

Here are a few quick impressions from a recently minted MBA gradu-ate's first year in the Human Resources Department at a well-established Rule Maker.

■ ■ ■

I feel proud when I tell people where I work. I'm a part of a business that is out to transform society.

I've noticed that people who work here take their special identity seriously, even outside the office. We've been kidded about walking taller, standing straighter, and even parking our cars more carefully—lest we reflect poorly on the company.

Sure, we occasionally are the targets of criticism. It just comes with the territory when you're the biggest, most successful player in the industry. A number of us were bothered by that antitrust inquiry a few years back, but that's long past. I can't imagine why the government would consider breaking us up. We're a national asset, one of the country's few shining stars able to stand up to those government-subsidized monopolies in Europe and Japan.

This is one of the few places I can imagine working where a job in the personnel department is not an assignment to Siberia. Top management listens to us. Major reorganizations aren't even con-sidered without pulling us in at the first planning meeting. We manage people's career progressions and job assignments as if people flow was as important as cash flow. We give as much attention to devising effective internal employee communications as other companies do to planning their next ad campaign. The HR function is growing, and I jumped at the chance for an assignment here. It's a great way to get some early visibility with the higher-ups.

I still can't believe all the training this place provides. Orientation lasted three weeks, none of the cursory "here's your PC and here's the

washroom" most of my classmates got on their first
day. Before the first class began, the instructor sent a

form asking every participant if we were left- or right-handed. It
seemed like a silly question until I got to the first session and looked
at the hardcopy in my notebook. I'm left-handed, and they specially
printed mine so all the blank pages were on the left—what a
convenience for note taking!

And it's obvious that someone has given a lot of thought to the best
ways to get things done here. Policies and procedures are well planned
and clearly laid out.

An added bonus is the built-in social life. When I moved from
grad school, the company housing office made sure I got a condo in a
building where a couple of my colleagues live. We all get memberships
to a nearby health club; it's great unwinding with people you know.

This is a great place to work. I'm looking forward to a long career
here.

This is the WORST place in the world to work.

*Here are some other impressions of the same outfit, also from a relatively
recent hire.*

■ ■ ■

I wish my friends would lay off congratulating me for getting a job
here. I feel like a bottled-up tiger. I came here last December after 15
years with two hotshot consumer products companies—both were
tough outfits that really knew how to fight for every scrap of business
they ever got. Here I've got to go around with a card in my wallet
written by our legal people telling me not to do this and not to do that
when I'm on a sales call. Mentioning how big we are in front of a
customer is grounds for quick dismissal. They might as well just turn
me into an order clerk.

I thought they hired me for my industry experience, but every time
I suggest doing something I've seen work outside, my idea's politely
listened to and then completely ignored.

Rule Maker   We have become so smug and complacent over the past couple of years. A "we can do no wrong" mentality seems to prevail through the company. All those great write-ups in *Business Week* and *Fortune* have gone to our heads.

I might be fired for admitting it, but where we really could use more outside scrutiny is from the Justice Department. Don't get me wrong; we're not dishonest—this is the most straight-laced place I've ever worked—but sometimes I think we're too damn successful for our own good. Look at how the telecommunications industry benefited when AT&T was broken up. The Baby Bells all had growth surges, and the old parent company is still holding its own nicely against MCI and Sprint.

At times I feel they treat me like a child. They've got rules and forms for everything. Even though I've had more business experience than half the people in the company, they still made me sit through a three-week orientation program with all the wet-behind-the-ears recent graduates. What a waste!

It hasn't taken me long to sort out what it takes to get ahead here: *loyalty.* That may be all well and good for some, but I'm more interested in finding a place that wants *performance!*

In the meantime, I'm going to work my tail off. This job's going to look great on my resume.

CHAPTER 7

Specializing

*Thrive through Focus
on Niche Markets*

"'ll personally break the neck of anyone who tries to veer us from the path we are on. We all know what business we are in. Love it . . . or leave it." Few Specialists are this direct with their employees, but most agree with the underlying sentiment: profits grow when everyone keeps to the straight and narrow.

The most heavily traveled path to growth is that of the Specialist. There are literally millions of these businesses throughout the world, ranging in size from multi-billion-dollar global energy giants to one-person software consultancies. Despite ubiquity, Specialists are frequently misunderstood, and their approach to growth is often unfairly discounted. These misperceptions are not all that bad, at least for many established Specialists. Being misunderstood can help mask opportunities and make it harder for competitors to discover what can be, for the right company in the right market, a great source of advantage.

Although companies that grow by specializing have similarities to those on the three other paths, they also have some key differences. Specialists are

- as *innovative* as Rule Breakers, without sharing these pioneers' high tolerance for risk taking;

147

- providers of *customer service* as flawless as any Game Player's; but more attuned to competing with themselves than with others; and

- holders of a *competitive position* in their particular market segment just as *strongly* as that which many Rule Makers control in the industries that they dominate. Specialists might be called, only in half jest, Rule Makers run by engineers.

Advantage That's Hard to Imitate

Specialists are companies with a unique talent. **They know how to seal off a portion of a market from other competitors.** Specialists define and protect their segment by providing high value, customer-pleasing benefits, usually including one or more of the following:

- Lowest prices.

- Highest service.

- Best quality.

- Broadest array of products and features.

- Most customized service or product.

Most Specialists choose one of these as their key point of differentiation and then position their business to deliver it. At the time the microcomputer chip market emerged, in the early 1970s, Texas Instruments (TI) was a sales leader because of its remarkable ability to race down the production cost curve faster than any competitor. This allowed TI to offer the lowest prices and gain the greatest market share with the raw material that fueled the personal computer revolution. During the same period, in another segment of the same industry, Digital Equipment Corporation used a different product attribute, quality, to win control—for a time—over the burgeoning minicomputer market.

Islands of Calm

Within their market segment, Specialists are able to create a zone of relative calm by controlling the pace of technology development and keeping competition at arm's length. **The best Specialists preempt direct competition by choosing market segments that are relatively unattractive to others.** Indiana's Batesville Casket Company excels at this. It created an initial strong position by introducing mass production to an industry once dominated by small artisans. The ongoing job of maintaining a leadership position in this business is facilitated by ongoing drops in the U.S. mortality rate and increases in cremations—statistics certain to frighten off any potential new entrant. Meanwhile, Batesville grows profit margins by judicious application of just-in-time delivery, flexible manufacturing, and maintaining its reputation for high-quality "fit and finish" by hiring skilled metal engineers laid off from the nearby downsizing auto industry.

Getting Rich Slowly

Specialists are willing to sacrifice product line breadth for stability and, when necessary, revenue growth for regular earnings increases. They believe in a "get rich slowly" philosophy. They first create a position of advantage through focus. Then their job is to avoid squandering the advantage by constantly improving their product and the processes they use to make it. These improvements, in turn, allow Specialists to aggressively maintain their prominence in their industry segment and make it harder for competitors to dislodge them—a nice way to grow a business. If, however, they fail to invest and reinvest in their segments, Specialists can easily become opportunity markers for more aggressive, growth-minded companies.

Specialists form the economic bedrocks of Germany's *mittelstand* and Japan's large network of suppliers and subcontractors, two of the world's strongest exporters. In smaller countries, Specialists provide a global reach for select industries, such as Finland (cellular telephones), Italy (ceramic tiles), and Switzerland (luxury watches and banking).

As with all growth strategies, there are dangers in excess. Too much focus and too much of the "looking inside" orientation that frequently accompanies it can lead to stagnation and eventual decline. While some well-managed Specialists have long stretches of unbroken growth, it is as hard to surround a market forever as it is to perpetually dominate it by controlling industry standards. Specialists, like all growth companies, require periodic course corrections.

Specialists Are Everywhere

It is almost impossible to imagine a market that does not include some Specialists. The identities of the leading Specialists, though, are usually well known only by those wanting to purchase their products. To other consumers, they are invisible.

- For industrial-strength door locks, the superspecialist is a company aptly called *Best.*

- More portable home spas are purchased from the *Hot Springs* Division of Watkins Manufacturing Co. than from any other hot tub maker.

- After a session in your spa, dry off in a hammock made in South Carolina by the *Pawley Island Rope Hammock Company.*

- The fastest growing natural food specialist in the mid-Atlantic states is *Fresh Fields,* operator of supermarkets selling only organically farmed, preservative-free products.

Two Connecticut Yankees

Specialists come in all sizes. How small can one be? For some businesses, one person, moonlighting, is just about right. Edward Tufte is a Yale professor. Being a statistician, he has a passion for educating people about the uses and abuses of charts—especially those used to display quantitative information. He has written two award-winning books on this subject: *The Visual Display of Quantitative Information* and *Envisioning Information.* Each is full of witty examples of skillful and deceptive uses of charts and graphs. They have become quick classics and have established Tufte as the undisputed master of this form of visual communication. What do you know as well as Tufte knows graphs and charts? Is there a market demand for your skill and expertise? Is meeting this demand a priority of your employer, or is your speciality something better to cultivate "on the side"?

Tufte has skillfully mined his niche. Following in the footsteps of other independent-minded authors such as Mark Twain and John Maynard Keynes, Tufte set up his own Cheshire, Connecticut–based company, Graphics Press. This one-person business oversees the printing, advertising, and distribution of both these books, giving him great control over his books' appearance. Tufte favors using an obscure hard-to-typeset fifteenth-century typeface—and ensures the books are exemplars of the graphic quality about which he writes.

Tufte avoids bookstore markups by limiting almost all of his distribution to mail order. He supplements direct mail marketing with advertising only in periodicals where a high percentage of the readers are likely customers: *Scientific American,* the *New England Journal of Medicine,* and the like. This disciplined focus has allowed him to earn millions of dollars and operate the business with pretax margins of over 50 percent.

Tufte always grows his revenues through ventures closely linked to his core competence and also through diversification. He uses his talents to prepare visually appealing evidence for jury trials, consults with New Jersey Transit on ways to make their train schedules user-friendly, and offers one-day seminars in the cities in which his readers commonly cluster. With the emergence of the "visual computing" industry, driven by Rule Breaker Silicon Graphics (see Chapter 4), the demand for Tufte's specialization is likely to experience quantum growth, and new competitors may emerge.

When this happens, Tufte may need some lessons in organization building from another Connecticut Specialist. Only a few miles from the Yale professor's highly successful home-based business is the headquarters of a company that has won worldwide renown by following this path to growth. General Electric, with over 200,000 employees and worldwide sales approaching $75 billion, is a blend of several growth strategies. The path that predominates, though, is that of the Specialist. As we can see, *niche markets are not necessarily small markets.*

Double-Digit Growth in Mature Markets

General Electric has mastered the art of achieving ongoing double-digit growth in mature markets. It is one of the most profitable companies in the world, frequently out-earning AT&T, Exxon, and Ford. Aside from a few detours into entertainment and financial services, GE operates almost entirely in very traditional markets: light bulbs, electricity generation, home appliances, plastics, jet engines, and railroad locomotives. GE is not a Rule Maker in any of these; all are highly competitive; and some are the homes of world-class competitors such as ABB, Hitachi, Philips, and Siemens.

GE has maintained its strong performance through a combination of focus and self-awareness. John Welch, its chief executive, likes to call GE the fastest elephant at the dance. Knowing the company is not the fastest dancer, he keeps it focused on slower-paced markets where its financial muscle and management genius can thrive. He avoids go-go businesses like computers and factory automation and tries to direct GE's vision toward big-ticket, technically sophisticated, capital goods.

Stretching Middle Management's Vision

Like most Specialists, continual productivity improvement is critical to GE's competitive survival. GE has been an early adopter of factory-floor-level innovations, such as

- best practice benchmarking to keep the company outward-oriented;

- involving suppliers and customers as participants in quality improvement task forces; and

- widespread use of the no-foreman, work-team approach to production.

To keep GE's managers focused on profitable growth, Welch replaced the traditional management-by-objective, lowest-common-denominator budgeting process with one that cuts through much of the double-talk and political bargaining that too often accompanies target setting.

Each manager has two, not one, primary targets to meet. One is a threshold annual profit number, what the unit must accomplish for the manager to keep employed. The other—the objective that top management really focuses on—is a "stretch" goal. It is a number frequently two to three times greater than the group's traditional level of performance in areas such as inventory turns, cash management, or new product introduction—the things that if improved today, would dramatically improve tomorrow's bottom line. A longer time horizon is associated with these stretch goals, and the manager is awarded a large cash bonus or stock options when they are achieved. Promotions also go to those who demonstrate the ability to repeatedly move their operation to the next level of performance. What stretch targets can fuel your company's growth by helping to avoid bottom-line myopia?

Like Edward Tufte, Welch has the Specialist's inbred instinct for sticking to what it does exceptionally well. Both also know that growth through continuous improvement is their only hope for survival.

Change Drives Specialization

GE is not the only global giant following the Specialist path. Specialization can restore growth to companies in industries subject to wrenching change. A number of America's largest corporations have been forced to rethink their approach to growth due to

- rapidly falling commodity prices,
- intense international competition,
- shortages of new product ideas,
- regulatory upheavals, and
- government spending cuts.

Do any of these plague your industry?

Renew Growth through Sharp Focus

Most of the major international oil companies—businesses that once defined themselves as being involved in every phase of the energy business—are refocusing their organizations around a particular competitive strength:

- Amoco is building around its marketing prowess.
- Exxon and Royal Dutch Shell are focusing on accumulating large reserves of oil and gas.
- Shell maintains a large shipping fleet, but its boats are as likely to be kept full and profitable by carrying a competitor's oil as they are to be transporting Shell's own products.
- Smaller companies, like Sun in Philadelphia, have stopped building their own oil tankers, have sold their exploration units, and are concentrating on refining and regionally focused marketing.

Get More People to Use What You Already Sell

The pharmaceutical industry is following a similar course. Drug companies are coping with unprecedented cost pressures as the practice of "managed" patient care has become entrenched in the American health system. Compounding this is a shortage of new products from the pharmaceutical R&D labs, the traditional source of the industry's profit growth. The net results of this upheaval are mergers and consolidations. One drug maker, Merck, even acquired a company that specialized in selling its competitor's products.

Medical product companies are increasingly following a hunkering down strategy for growth: *getting more people to use their existing products.* The makers of drugs to treat high blood pressure know that only a third of the Americans with this problem are using their products, and only 15 percent of people with high cholesterol take the medications available to reduce it. These statistics represent great market opportunities for companies like Bristol-Myers Squibb and Pfizer, provided they focus their resources around treating existing diseases, leaving the more glamorous rule-breaking discovery of new, blockbuster products to others.

Game Players grow by increasing their market share. Specialists can grow by increasing the size of the market they serve. How many potential customers need your products but do not yet know they should be in the market for them?

Look for Sardines, Not Whales

Concentrating resources on marketing is a specialization tactic a number of smaller, high-growth drug companies have used with great success. Medeva Plc., a decade-old British pharmaceutical firm, prides itself on spending zero on basic research. Instead, it buys smaller drug companies and slow-selling medicines and vaccines from the global giants of its industry. It even acquired its chairman, Bernard Taylor, from a major-league drug maker, Glaxo, where he was once chief executive. Over the past several years, Medeva's sales have doubled by concentrating on acquiring products that treat a narrow range of conditions, like influenza and asthma. This also allows its sales force to focus on visits to doctors who specialize in these ailments, making them more productive than salespeople promoting a broader range of products.

Another small drug Specialist, Forest Laboratories of New York City, takes a similar approach. Its sales force is among the highest paid in the industry as well as the most efficient. Every salesperson is eligible for stock options. Forest has a knack for taking outcast products from larger companies—drugs that never received significant attention—and turning them into strong sellers. This strategy is driven by a realization that there are many more 50 million revenue dollar unique drugs available than billion dollar ones, or as Forest's president puts it: "There have always been far more sardines than whales." Does your company fish for sardines or whales?

Similar transformational changes are at work in the defense, health care, and steel businesses. Many of the companies best positioned for future growth in these industries have shifted to the Specializing path.

Thrive among the Giants

Specialization can be an effective way to survive and prosper in industries dominated by game-playing giants. Midwest Express, a business class–style airline that serves 23 cities from its hub in Milwaukee, has earned profits each year in a business littered with bankruptcy filings from less-focused new entrants. Most of Midwest's failed look-alikes, Ultra Air, Air One, and Air Atlanta, set up their operations in the shadow of a major airline's hub—places the majors fight to the teeth to defend. Instead, Midwest chose to go where others were not: Milwaukee. Midwest is also very aware that its advantage lies in distinctive customer service—it was the first air carrier to bake chocolate chip cookies in flight. It carefully stays away from markets where frequency of flights is critical and has avoided most of the ruinous fare wars that have crippled so many upstart carriers. **"Know yourself" is the first rule of successful Specialists.**

The Dutch airline, KLM, has reinvigorated its profit growth with a different form of specialization. It is *the* airline to use if you own a horse and need to travel globally. Every year KLM transports thousands of the world's top breeding and racing horses in self-contained stalls—kept in KLM's 747 cargo compartments, of course. Charging up to $9,000 for a transatlantic crossing, amenities include an animal steward who keeps the horses calm during takeoffs and landings and an equestrian hotel at KLM's Schipol hub to help them recover from jet lag.

In another crowded industry, telecommunications, MFS Communications Co. has found a profitable niche. It provides "bypass" service to businesses in 24 cities, allowing them to route long-distance calls directly to a preferred long-distance carrier, without ever going through the local phone company and often at a significant cost savings. MFS has fueled its growth by the do-one-thing-and-do-it-well philosophy and plans to steer clear of the hotly contested residential phone market.

Defragment the Industry

Sometimes the best way to find growth is to look in an industry that has fragmented itself into hundreds of tiny pieces and *put the best of these together.* Make sure, though, there is an about-to-emerge trend that promises to energize the industry. Martin Franklin, 30-year-old chief executive of Benson Eyecare, did just that. The underlying trend is demographic—almost all adults over 45 wear some form of corrective lens, a market poised for double-digit growth by the end of the century as aging baby boomers require reading glasses and bifocals. Franklin consolidated the eye-care industry by acquiring ten companies, including Foster Grant sunglasses, a maker of lens blanks, and another lab that grinds the blanks into optical lenses. Creating this eye-care empire has earned Franklin the honor of being the youngest CEO of a company listed on the New York Stock Exchange.

Go Where the Growth Is Hottest

At their best, Specialists excel at *finding growing segments even when the overall industry is contracting.* This is a hunt that requires vision more intensive than expansive. Beer drinking may be slacking, but business for microbrewers like Anchor Steam Beer and Sam Adams has never been stronger. The mass market for wine in the United States has slowed as consumers are drinking Calistoga Water instead of California chardonnay, but Jason Pahlmeyer still complains about his phone ringing off the hook with calls from people wanting his speciality premium wines. He is the producer of the Napa Valley chardonnay ('91 Pahlmeyer) that actress Demi Moore offered to Michael Douglas in the movie *Disclosure.* The wine's rarity, only 400 cases of that vintage were made, plays a key part in the film's plot. It is also key to Pahlmeyer's business strategy.

Pahlmeyer is an example of how the Specialist trend is changing the face of American wine making. He does not own a vineyard or a winery. Pahlmeyer's only capital investment is the barrels in which the wine is aged before bottling. Investors own the land on which the grapes for his wine are grown, and he contracts with a "custom crush" company (the Napa Wine Company) to make, age, store, and bottle the product. Pahlmeyer concentrates on the formulating and marketing of his chardonnays and cabernets. Napa Wine and its competitors, such as the Associated Vintage Group, handle the capital-intensive, expensive production details for him and many other California wine boutiques. These "wineries without labels" are able to spread the high fixed costs of wine making over a much higher volume than any small boutique could.

Some larger wineries also stay focused by having others handle the production. The Codera Wine Group's business emphasis is on building the identities of its medium-priced brands and on efficiently managing their sales and distribution. With the help of the Associated Vintage Group, it is able to sell over 200,000 wine cases a year with only *eight employees*—true bloatless growth!

Ride the Outsourcing Wave

Outsourcing is far more widespread, of course, than the wine business. In many industries, the large successful firms are pulling back to emphasize their core competences, creating a seemingly unending variety of niches for smaller suppliers. **An unwanted side dish for an industry giant may be a healthy main course for a focused Specialist.**

An even more radical change is the increasing willingness of many companies to subcontract—as in the wine industry—the complete manufacture of products on which they still put their own name. Examples of this trend are everywhere:

- Apple's Power PC's are fully assembled and packed in a box with Apple's logo on it by the Solectron company; Apple's first notebook computers were made by Sony.

- Heilman Brewery makes Arizona Iced Tea.

- Coosa Baking produces General Mills' granola bars.

- Many Asian car makers build the General Motors Geo line.

- Most of Sam Adams Boston Lager is brewed in Pennsylvania by Pittsburgh Brewing.

Specialists that concentrate on providing outsourcing or contract production are in the most rapidly growing segment of that path to growth. Acting as both manufacturers and service providers, these Specialists have found a new way to add value: freeing customers to specialize on the talents that will add the most value to *their* customers.

Car manufacturing used to involve putting iron and coal into one end of a plant and watching for a car to come out the other end. Now industry profit-per-vehicle leaders like Chrysler rely on Specialists like the Lear Seating corporation to make what it once produced for itself. When BMW decided to produce a two-seat convertible roadster in the United States, it carefully sorted out what components of the car provide the "unique BMW experience": the power train, the suspension, and the cockpit. Everything else in the new luxury cars will be made by Specialists such as Spartenburg Steel (metal body stampings), ASC (roof tops), and Hayes Wheel (the aluminum alloy wheels).

Hallmarks of the Specialist

More than most types of growth companies, there is great diversity among Specialists. By their nature, each is *sui generis* (in a class by itself), but there are characteristics that many on this path to growth share. Some of the most common are addressed in the following sections.

High Margins

Successful Specialists should be profit leaders. Though these margins might not reach the stratospheric heights of Rule Makers' financials, Specialists operate in markets less competitively intense than Game Players' and slower paced than typical of Rule Breakers'. Both are situations usually very favorable to profit generation.

Keeping this level of profitability requires sustaining high customer regard. Specialists need, even more than other growth companies, to carefully monitor their operations. Many operate in unforgiving markets, with only stable or declining demand. Once credibility with customers is lost, it may be extremely hard to regain, unlike the situation in the more

rapid growth markets of Game Players where fast-changing buyer preferences allow recovery of image and reputation much more easily.

For many years, the Caterpillar Tractor Company was renowned for
its high level of customer service. It guaranteed customers replacement
part delivery within 48 hours—regardless if the broken tractor was in a
nearby Peoria farm yard or a construction site in Australia. Service like
this built strong customer loyalty and the industry's highest margins—
for a while; however, in the 1980s, Caterpillar's market became much
more turbulent. New competitors and changing customer preferences
caught Caterpillar off guard. The meaning of "quality" was redefined to
stress product variety, and Caterpillar found itself trying to sell too few
of the types of tractors that were in most demand.

Quality is highly correlated with Specialists' profit-making ability.
In a study of 800 businesses operating in mature markets, researchers at
the Strategic Planning Institute found that all the profit leaders were
ranked in the top third of the group for product quality as well. The
money losers all received scores for quality well in the bottom half of the
rankings.

Process Improvement Leaders

Specialists are frequently the kings of process improvement innovation—keeping on top of the latest ways to produce their products or services. They have been the earliest adopters of quality circles, zero defects
programs, and business process redesign. These techniques have value
in almost all companies, but their relative payoff in businesses growing
through specialization is usually much greater. Process improvements
directly lead to greater quality or lower costs, the two strongest drivers of
a Specialist's competitive advantage.

Ironically, despite the vital importance of ongoing innovation, too
many Specialists fail to take full advantage of the techniques available.
Instead, they devote most of their attention to keeping their production
processes *stable*. Specialists just seem to innately prefer fine-tuning to
radical change: "I'm making so much money doing things this way, why
should I be bothered with changing?" **Specialists expend great energy in building buffers between their well-oiled operation and
the outside world.** They look hard for stable sources of supply, give
great attention to managing inventory, and prefer steady demand for

their products over higher but less predictable sales. Specialists are very tempted by vertical integration, owning as many of their suppliers and distributors as they can. Unfortunately, **the hidden cost of this quest for stability is often diminished attention to the real value they provide for their customers, their particular hard-to-imitate advantage.**

Centralizers of Control

Specialists are bastions of strong, centralized management control: "Do things my way or not at all" is often the message from the top. A small top management group often makes most of the key decisions. The controller or head of production usually has more sway over decision making than do the executives in charge of marketing or new product development.

Specialists are most likely to have the clearest separations between line and staff roles, that is, between the doers and the thinkers. "I set the course; you execute it" is standard operating procedure. They tend to manage expertise by first compartmentalizing and then delegating it. The approach they take to growth in their outside market—specialization—is also tightly reflected in how they manage themselves internally.

Unlike the cross-functional job hopping common in Game Players and Rule Makers, successful careers in Specialists often involve holding a sequence of jobs entirely within one functional speciality. "Don't take a particular job at a specialist unless you are 100 percent sure you like it, because your reward for doing well will be more of the same" is apt career advice for many Specialist employees. Salespeople tend to stay salespeople, engineers work in engineering, and human resource specialists confine their career to the personnel department.

Companies or Machines?

At their worst, Specialists operate in a manner as machinelike as what they may be producing. Some, after a long stretch of stability, give the impression they are businesses running on autopilot. Specialists share a fixation on control with Rule Makers, but their approach to control is qualitatively very different from those businesses that set out to dominate an entire industry:

- Specialists focus more on *today's* operations and customers rather than on what is needed to do to guide *tomorrow's* evolution of the industry.

- They are willing to settle for a business of a *smaller scope* than a Rule Maker may aspire to, if that is what is necessary to *maintain* a strong market position.

- If forced to choose between keeping a *tightly controlled internal operation* or achieving rapid growth through adjusting to new market conditions, most Specialists usually walk away from the rapid growth.

Functionally Organized

The organizational structure of a Specialist is designed to *provide control through stability.* It is almost invariably a functional structure, characterized by a sharp division of labor. Compare this with the typical structures of other growth companies:

- *Game Players* are usually able to achieve fast market penetration by organizing employees primarily around customers or geography.

- *Rule Makers* tend to structure around entire markets.

- *Rule Breakers'* structures tend to reflect the individual idiosyncrasies of their visionary leaders.

Job Titles Mean Something Here

An employee's rank or level in the hierarchy usually means more in Specialists than in companies on other growth paths. A sense of working in a quasi-government bureaucracy may set in, with employees frequently referring to themselves and others by their salary grade: "I'm a 22, and he's only an 18, so why should I bother listening to him?"

The structures and personnel systems of Specialists often get in the way of adopting participative management practices. Strong functional walls and tall hierarchies limit the effectiveness of reengineering and other forms of process redesign. When Specialist employees are assigned to cross-functional task forces, they commonly follow the unwritten rule: make no changes that will diminish the role and power of the department in which they are based.

Watch Every Bloody Detail

There is an upside to Specialists' functional organizations, though. It is a benefit that should not be totally ignored in the wave of current frenzy to reengineer operations and obliterate old ways of doing things. *Specialists are native-born cost controllers.* This is reflected in the industrial grade carpeting, metal desk tops, and cinder block walls often visible in many of their headquarters offices. It is reflected in their ability to manufacture products more cheaply than companies on other growth paths. They do this by what Harvard Business School researcher Richard Hamermesh observes as intense attention to every bloody detail.

The Specialist's functional orientation allows them to excel at tasks involving detailed analysis, like operational planning. A Specialist will always carefully *aim before firing.* They may not be best at spotting a new market trend or unresolved customer problem, but when an opportunity is put in front of them, they are very likely to find a good solution. When a Specialist is in a business, it is fully engaged in that business.

Know Who Fits In

Specialists also tend to have better ideas than most about who will fit into their particular company. Stephen Ardia does not waste his time recruiting at Harvard Business School. He is chief executive of Goulds Pumps Inc.—an industrial and commercial pump maker in Seneca Falls, New York. *He wants people who know pumps.* Model railroad builder Kato, in Tokyo, wants train-crazy new recruits, and Germany's Silberstrand prefers hi-fi fanatics. Do you eat, sleep with, and dream about your company's products?

Some Specialists are very aware of the insularity problems that functional organizations produce. Worthington Industries—a Columbus, Ohio, steel-processor—goes out of its way to hire former football players, people who have already proven an ability to be team players. For Worthington, this approach is a lot simpler than expensive selection consultants and teamwork training. The company seems to be on the right track, though for diversity's sake, they might want to consider some other ways people exhibit collaborative abilities.

Pay for Stability and Performance

For some Specialists, higher-than-average wages are an important part of the business strategy. This may seem odd in such cost-conscious companies, but many justify the higher pay scales by the benefits they receive from a more stable work force: low turnover-related costs, ease in conserving a proprietary knowledge base, and less labor strife. The best specialists also make liberal use of incentive pay, both to reward high customer service and to encourage everyone to wring out operational costs.

In general, Specialists' pay practices heavily rely on profit or productivity gain sharing, while Rule Breakers will, for example, use stock options to focus attention on the company's future performance. Game Players are more likely to incentivize revenue increases and market share gains, while Rule Makers often encourage development of the next generation of products with their bonus and stock plans.

When Specialists set performance targets, the orientation is frequently to beat themselves, to do better next year than they did last year. This *rear-view-mirror* type of appraisal is fine to encourage continuous improvement, but it can create *blind spots* by not paying enough attention to what competitors are doing. It can also reinforce dangerous tendencies toward smugness, a problem shared with some Rule Makers, and compared to Game Players, Specialists are chronic *under users* of benchmarking. Regardless, while a Specialist is on a long winning streak, little else may really matter but bettering last year's results. Since the 1970s, Giant Food Inc. has dominated the market share battles in the Washington, D.C. region's supermarket business. It has also successfully fended away larger food retailers with a blend of astute management, high customer service, and vertical integration. Izzy Cohen, its chief executive and son of one of Giant's founders, never admits to chasing anybody in his market. He very firmly believes that *nobody beats Giant, it only beats itself.*

The Specialist Persona

Examine the inner workings of a Specialist more closely. If a Specialist company was an individual, rather than a company, what would be the character of that person? How would that person describe himself or herself? Such an individual would probably say something along these lines:

I'm a person who is cautious and prudent, maybe a little slow in making up my mind. People tell me I'm conscientious and reliable, which is music to my ears. I like to trace my lineage directly back to yesterday's family farmers, craftsmen, or master artisans. I've never lost my work ethic.

I usually keep my cool, restrain my emotions, and stay on an even keel.

I'm detail oriented, sometimes even called a perfectionist. I am efficient and well organized—and really bothered by people who aren't. If I arrive for appointments on time and get projects finished, then why can't everybody else? Deadlines are commitments carved in stone—never starting points for a negotiation, the way some people like to treat them.

I am usually more comfortable with things I can get my hands on than with abstract intellectual concepts. I attended an engineering school and never had much patience with liberal arts types.

I'm fairly conservative and never have problems thriving in a defined structure. I go along with what the psychologist Erich Fromm once said about freedom. True freedom, according to him, is not the total absence of structure. Letting people go off and do whatever they wish seldom accomplishes much. Instead, most people, Fromm believes, prefer a clear structure, one that allows them to work within defined boundaries in autonomous and creative ways. I share this belief.

Intrinsically Motivated

The Specialist is intrinsically motivated and may say something like the following:

I'm happy to pursue creativity and technical excellence for its own sake. I get turned on by problems that need to be solved and challenges that need to be met. I'd rather prefer to receive recognition for climbing a high mountain than for developing a new theory.

I want to do work I like, even if it means taking a pay cut now and then. I get a lot of satisfaction from putting something together and seeing it work.

Maybe my range of interests are a little narrow, but they run very deep. **I want to know everything there is to know about the things that most interest me.**

I bet I'm more at peace with myself than most people. I seldom brood over existential questions. Why bother, they never have a clear answer, anyway. I'm not a person plagued with deep doubts, my sense of confidence comes from my ability to *get things done.*

Accepting People's Limitations

In his business classic, *The Gamesman,* Michael Maccoby noted that individuals who do well in Specialists cultivate a strong sense of limitations—their own and others. They work well within constraints, whether they be related to materials, techniques, energy, time, or available knowledge. You can feel safe on an Alpine ski lift knowing it was most likely designed and built by Specialists. This appreciation for limits also carries over to a respect for most moral and societal norms.

Specialists are less likely than others to be disappointed in people because they try hard to be realistic about others and about what they can expect from them. They quickly take the measure of new acquaintances; they are seldom disillusioned because they work so hard to free themselves from anything they consider an illusion. If interested in psychology, Specialists would more likely be users of tests and measurements or followers of Freud. They have little patience with much of today's achievement-oriented pop psychology or the human potential movement.

Specialists are usually content to work within a paradigm, unlike Rule Breakers who seem happy only when defying established conventions. Specialists are lower-keyed than most Game Players and less domineering than Rule Makers.

Blind Sides

Some Specialists pay a price for living such a stable and focused life. At their worst they may be obstinate or dogmatic: "Don't distract me, my mind's already made up" seems to be the message they project. Specialists may have a fairly limited degree of sensitivity, finding it difficult to reach out to others with different ways of doing things. A weakly developed antenna for other people's feelings may limit Specialists' ability to sell themselves or their ideas. Some make better senior individual contributors or high-level troubleshooters than supervisors or managers.

Competent Specialists may be—justifiably—very proud of their accomplishments. They may also be able to be seduced or misled by appeals to their pride.

Many Specialists give the impression of always intensely concentrating. For some Specialists, this can be a problem-solving strength, but it can also lead to missing out on more subjective experiences, the ones only noticed when in a more receptive mode. Specialists can easily miss nuance. Unlike Rule Breakers and Game Players, Specialists seldom respond to emotional appeals. It may even be hard for some Specialists to experience feelings of deep conviction—they respond better to calls to their sense of cold logic. They are glad to do something, as long as it all adds up.

Where Specialists Thrive

If a corporation had characteristics similar to those, where would it most thrive? **Specialists can do exceptionally well when the world of tomorrow is highly likely to be similar to that of today.** Or, in industries experiencing more turmoil, growth through specialization is appropriate when pockets of stability can be found among the chaos. Specialists search for the "eye of the hurricane."

Specialists are the kings of mature and aging industries, in markets that can be sealed or niched. These industries

- grow in pace with the economy as a whole;

- display only moderate or limited potential for dramatic upheavals;

- have companies with well-established product lines;

- host competition among a well-defined group of businesses, with relatively stable market shares, and few new entrants;

- serve customers with well-defined needs and long-established purchasing patterns; and

- are driven by tried and trusted technologies.

Financially, businesses in these industries have high returns on their assets, decreasing needs for working capital, increasing cash flows, and diminishing unit costs for goods sold—or in other words, a very favorable economic position!

If this profile fits your company's or division's external situation, consider specialization as a path to growth. If the persona of the Specialist matches your own and that of your colleagues, you might have a good chance to ably lead the business in this direction.

Cash Cows or Long-Distance Runners?

Specialists, especially successful Specialists, have frequently been labeled "cash cows." This may sound apt, considering their strong financial position, but it is also dangerous and misleading. **Specialists are not cows to be milked, they are businesses to be grown!** For many years the conventional wisdom of what to do when an industry matures was to "cut and run." Manage the business to generate a lot of cash, use these proceeds to diversify into a different industry with greater growth prospects, and then eventually divest the tired "cow" when its milk starts to run thin. This is good advice for *others* to follow.

Specialists often do very well in situations where competition follows a path of slow-motion liquidation. There is often a lot of money to be made in markets that others are exiting. Earning it requires an ability to dig in and tough out the temporary glut of competitors. Some companies lack this perseverance (out-of-place Game Players, for example). These non-Specialists are prone to do what they do best: fighting pitched battles for market share. This makes sense in rapidly growing markets; in more mature industries it is likely to lead to fatal, profitless price wars that only accelerate the departure of those not totally committed to the particular business. Mature markets require a mature, disciplined mind-set.

Threats to Future Growth

While mature markets favor long-distance runners, the industrial equivalents of earthquakes and volcanic eruptions (i.e., Bill Gates deciding to enter your business) require more than the abilities of the sprinter. Unlike human life cycles, industries can evolve in reverse. Today's mature and settled market may be tomorrow's fast-paced growth industry. When sea changes occur, old niches and long-standing market segments collapse like sand castles. Specialists in this situation risk rapid extinction if they gamble on the continued viability of what worked in the past.

Until recently, Ginns was *the* company to go to for office supplies in Washington, D.C. In a city fueled on yellow legal pads and Bic ballpoints, there was a Ginns store in sight of almost every office building. Ginns' only competition was another, look-alike Specialist, Jacobs Gardner. But in the past several years, office superstores—Staples and Office Depot—arrived into this market, with warehouse-sized variety and deeply discounted prices. Last year Ginns closed its last retail store and joined Jacobs Gardner in a new specialization: selling stationary under long-term contracts and office supplies by mail order. Ginns and Jacobs Gardner were lucky. Most of their peers have either closed completely or been merged out of existence.

Functional Myopia

Why do so many Specialists succumb to rapid change? Ironically, the same functional organization that keeps them focused on costs and quality *limits their ability to notice and adapt to rapidly changing business conditions.*

Specialists tend to *overrely on the person at the top* of their hierarchy for early warnings about major change. Specialists frequently have little choice because this is often the only job in the company that integrates the views of the senior functional managers (production, sales, finance, etc.) into the "big picture." Often the detailed work of coordinating and integrating leaves little time for focusing on what is happening outside the organization—changes that may reshape the industry in which the Specialists operate. Who in your company keeps closest watch on changes outside?

Specialists notice change the way the proverbial blind men observe the elephant—each sees only a part of the whole through his "functional blinders." Functional organizations and the hierarchies needed to coordinate them tend to require information to pass through many people before it is acted on. This as well as a paucity of windows to the outside world can make a business dangerously myopic.

Ask the Right Questions

The sense of stability many Specialists work hard to cultivate is also dangerous. It can lead to taking too many things for granted for too long. An analysis of a Specialist's board or management committee meeting minutes will most likely show that questions related to "doing things the right way" are asked much more frequently than those pertaining to "doing the right things." Too strong an emphasis on efficiency drives out considerations of effectiveness. What kinds of issues are raised most often in the meetings you attend?

Plans Masquerading as Strategy

Missing the forest for the trees is easy for a Specialist—it seems to come with the territory. Its field of vision is just like that of a high-powered electron microscope: very narrow. Fine-grained details are observed closely, whereas broad basic changes disappear into the background and are missed. Developments occurring outside the Specialist's particular niche may be completely ignored or discounted.

Strategic planning is supposed to cure this kind of narrowness, but what many Specialists proudly call their "strategic plans" are primarily agglomerations of unrelated details. One Specialist executive proudly showed me a three-volume planning document. He obviously felt so much information was gathered that the company must be safely on top of the situation. Upon further inspection, the plan consisted of stapled-together collections of individual departmental plans, with minimal examination of the real key issues that cross-cut the company. These were really plans for sales or manufacturing, *not a vision of what the business as a whole* must become. These multiple volumes were primarily a source of dangerous false comfort. How thick are your strategic plans?

Some Specialists succumb to management by autopilot, allowing the planning process itself to become a paper-shuffling ritual. All the forms are properly filled out, but little effort is given to obtaining new insight about customer or market dynamics. After the founders of Polaroid and the Walt Disney Company died, both firms drifted from the rule-breaking to the Specializing orientation. Instead of applying a fresh creative approach to planning their futures, managers in both responded to business challenges by asking "what would Walt [or Ed] do now?" Good strategy seldom flows from exegesis.

Management by Imperialist

Specialists are also susceptible to a problem much more serious than excessive ritualism: executives who believe that absolute control is the only answer to the challenges facing the company. These individuals fear losing their position of power more than threats in the marketplace, so they dominate—or attempt to dominate—all aspects of the company's operation. They insist that employees completely submit to their ways. Relationships among managers and subordinates are characterized more by dominance and submission, not colleaguality and mutual respect. These situations become poisonous quickly. The strong human ties that often bridge the gaps caused by a Specialist's functional organization become almost impossible to maintain, and civil war among departmental fiefdoms becomes rampant.

A. Robert Abboud, once chairman of First Chicago Corporation, ran the bank that way. A competing banker characterized Abboud's attempts to run everything and to know what everyone was doing all the time as more appropriate for a branch manager than chief executive. This style was effective during Abboud's initial years at First Chicago when he turned around a serious financial loss situation; however, as the bank matured, Abboud did not, and over 100 officers resigned before Abboud finally left. This situation is too common in U.S. businesses. World War I fighter ace Eddie Rickenbacker later led Eastern Airlines and started its long slide to decline with similar behavior. Similarly, Henry Ford's drive for absolute control almost destroyed the automaker he created.

Sustaining Specialists' Growth

Sustaining the growth of a company on the Specialist's path is not easy. Excessive control and functional myopia must be avoided, and the "cash cow" mentality must be left for those Game Players who have strayed into markets where they do not belong. Oversimplifications tend to stunt, rather than deliver, growth. Phrases like "sticking to one's knitting" have a nice ring in a management seminar, but staying with only what you are good at today seldom leaves much room for growth. It is more likely to diminish a business by *only encouraging variations on a theme.* Attempting to fuel growth through tinkering is the equivalent of the Detroit automaker's bygone practice of limiting product development to annual redesigns of a car's tail fins during a time consumers hungered for the smaller, fuel-efficient cars made in Japan.

The road to recovery for a Specialist that strays from the growth path can be a long one. *The core capability of Specialists is knowing how to focus on a particular market segment and seal it off from others by providing customers with a hard-to-replicate advantage.* When Specialists move into markets that require other competences, their performance is likely to diminish (unless they also transform their capabilities, organization, and people to fit the new situation). This is what happened to Goodyear Tire & Rubber, Owens-Corning, and Union Carbide. They all blurred their focus.

Returning to Growth

Union Carbide is a good example of what straying Specialists need to do to restore growth. This multi-billion-dollar chemical maker was once the quintessential American growth company. It was a charter member of Dow Jones Industrial Average of Stock Prices, and it has won more awards for innovation in chemical engineering than Du Pont and Dow Chemical combined. But in the 1970s and 1980s, it found its base petrochemical business under attack from foreign competitors. Rather than stand and fight to retain its position as the industry's low-cost chemical producer, Union Carbide surrendered market share and diluted focus by branching off into areas it knew little about. These diversifications, all touted at the time as "great growth businesses," included synthetic gemstones, salmon farming, integrated circuits, and even diaper making (the baby boom generation was just reaching its childbearing years).

Then the inevitable happened. These cash-hungry new businesses consumed the dollars and top management attention that should have gone into the chemical business. Carbide's American rival, Dow Chemical, had the courage to borrow money to expand its core business and soared ahead in the petrochemical market. Dow attacked the foreign competitors aggressively, often abroad where its massive investments in new capacity made it the most reliable supplier in an industry too afraid of the OPEC cartel to invest in new plants. Carbide and others tried to win overseas business through low prices, but security of supply made Dow's higher prices easily palatable. Carbide's weakened position was compounded by the Bhopal tragedy and a well-publicized leak at a plant in Institute, West Virginia, and it attracted the attention of a Wall Street raider.

Downsizing Isn't Enough

Fending off the raider's attempted takeover forced Union Carbide to do what it probably should have done long before:

- Its marginally related diversifications were sold off.

- Its monumental, conglomerate-era, headquarters building was also sold, and its staff was pared from 3,000 to 500.

- Costs were squeezed out of every part of Carbide's remaining operations, starting with the elimination of two corporate jets and the chief executive's chauffeur.

These changes alone are never sufficient to restore real growth. At Union Carbide they were only prerequisites to *free up management time and to get the most from the company's real genius:* its competitive advantage in using advanced technology to make chemicals cheaply. Carbide's growth is now fueled by selling both its chemicals and the processes it uses to make them. Carbide keeps some of its technology enhancement to itself (so it retains lead as a low-cost producer) but licenses still-attractive techniques to others so that it grows profits even when competitors steal away an order.

The Critical Role of Top Leadership

Specialists, by their nature, are companies driven from the top. A lot of the credit for Union Carbide's strong return to profitability and growth belongs to Robert Kennedy, its chief executive since 1986. A lifelong Carbide employee, Kennedy had enough appreciation for and confidence in the Specialist's underlying strengths to turn the company almost upside down to restore these capabilities to prominence. **Growth-oriented managers in Specialists have two hard-to-combine skills:**

- **insisting that things be done right** (this is the Specialist's stock-in-trade, keeping the craftsmanship ethic alive) and

- **keeping alert for new things to do** and new sources of growth *rooted* in the Specialist's particular core skills.

At Union Carbide, Robert Kennedy's approach to the second skill involves encouraging researchers to apply their proprietary process technology to produce products priced higher than the mundane commodity chemicals that Carbide is so good at making cheaply. Synthetic rubber, used to make window frames and auto parts, is one of these possibilities. These new products may take Carbide toward markets where Specialists do not belong, but Kennedy's memories of its recent painful restructuring should provide navigational lessons to find the right new niches. Effective, not just efficient, Specialist managers keep growth high on the company's agenda.

Growth Options

There are a wide range of growth strategies available to Specialists:

Go for share of customer.   Leave pursuit of market share increases to Game Players. Instead, find growth through increasing "share of customer." Look for logical ways in which well-established relations with existing customers can provide conduits to sell them other things you have credibility providing. Crown Cork & Seal specializes in bottle tops and metal cans. It recently purchased the largest U.S. maker of plastic bottles. Noting that the same customers who buy metal cans also purchase plastic containers, Crown quickly put plastic-making machinery from its acquisition into its existing plants and now efficiently makes and sells a full range to each customer.

Let the customer find new uses for your products.   Kellogg originally was a health food company, making breakfast cereals for people with digestive ailments. The product soon caught on and became a mass market item. Some markets come full circle, though, if you wait long enough. Contemporary concerns about fiber and nutrition are bringing Kellogg back to its health specialty roots. 3M is another company that grew from a lackluster maker of industrial abrasives to a consumer giant by fusing a Rule Breaker's sense of creativity with a Specialist's focus on a handful of technologies it knows inside and out.

Segment out of commodity markets.   The key to growth in a mature market or survival in a rapidly growing one is segmentation. Let others turn products into commodities, while you stay alert for the most profitable pieces of the industry. The American message-paging business is a battlefield in which a dozen Game Players compete, primarily on price. In the midst of this chaos, Skytel plays the game in a more focused manner and is able to charge customers a third more than its main competitors. Skytel concentrates on the business paging market and has grown to be the dominant nationwide beeping service. It continually innovates to protect its niche, creating a cross-country two-way wireless network for E-mail and offering pagers that display over 200 alphanumeric characters. Don't get into the commodity mind-set! You will only relegate yourself to the low end of your business.

Innovate! Innovate! Innovate!   Innovation is key to the survival of most Specialists, even those operating in industries long on tradition but short on fresh thinking. Several years ago, American President Line was an endangered species, a high-labor-cost shipping company struggling in an industry of cheap foreign competitors. Rather than shut down, APL innovated. Knowing it could never ship goods from Asia, through the Panama Canal, to the East Coast as inexpensively as its competitors, it decided to create a land bridge from Asia. Its ships carrying New York-bound goods end their journey in Oakland, California. Then the containers they are carrying are put on an APL specially designed, double-stack container train that speeds them to New York. This service is two weeks faster than port-to-port competitors, which allows APL to attract higher value, higher margin cargo.

All innovations create problems; APL's was no exception. Most of its traffic went one way, from the Orient to the East Coast, but the special rail cars it used had to be returned to California for more containers. Rather than send them empty, producing no revenues, APL managers took off their seafaring blinders and learned that most domestic U.S. cargo moves—a lucky coincidence—east to west. Soon deals were made with United Parcel and the U.S. Postal Service to fill the empties, and APL's margins received another healthy boost.

Become the global specialist.   Nokia used to be a small Finnish company that sold a little of everything—from television tubes to toilet paper. While this range made sense for a company serving a small Nordic economy, it did not fit the global aspirations of Jorma Ollila, its chief executive since 1992. In true Specialist style, he sold off most of Nokia's product lines and concentrated on developing the mobile telephone technology it had once pioneered. Ollila knew this focus would require selling in markets beyond Scandinavia, so he pulled all the stops and focused all his engineering talent on producing cheaply the latest technologies. This single-minded focus allowed Nokia to steal the technology lead in cellular phones from Motorola and become the number-two company in this high-growth industry.

Broaden the Field of Vision

Capitalizing on growth options such as these is heavily dependent on Specialist managers with a *willingness to broaden their field of vision* while *keeping their core strengths.* They have to actively resist the natural tendency not to want to be distracted from the straight and narrow. Some steps growth-minded Specialists can take to stay attuned to future opportunities are as follows:

- Expand the number of employees with *broad, multifunctional jobs.* Organize in ways that pull together functional teams around specific customer groups *below* the chief executive and senior management levels.

- Seed the business with *senior individual contributors* responsible for the "white space" on the organization chart—the promising markets, technologies, and customer needs not currently the responsibility of an established organization unit.

- Encourage *widespread involvement* in industry and professional associations. Make sure that functional specialists actively use the industry associations to broaden their personal perspective. Then use the information obtained to actively challenge the company's conventional wisdom.

- Organize *cross-departmental/cross-organizational level networks* throughout the company to generate the strategic plan. This is too important a process to delegate to planning specialists. Consider ways to actively involve suppliers and customers in preparing the plan.

- Incentivize employees on *company-wide*, not solely departmental, *performance*.

- Use tools such as *360° evaluations* of individual performance (appraisals in which employees are rated not just by those above them but by peers and subordinates as well) to lower the walls around functions and levels. Be willing to retrain or remove strong performers who will not support others or play as part of the team. Their debilitating effect on the organization overall will outweigh the benefits of their individual talent.

Follow John Welsh's lead at General Electric: "The two quickest ways to part company with GE are," says Welsh, "one, to commit an integrity violation, or, two, to be a controlling, turf-defending, oppressive manager who can't change and who saps and squeezes people rather than excites and draws out their energy and creativity." This is good advice for managers on any growth path.

A Fifth Path to Growth

Matching a *situation* with its appropriate *strategy* and the right kind of *people* needed to carry it out is the first step to growth. There are many paths a business can take to successfully grow. Mastery of one, however, does not imply success on the others.

Some paths are mutually exclusive. Rule breaking would be counterproductive, bull-in-a-china-shop behavior in a Specialist's natural market. Few Game Players successfully unseat a reigning Rule Maker, although some Rule Breakers have.

Successful Specialists hate to feel they are at the mercy of events in their marketplace. They will work overtime, if necessary, to control everything affecting them. Specialists do well in situations stable enough to allow such behavior—but not all growth situations are amenable to focus and defense. Some markets are so volatile and some rules of the game so up in the air that the only way to *move forward is by giving in*. These chaotic industries are the most challenging in which to grow. They are the realm of the Improviser.

What Is It Like Working for a Specialist?

This is the BEST place in the world to work.

Here are some observations from a Specialist's chief technology officer. This company has a reputation as the *place to buy the electronic components it manufactures.*

■ ■ ■

I feel as though this is the job I've been preparing for all my life. I'm in charge of microchip technology in a company that lives, breathes, and eats microchip technology.

I studied chip making and IC circuits when they were just a glimmer in some Bell Lab's research project. I probably know more about how to put electronic circuits on silicon wafers than anybody in the country—maybe the whole industry.

I've got absolute control over the production process here. All the quality people report directly to me, and nothing ships unless it meets my standards.

I'm no slouch in the cost department either. I got my last promotion to technology czar because of the campaign I spearheaded to drive down our production costs. I've just about eliminated scrap and rework, and we can now produce silicon chips for less than it would cost to find it on the beach.

If only our sales force were half as efficient as we are. They're always away from the office, and nobody has any idea what they do, aside from eating expensive expense-account lunches. I don't even know what we need them for anyway—the engineers at our biggest customers all call me when they need something.

The company is doing better than ever. We are just finishing another record revenue year, and profits are at a historical high. The way things are going I won't have to worry about touching my 401K plan until retirement.

Specialist   We've just signed a big production contract with IBM, making all their new high-performance chips. Years ago I worked there in manufacturing. It was just like I was in career Siberia. Talk about being the low guy on the totem pole—all the glory and big bonuses went to the sales and marketing people.

Here, it's a different world. My work is watched closely by the top brass, and I'm paid more than anybody in my salary grade. I guess I've found my niche.

We still need to be careful that we don't let our success go to our heads. Just a few months ago one of our sharpest competitors went nose under. Its quality had been slipping over the past years, and a big snafu with a new product—using a technology never tried in this industry—brought even its most loyal customers to our doorstep. I'm no management consultant, but it's obvious the troubles began when its bright founder let all his success go to his head.

He abandoned engineering to become a jet-setter. I even saw him on TV sitting two seats away from the first lady at last year's State of the Union speech. Hobnobbing with the president is fine, but not when it takes your eye off your business. He overdelegated—I call it abdicated—and let his bloated marketing staff take the company into businesses where they didn't belong. He's flying coach now. His stock's not worth much, and the bankruptcy referee made sure he isn't paid a cent until the company's turned around.

That'll never happen here. Our top management is lean and focused. They believe in the straight and narrow. So do I.

This is an engineering company, and I'm its chief engineer.

This is the WORST place in the world to work.

At the same component-making Specialist, here is the perspective of a woman who was last year's sales superstar.

■ ■ ■

This company's like a walled castle, moat and all. The drawbridge is up, and I'm out on the wrong side.

I left a copy of *The New Yorker* on my desk last
week, and the techies stared at it all day—like it was █ Specialist █
some alien icon. Well, for them it probably was. I don't mind if I never
read another one of their tech manuals again.

I've never worked in a place with so many narrow-minded people.
Everyone seems to live, breathe, and eat computer chips. I'd like to tell
them to go out and get a life, but I've got enough problems getting
people to listen to me already.

Which is surprising, considering I sold more of our micropieces
than anyone else did last year. Fat lot of good it did me. I got one "pat
on the back" memo for my personnel file from the marketing manager,
and a nanosecond mention at the big deal, black tie Annual Technology
Awards Dinner.

You know, I bet senior management doesn't even track sales
statistics. They're too immersed in how close we are getting to
achieving six-sigma quality nirvana. They should though. If they
looked closely, they'd see that while sales keeps climbing each year, our
best customers are buying more and more from other sources, and the
new generation IBM has on the drawing board won't even use any of
our chips. If only I had a way to get our execs to stand back and look at
the big picture, I'm sure it would convince them to put more dollars
behind new product development. All they seem to want to do is keep
tweaking the old stuff we've made forever.

Management wants everything to go through "channels"—they
say it allows them to keep focused on our core competences, but every
time I share my latest intelligence about IBM with my boss, he shud-
ders and swears me to tell no one. I can see he doesn't want to be the
bearer of bad news.

A lot of our recent growth has come from a few big contract
production jobs. We've relegated a lot of our growth to this outsourcing work—picking up somebody else's scut work. I just can't
understand that if this stuff is so profitable, why our customers don't
just do it themselves.

It's also a personal thing. I really get excited when I see the name
of the company I work for out there on our products in the

Specialist   marketplace; you know, like those "Intel Inside" ads.
But we're moving in the other direction—making other people's stuff and then putting *their* name on it. It just doesn't seem right, but it's the way the wind is blowing.

And it will probably blow me elsewhere. I was last year's star seller. I expect to be top seller next year, too—just not here.

CHAPTER 8

Improvising

Profit from Change
by Rolling with the Punches

Imagine working in an industry where everything seems up in the air—almost all the time. Whenever a company advances two steps, it falls behind at least one. How can a business possibly grow when the following occurs?

- Many *aggressive competitors*, from a variety of industries, are preparing to enter its market.

- Its *largest customer* plans to be its biggest competitor.

- Smaller competitors are *skimming off the most profitable customers* and lines of business.

- Some of the most promising growth possibilities are industry segments dominated by its *biggest customers.*

- The *technologies* underlying its products are *in a state of near-complete flux.* New, competing technologies are being announced monthly, and no one is certain what the new industry standards will be. It has a multi-billion-dollar investment in fixed assets that may lose much of its value if several emerging technologies live up to their promise.

181

This, in a nutshell (if you have not already guessed), is the competitive situation of *America's local telephone companies*. These businesses, the seven Baby Bells and a score of independent companies, are facing a battery of pressures—each sufficiently strong to topple well-established corporate giants. However, they have not gone under, and several have made impressive gains, growing both revenues and profits. How does a company grow while facing threats, uncertainty, and inconsistency on all sides? It improvises.

A Growth Strategy for the Future

Improvisation is the growth path to choose *when no other good choices are available*. Improvisers lack the sharp focus of Specialists and for good reason. Improvisers' target markets are in such flux that any attempt to zero in on a particular segment is pointless. Yesterday's promising niche too easily becomes today's cash trap and tomorrow's dead end.

Instead, **Improvisers make up for a lack of concentrated effort with an organization built around speed, cunning, and flexibility.** They have a great gift for rolling with the punches, that is, for shifting strategies to meet whatever immediate challenges must be faced. Improvisers can be very exciting places to work—for the right person—but for many individuals, this is a path to be avoided. While exhilarating for some managers, others are sure to find it only a source of depression, burnout, and ongoing frustration.

Improvisation is the least appreciated, most misunderstood path to growth. It is the one most likely to cause a company to stumble, but it is also a very important path. Along with Specialization, it is likely to be the most traveled path by the turn of the century.

A Blue Chip Growth Strategy

There are, as is true with rule breaking, many easier ways to make money. Leaders of Rule Breakers, though, choose that path because they feel an *inner* compulsion to follow it. In contrast, Improvisers seldom volunteer to take this approach to growth. They are driven to it, instead, by strong, *external* pressures. At least Improvisers find themselves in good company with organizations such as *American Express* and *Kodak;* many *Madison Avenue ad agencies;* industry giants like *AT&T* and

General Motors; Westinghouse (the Specialist General Electric's historical rival); *IBM;* many of IBM's rivals such as *Apple, Digital,* and *Unisys;* and most of the world's airlines.

B.F. Goodrich, an Akron, Ohio industrial company, is a classic Improviser. It has demonstrated a remarkable ability to change course— from spinning off its traditional tire business, so it could focus on making polyvinyl chloride, to selling the PVC operation, to allow it to emphasize other chemical products and to, eventually, enter the aerospace business—all within ten years!

A Strategy for Both Pioneers and Latecomers

Improvisation is the path followed by the original pioneers of on-line services: America Online, CompuServe, and Prodigy. Their businesses are caught between a rock and a hard place. They operate in the wake of Rule Maker Microsoft's entry into the on-line market. They also face challenges by the less tightly organized but rapidly growing Internet.

Improvisation is a path that has opened many opportunities for entrepreneurs like Kathy Haycock. A former dental hygienist, she took advantage of the chaotic changes in the telephone business to start Call-America in Mesa, Arizona. Her company buys discounted long-distance service in bulk from AT&T and resells it at higher rates to 20,000 customers. Haycock mortgaged her home to start up what quickly became a 25-employee organization. It is a niche player in the telecommunications industry, but Call-America lacks the protection most Specialists provide to their segments. Haycock is at the mercy of all the competitive pressures buffeting her major supplier and may quickly be victimized by new wireless technologies that allow competitors to steal away her customers.

Hallmarks of Improvisers

Improvisers do have some consistency behind their inconsistency. For them, strategy and tactics often blur. Survival and growth are synonymous, and they are driven by both being fast on their feet and being able to do whatever it takes to remain competitive at the moment. Shifting gears from emphasizing product quality to service delivery to low cost is all in a day's work. Long-range planning, for some Improvisers, means having a good fix on how the next quarter's likely to turn out.

Guerrilla Warfare

When at their best, Improvisers are like guerrilla soldiers. Both move fast, get off a few shots quickly in the general direction of their opponent, see where the shells land, and keep improving their accuracy by trial and error. Then they go into hiding, lest they attract too much attention from more powerful enemies. Both Improvisers and guerrillas avoid fixed positions requiring defense and live off the land as best as possible.

Even in asset-laden businesses, such as telecommunications, this philosophy holds. A "the best defense is a good offense" spirit characterizes both the moves of cable TV companies into telephony and experiments by local telephone service providers to offer home movies on demand through existing phone cables. In addition to poaching, each competitor is racing to develop interactive video shopping systems—not so much because consumers have signaled a deep desire for this service—but to preempt other companies from offering it.

The Concentrating Effect of the Hangman's Noose

Some Improviser chief executives, like Apple's Michael Spindler and Digital's Robert Palmer, are aided in building flexibility and cunning into their organizations by the need for a quick turnaround in profitability. The job of managers in these companies is very focused: helping employees abandon fantasy-prone tendencies toward long-range planning and, instead, relearn how to live in the moment. Doing this requires the simple focusing on specific, immediate goals and doing whatever it takes to achieve them. At Bell Atlantic this is called "being here now," a key tenet of the value-inculcation effort called the "Bell Atlantic Way."

Most Improvisers operate in industries with many interesting distractions—new customers, competitors, and technologies, all good excuses for avoiding current performance problems. An important management priority is to keep everyone's attention on the straight and narrow. This, an easy task in Specialists, is like pulling teeth in Improvisers. Sometimes only an immediate crisis makes this kind of focus possible. Improvisers are living examples of the eighteenth-century

English author Samuel Johnson's observation: when a man learns he is to be soon hanged, he also receives the wonderful gift of a concentrated mind.

Naskapi Indian-Style Planning

Even when awaiting the hangman's noose, it helps to have a plan. Let's start at what might seem like an unlikely place, the Naskapi Indians of Canada's northern province of Labrador. These Native North Americans are born Improvisers. Like many of their counterparts in business, they are hunters. Their land is not especially fertile, and they move around too much to be disciplined crop tenders. So they are faced, very frequently, with the need to decide where to go next to hunt for game. The Naskapi set their course with a well-established methodology. They obtain some dried caribou bones, remains from a previous successful hunt, and build a fire. Then they hold the bones over the flames until cracks appear. These cracks are then "read" by the tribe's designated strategic planner. He interprets the cracks to indicate the direction the hunter should take to find game.

The Naskapi practice has a lot of credibility because it allows a place for their gods in the planning process. Its application is also popular because it works. Though not every hunting trip is successful, enough are that the Indians are reasonably well fed.

Planning for an Uncertain World

Karl Weick is the Cornell University theoretician who has had a great influence on much of Tom Peter's thinking. He has analyzed the Naskapi planning process, finding a number of useful features that are applicable beyond Labrador.

- *No person or group is blamed* if game is not found. The gods are considered at fault, and team cohesion is maintained.

- The location chosen has *no relationship to* places where game was found to be plentiful in *the past*. This is good; otherwise, the most likely place the tribe would return to hunt would be where they had best luck before. This may seem like an obvious course of action, but it is also very counterproductive. Revisiting past successes is a way to guarantee future failure—the animals there would soon become depleted. (Refer back to Chapter 2.)

- The Naskapi's *actions did not follow any set patterns.* Irregularity is extremely useful—whether chasing game or battling tough competition. *Regular patterns will, over time, serve to sensitize the prey to the hunter's habits* (just as antibiotics eventually induce bacteria to breed resistant strains, rendering the once-miracle-drugs impotent). Game animals, like their hunters, like to survive too, and they will just move to a more distant feeding ground.

Avoid Predictability

What this tribe has done, Weick observes, is to intentionally complicate human behavior. It would have been much more straightforward for the group to vote on the direction to hunt or listen to the hunter with the best practices or greatest number of past kills, but in this situation, just as in the constantly changing competitive positions held by many Improvisers, there are real advantages to avoiding predictable or fixed patterns of activity.

Improvisers must also thrive in inherently unpredictable environments. Their chances of accomplishing this are greatly diminished if they approach planning and decision making with the deterministic rigor appropriate for Specialists or Rule Makers. This is not to suggest the planning department be replaced by a table of random numbers, but **planning in a way that surprises and throws the competition off balance has a lot to recommend to it** in the world of the Improviser. When everything is up for grabs in the marketplace, a company is not likely to be worse off by behaving randomly than attempting to follow a lockstep plan. It is not especially productive to follow traditional planning techniques in an unplanable industry.

A management style based in part on randomness has some key advantages. It helps a business *forget* what made it currently successful. *Managers tend to remember only what is producing results today.* Using recent memories is a good way to be efficient but a poor approach to coping with uncertainty and the need for constant change. **It is easy for an Improviser to stumble when it is too adapted to its situation.**

Benefits of Improvisational Planning

Karl Weick found many advantages to the Naskapi planning approach. These also can serve as a checklist to judge the appropriateness of a planning process to the unique situation of an Improviser. These benefits, to paraphrase Weick, include the following:

1. Mistakes have few consequences (the hunt can begin again tomorrow).

2. Decisions can be made when facts are otherwise insufficient.

3. A choice can be made among look-alike alternatives.

4. Competitors are confused; employees are not—they know how the course of action was arrived at.

5. A near-infinite number of alternatives are available (thinking out of the box is built into this method). Real novelty is introduced into the plan.

6. Decisions can be made swiftly, without a lot of debate (why argue about something with no knowable answer?)

7. It is easy to change a streak of bad luck.

8. This is a low-overhead technique, requiring minimal data collection and record keeping.

9. Bias is eliminated; all possible choices are weighed equally.

10. The process is fun.

Insightful Improvisers know absolute control is an illusion. They leave this practice to Rule Makers and Specialists (whose natural markets are less dependent on serendipity). Improvisers can do a lot worse than following the principles that guide the Naskapi's tactical planning. Taking small steps this way helps Improvisers avoid being bet-the-business companies. Improvisers like to survive.

Fresh Thinking, Outside Leadership

A key to successful improvisation is fresh thinking about the company and its situation. Creative planning procedures can provide some insights, but many Improvisers also require a change of leadership to move them forward.

- George Fisher, ex–chief executive of highly successful Motorola, replaced generations of inbred leaders at Kodak. Like many of his predecessors, Fisher has a technical background. But his Ph.D. is in math, not Kodak's traditional core competence of chemistry, and he learned how to manage in an electronics environment.

- IBM's new chief executive, Louis Gerstner, came from RJR Nabisco, a consumer products company.

- 25 percent of Nynex's top management group were hired with no telephone business experience. The head of Ameritech's endangered residential phone service monopoly, James Firestone, came from a successful career managing American Express's travelers cheque business.

There are some exceptions to bringing in outsiders but not many. B.F. Goodrich's multiple, chameleon-like business reinventions were all led by one chief executive, John Ong. General Motors' chief executive, John Smith, spent his career at this Detroit car maker, but the company's senior change agent, board chairman John Smale, was the former Procter & Gamble CEO. GM also brought in a senior manager from Bausch & Lomb, a BMW owner to boot, to revitalize its worldwide marketing operation.

Forget the Organization Chart

Official versions of an Improviser's organization chart are even less useful than in most companies. Improvisers' organizations have only coincidental correspondence to the rapidly evolving strategies they follow. These structures—and on-paper depictions of them—both *lead* and *lag* current reality.

Some organization units shown are, in reality, empty boxes, divisions that have been announced but not yet staffed. The value of these departments is primarily aspirational. Other departments may exist and be populated but are more a memorial to a past business plan than the current strategy. Individuals working in these functions are sometimes called "the walking dead." Their jobs are redundant, but their employer has been too distracted with other matters to redeploy or outplace the individuals in them. How accurate is your company's organization chart? How useful is it?

Restructuring Can Be a Substitute for Real Change

Improvisers seem fated to be on the receiving end of frequent reorganizations—each usually occurring before the dust has settled from the last wrenching change. Even though these are often intended to signal significant directional shifts, reordering lines and boxes is seldom sufficient to establish a new growth path. Too often it is *a substitute for the real, deeper changes* that are needed for a business to thrive as an Improviser. John Scully was known for his frequent reorganization of Apple Computer (an environment where you would check your E-mail each morning to see what department you're working in that day). Kodak's employees, before George Fisher arrived, experienced *five* major restructurings, none going far enough to reenergize growth.

Catching the Disease of the Market

A problem too-frequent organization changes bring—along with their seemingly unending waves of downsizing—is the importation of the turmoil and uncertainty of the market into the Improviser's inner workings. **While it is vital to roughly align organization with marketplace dynamics, too close a coupling with an industry lacking clear direction can become very debilitating.** Employees tire of the constant change in their work, and they hunker down and cling even more tightly to the old ways as a way to cope with their fears. Effective improvisation requires discovering ways to erect a "zone of relative stability" between the company and the maelstroms in which they operate.

Some Improvisers keep their structures simple and stable but accommodate change by more-frequent-than-usual personnel reassignments. Others

- establish several *senior-level troubleshooter or coordinator positions* to oversee the key business processes of the moment;

- give departments *intentionally overlapping charters*, acknowledging the need to continually develop alternative approaches to meeting market needs; and

- manage key operations through a structure of *temporary teams*, drawn from employees in the ongoing departments, *overlaid on the existing structure*, and set up and disbanded as needs arise.

Today Is What Counts Most

Regardless of contemporary trendy talk about managing for the long haul, creating the markets of tomorrow, controlling your destiny before someone else does, and the like, it is important to keep in mind the two kinds of companies for whom these injunctions are counterproductive, even toxic. One is a company whose current operations are hemorrhaging to such an extent that rapid and ruthless turnaround management is the only chance for survival. The other is an Improviser.

For Improvisers, a focus on the short term is pervasive and vital. Cycle-time improvement is treated as a religion, not just the latest management gimmick. When reengineering is undertaken, great emphasis is given to its "obliterate the old, start with a clean sheet of paper" techniques. Three-years-until-results-come-in projects are shunned in favor of investments that pay back during the next quarter.

Pay for the Here and Now

The here-and-now orientation should also be reflected in and reinforced by the compensation system. Pay is more variable than fixed; pensions are funded through profit sharing—when there are profits to share. The entitlement mentality is minimized, starting with top management. Executive perks are few, pain is shared along with gain, and stock options are *never* repriced. Top management is held accountable for keeping a vigilant eye on operational basics: 50 percent of Apple Computer boss Michael Spindler's compensation is pegged to annual success in delivering and managing products.

Heavy Dose of Reality

To earn his bonus, Spindler has cut Apple's average development cycle from two years to nine months. New projects now begin and end within one pay cycle; bonuses are not awarded for milestone achievement or good tries. More than half of Apple's R&D projects are expected to turn into products in less than three years. Apple's previous chief executive, John Scully, was trained as an architect and was considered susceptible to being "snowed" by the company's top technical talent (although Scully also held the "chief technical officer" title). Spindler, even though himself an engineer, keeps from getting caught up in debates about visionary products. Engineers now present their pet ideas for review to a board of Apple's top technologists. Each member of this board is distinguished by having already created at least one successful Apple product.

"War rooms" are used at Apple and other Improvisers to plot the launch of new products. Customer and competitor reactions are closely monitored, and mid-course corrections are made in rapid, commando style. The atmosphere in some reflects an "us vs. them" siege mentality, and depending on the Improviser's immediate competitive position, pure survival may be the management team's only objective.

These forms of "reality-based management" may force an Improviser to abandon long-held tenets:

- Apple once shunned offers to clone its Macintoshes; now licensees are actively sought. Improviser executives mutter "Never say never" in their sleep.

- IBM was once Apple's main market opponent. Now Apple and IBM jointly develop products to compete with Microsoft.

- Apple's latest computers acknowledge market realities. They all run software made for Microsoft's Windows as well as Apple's original graphically oriented programs.

Has your business ever "strategically backpedaled"?

Hockey Stick Projections

A few Improvisers try to deny the need for immediacy. They hunker down, avoid risks, and spend long hours developing elaborate ten-year plans. While this approach to planning runs completely counter to the wisdom of the Naskapi, it fits into another Indian tradition. These plans are the business equivalent of *tribal amulets;* they are expected to ward off an evil future. Successful Improvisers who go through these rituals are usually savvy enough, though, *to ignore them* when quick decisions eventually need to be made. A few years ago a manager at one troubled steel maker responded to headquarter's request for a new strategic plan by sending a copy of last year's plan with an updated title page. No one at headquarters ever noticed!

Hockey stick–like, wishful-thinking projections, showing a quick reversal of a long negative trend, abound in many long-range plans. Prosperity (and stability) is foreseen just around the corner. Hope springs eternal. For some companies, these are appropriate expectations, but Improvisers endanger themselves when they view their path as only a temporary detour, a transitional stage requiring only holding one's breath until stability returns. The reality, for many Improvisers, is that they will be on this path for many years. They need to know how to manage themselves to thrive through flexibility. Setting realistic expectations is a good first step.

Seesawlike Financials

Until the dynamics of an Improviser's market slow down, its financials are likely to reflect the ups and downs of a child's seesaw ride. Sales may be well below all-time revenue records. Kodak's planned divestitures changed it from a 20-billion to a 12-billion-dollar company. Its debt has been paid down, thanks both to the proceeds from asset sales and also to the enhancing of its strategic flexibility.

Having solidly positive cash flow—the money used to pay suppliers and meet payrolls—is more important for some Improvisers than the size of year-end profits. America Online, when it was its industry's fastest grower, earned a measly $6 million on sales of $104 million. Part-Improviser, part-Specialist CompuServe did better, with before-tax margins of about 25 percent. Prodigy, pioneer of this industry, had ten earningless years (and a billion dollars of investment from its deep-pocketed co-owners, IBM and Sears) before finally turning a modest profit in 1995.

In keeping with a pattern of low or erratic earnings, Improvisers' overhead and administrative costs need to be at record lows. An Improviser's controller once observed that the only increases in the human resources department's budget were for outplacement and survivor training.

Is improvisation really a *path to growth,* or is it only a *holding ground* for a company while retrenching, turning around, and searching for one of the other four paths? It can be both, but improvising should not be written off because it lacks some of the traditional positive expectations about growth exhibited by companies on the other courses. For many companies, the only good alternative—because of their market and competitive situation—is to remain flexible and improvise. Let's look more closely at these typical situations, ones where Improvisers are likely to outperform most others.

When Improvisation Makes Most Sense

Improvisation is especially useful in two situations:

1. When a market is on the verge or in the midst of a *massive, hard-to-predict-how-things-will-sort-out change.*

2. When a company's competitive position has slid to the point where *just doing the customary things better* is unlikely to improve prospects for growth.

Confronting Massive Change

The situation faced by the U.S. local telephone companies, described at the start of this chapter, is a classic, requiring all the talents of an Improviser. Improvisation is their best strategy to cope with the melange of an industry reshaping itself around providers of local, long-distance, cable, wireless, data communications, home shopping and movies on demand. In addition to being threatened by its biggest customers, the Baby Bells'

- customer preferences are open to widely differing interpretations;

- stockholders frequently are up in arms at reports that the dividend might be cut to fund growth initiatives;

- costs are the highest in the industry;

- hope to thrive in new, go-go markets with an organization that has traditionally operated along the lines of a military or government bureaucracy; and

- prices and services are subject to both federal and state regulation, entry into new markets is controlled by court judgments, and all of these are changing in a disjointed manner at an unpredictable pace.

These phone companies are operating in the nebulous state of neither having a complete monopoly nor having freedom to set prices and enter new businesses. One Forbes writer summed up this state of slow-motion deregulation as one in which these Baby Bells are praying to become competitive, but just not yet. This uncertainty exacts a severe price in businesses accustomed to being, in their local markets, quasi–Rule Makers.

The situation of the phone companies has parallels to that of the American auto industry in the early 1970s. Japanese car imports started entering the market but had not made much of a dent in Detroit's market share. A more pressing worry was the plans of Volkswagen to begin production in the United States. In a few years, the Japanese had won much of the market for small cars—and the German beetle maker turned out to be a minor distraction for Detroit and eventually closed its Pittsburgh plant.

Executives of the regional phone companies do not want to be caught off guard. Nor do they want to be distracted by threats that never seriously materialize. Many, often at odds, views of the future are expressed. The chief executive of Southern New England Telecommunications Co., Daniel Miglio, feels flatly that there is no future for the traditional local phone business. His counterpart at Bell Atlantic, Raymond Smith, is more of an optimist. Smith feels lucky to be living in an era when almost every company in his industry seems destined to do well. For Smith, the mid-1990s are like the mid-1890s, when almost everyone who started a steel mill died rich.

Similar uncertainties and divergences of opinion about how to deal with them plague other major industries, including air travel, banking, electric power, and health care. Is your industry facing a major sea change? Is there any consensus in your company about how to cope with it?

Improvisation, an Unintended Detour

Companies frequently follow the Improviser's path when their previous approach to growth reaches a dead end:

- *American Express* struggled to turn from Game Player to Rule Maker (with its failed concept of becoming a "financial supermarket") and is now a rebounding Improviser.

- Dethroned Rule Makers, such as *IBM* and *Kodak*, find improvising a useful way to rediscover latent market strengths.

- Specialists, like *Digital Equipment*, use improvising to find new market niches, such as computer networking.

- One-time Rule Breakers, *Apple Computer* for example, shift to the improvisational mode to search for a new vision to run with, find a speciality niche to serve, or—possibly—seek a business partner with whom to merge.

Look Abroad for "Natural" Improvisers

This path to growth is not an American-only phenomenon. Its logic is deeply ingrained in many businesspeople who have long coped with adversity, including Beruit's merchants and the Palestinian leaders of the emerging industries of the Middle East. India's fast-moving business class favors improvisation as a way to cope with a rapidly growing but only partially deregulated marketplace. Improvisation was the only way Russian plant managers coped with the irrationalities of communism; it is now their best tactic for survival in the former Soviet Union's rough-and-tumble capitalism.

Brazilians are probably the world's champion Improvisers. Their hard-won experience managing roller coaster inflation, loss of protected domestic markets, and the social challenges of high population growth will serve them well as Brazil becomes one of the export powerhouses of the twenty-first century. Have you met with businesspeople from any of these countries? Are there lessons from their management style that have applicability in your company?

Persona of an Improviser

What is the personality of a company as fast at making tactical shifts in the marketplace as Pele was scoring goals on the soccer field? Here's what an Improviser might have to say for him- or herself, assuming as in previous chapters that it is useful to understand an organization better when it is thought of *as if it were* an individual.

I'm a consummate realist. I deal with the world as it is and avoid being distracted by the world as somebody might want it to be. I've never been much for fairy tales.

I do get excited by the unknown. Ask my friends, and they will tell you I'm chronically dissatisfied with the status quo.

But my approach is different from most reformers'. I'm a take-charge pragmatist. I'm good at making do with what I've got, and I'm capable of rapid and unhesitating action. I may be hard to pin down, to be cornered, but that's what works best for me.

I like to master challenges quickly and then move on. Non-Improvisers may need to clean up after me. I have little toleration for endless debate. My motto is: "Life is short, let's get on with it."

I may be a bit egocentric, but I'm never too proud to roll up my own sleeves when the situation demands. I keep trying until I get what I'm doing right.

Watch out if you and I ever play poker. I'm great at bluffing my way around a weak hand.

Many Improvisers have a broad repertoire of behaviors. They will act, in true Rule Breaker fashion, like adolescent rebels when it suits the situation or as loyal, game-playing supplicants when necessary to win the support of people more powerful. Few Improvisers enjoy being at the mercy of others, but frequently, they have no choice.

Improvisers can be strongly committed to a particular course of action and then are able to change plans and go off in a different direction without any signs of remorse or second guessing. They can also return to an abandoned plan and be totally immune to I-told-you-so criticisms. Improvisers' plans and egos are kept separate. Mid-course corrections are, for Improvisers, a way of life. Their ideas and strategies are always subject to last-minute changes, especially when new information arrives. They can easily hold two contradictory ideas in their minds at once and not feel paralyzed by uncertainty.

Most Improvisers prefer procrastination to being forced to make an unalterable decision. At their worst, though, Improvisers can be impulsive, too quick to react. They may act before having sufficiently thought through what they are doing. They may try to use the need to be flexible when faced with uncertainty to mask their own mistakes and indecisiveness.

Improvisers: The Dark Side

All paths to growth have their strengths and weaknesses, a light and a dark side. At their best, Improvisers are industry's true "learning organizations," businesses capable of advancing forward, stumbling, figuring out what went wrong, and investing their energies into renewed forward movement, not into apportioning blame and punishment for the initial misstep. This is a process, however, that eludes many Improvisers. Instead, they become prisoners of improvisation's *dark side* and succumb to near-constant stumbling and economic performance that is marginal, at best.

Growth eludes Improvisers when they fall into one or several of the traps that almost inevitably line this path. The five most dangerous pitfalls include group think, pulling back from reality, avoiding what needs to be done, impulsively winging it, and just giving up. These dangers can affect any company, but Improvisers, with their limited margin for error, are especially prone to the problems they cause.

Group Think

Working in a high-pressure, high-uncertainty business environment requires managers and employees able to cope with a great deal of anxiety. Banding together in teams is one, increasingly common, way to do this. Teams, especially ones that include employees with a mix of organizational and functional backgrounds, can be very valuable. But they also can, in Improvisers, be equally as dangerous.

In pressurized situations, teams begin to value their own cohesion—an antidote to the chaos the company is in—**over dealing directly with the conflicts that naturally arise from differing perspectives and opinions about courses of action the business needs to consider.** This reaction to stress tends to make a bad situation worse. Team or department members lose contact with outside sources of information—especially information that may threaten their unity—and are very susceptible to delusions about the company, its markets, and competition.

Not all shared visions are good shared visions. An "us against the world" mentality may ensue, making the situation even harder to correct. These dynamics were common in the Pentagon during the Vietnam War and in Detroit in the early 1970s as Japanese imports started to trickle into the United States.

Companies where group think is entrenched tend to make things worse for themselves by perpetuating a sense of isolation. They discount the value of thinking that does not harmonize with their own. Independent-minded subordinates, they fear, will only make matters worse, increasing through dissension and confrontation the already high level of anxiety. So managers in these Improvisers tend to hire in their own images and weed out or exclude from decision making any nonconformers. All of which limits the diversity of options considered, constraining the Improviser's ability to easily adjust to its changing environment.

Pulling Back from Reality

The delusions generated from "group think" can lead some Improvisers to experience an even deeper problem: individuals or groups "detaching" themselves from the ongoing operations of the business. Managers acting this way may be very involved in life outside the office, but inside they are withdrawn and uninvolved. They, almost Howard Hughes–like, seem to have lost interest in both the company's day-to-day and future concerns. These managers are often indifferent to either praise or criticism, acting along the lines of Nero while Rome burned. This is most commonly the behavior of entrenched senior executives and can easily leave the rest of the company feeling leaderless and adrift. Managers in the next tier can either use this withdrawal as an opportunity to fill the breach with their own involvement and sense of direction or they can take advantage of their bosses' distraction and use their positions solely for personal gain.

Before George Fisher arrived at Kodak, the company "detached" itself from action by a great willingness to study, almost forever, whatever problem had arisen. A symptom of this behavior in other Improvisers is the tendency for managers to miss performance targets by a mile but suffer no ill consequence.

Avoiding Reality

It is an open issue whether detaching from reality is worse than another tendency of Improvisers in decline: avoiding it altogether. Companies that act this way seem to have given up on maintaining any single sharp focus of attention. Executives make decisions based more on hunches than facts or disciplined analyses. The situation is often even worse than "my mind's made up, don't bother me with the facts." Managers in these companies have so internalized the vicissitudes of the market that "whom they talked with last" is likely to be the voice having the greatest influence. These managers cope by being impressionistic. Any long-range vision for the company they have is vague, romantic, and based on a "when the ship comes in everything will turn out all right" form of logic.

Employees of Improvisers that foster this kind of denial also tend to have a very nostalgic or idealized view of the company's past. And they exhibit genuine surprise when things turn out unfavorably—even though the business press has long before predicted rough waters for their company.

Winging It

The opposite of ducking or detaching from reality is giving it too fond of an embrace. Some Improvisers attempt to match the dizzying rate of change in their outside world with equally rapid changes in the way the business is operated. These companies give the appearance of being out of control or acting on whims, rather than searching out facts and judging actions based on any assessment of consequences to the business. The time between a manager having a thought and taking action on it is minimal and seldom integrated into any view of where the business is headed or what it must do to get there.

Some executives prefer this kind of impulsiveness to its direct opposite, feeling immobilized by indecisiveness. In reality, impulsive behavior is more likely to amplify the uncertainty in the marketplace than to provide a way to manage it effectively. When winging it becomes ingrained into the corporate culture, it easily leads to temptations to cut corners, and attention to product quality, or concerns about legal or regulatory restrictions are abandoned. The eventual result: spilled toxic wastes, tainted pharmaceutical products, or planes taking off with insufficient fuel—all behaviors likely to accelerate a would-be Improviser's downward spiral.

Giving Up

A final, too-common response to chronic uncertainty is simply throwing in the towel. When companies do it, it is called bankruptcy; for individuals, burnout. Without strong, positive leadership, it is especially easy for an Improviser to attempt to run on "autopilot," letting habit and routine drive the business instead of flexible adaptiveness. The result: a depressed corporate culture. Feelings of hopelessness and inability to change the course of events plague managers and employees. No one seems able to produce positive change, and much like the situation at the Walt Disney Company in the years after its founder's death, the business loses its edge, its ability to follow any path to growth.

The path of improvisation has ample potholes. How many of these traps has your business fallen into?

Improvisers: The Light Side

At Disney, deteriorating financial performance led to an attempted takeover and the eventual hiring in 1984 of Michael Eisner to reenergize the entertainment empire's growth. His success, and shift of the company from the Improviser's to the Rule Maker's path, is the stuff of modern business legend. Eisner knew that Disney's employees craved returning to the growth track but that memories of the company's dead founder were not sufficient to take them there. **Eisner did not attempt to become the "new" Disney, replacing one cult figure with another. Instead, he led by holding the company to applying its founder's values in a way relevant to the company's current situation.** Full-length animated feature films were again made, Disney's genius at "total control" was rediscovered as a strategy for re-releasing classics from the company's film library in a contemporary video format, and advanced technologies were used to add thrills back to the amusement parks.

Going Back to the Future

A similar approach to revitalization is happening at Kodak. Chief executive George Fisher is moving this Improviser away from its dark side by reemphasizing the growth-oriented, inventive ways of its founder, George Eastman. Rather than spending his energies fighting Kodak's dysfunctional habits, Fisher reaches around them, putting the spotlight on even older traditions. Kodak, Fisher discovered, was once a genius at mixing technology with market savvy. This historical mix, refreshened with digital imaging technology instead of 100-year-old silver halide–based photography, is the basis for Kodak's renewed growth as an Improviser.

Before Fisher took charge, Kodak had already invested $5 billion in research on electronic imaging, with minimal results. Fisher realized that the missing element was the kind of marketing orientation Kodak used a century before to build consumer interest and acceptance for the then new technique, amateur photography. Kodak, Fisher found, was amply staffed with technical types. He added the missing piece, marketing, by bringing in managers like Carl Gustin, an ebullient ex-advertising professional to pull together the vast array of new technologies that were languishing in Kodak's labs.

Fisher symbolized Kodak's need to "go back to its future" in a very personal way. When he moved to Rochester, New York, he and his wife made a point of buying a house on East Avenue, the same street on which Kodak's founder lived during the company's first golden era.

The Present Value of a Company's Past

This kind of search for a corporation's "roots" can serve Improvisers well. Understanding a company's past history and extracting from the past what is missing today can *restore a missing sense of integrity* to an Improviser long buffeted by change.

Improvisers having problems coping with change frequently misunderstood the source of the difficulty. **It is not so much their habits and traditions that give them problems, it is that these old mindsets have become disconnected from their original context.** When so detached, traditions take on a life of their own, unconnected to current market realities. They appear to drive employees' current behavior but only in a hollow, ritualistic manner.

The trick to successful change is not so much to abandon the past (an impossibility, anyhow) but to reinterpret it to serve the needs of the present:

- Discover *what* used to work when the company was last on a growth trajectory.

- Examine the business history closely to understand why it worked then.

- Then look hard at the company's current situation to see what *new role* these past practices can play in generating today's growth.

This approach is what historian Alan Kantrow calls an intelligent mining of a company's past. He sees the challenge for Improvisers, such as AT&T and General Motors, as not so much trying to become something they never were, but rather "to recapture part of what [they] used to be and [have] been all along." Investigate your company's past. What did the business "used to be" that has some relevance for "where it needs to go"?

Never Declare War on Yourself

AT&T and its Baby Bell spinoffs are at work overtime to abandon what they like to call their old "Bell-shaped head" mind-set. This may be a mistake. Rather than putting efforts into discounting the past, the regional phone companies may do much better as Improvisers if they rethink the values behind past traditions and use them as a core to build their futures around. Even "Mother Bell" AT&T was not always a slow giant in a low-growth business with minimal competition. It was once a Rule Breaker in an industry it had to define for itself, without a stable base of competitors and with customers unclear about what value its services would ultimately provide. AT&T's past as a scrappy upstart battling Western Union in the early 1900s may hold many clues about how it needs to operate in the information age of the twenty-first century.

Unfortunately, many companies on the Improviser's path lose continuity with their heritage, preferring to declare war on themselves rather than taking possession of their history and reinterpreting it the way Disney and Kodak have done. IBM could do much worse than rediscover its past successes at smothering customers with kind attention, an aspect of its corporate culture that will always be warmly welcomed in the marketplace. Many managers can recite the philosopher George Santayana's famous phrase about those not remembering their past being condemned to repeat it. Santayana is only half right. The real trick is not just to remember a business's past but to *make good use* of it.

The ability to find pay dirt in a business's past requires the same skill essential for an Improviser to find growth opportunities in its present. Improvisers must know how to do *organizational learning*.

Organizational Learning or the Learning Organization?

Since Peter Senge's book, *The Fifth Discipline,* popularized the idea of the learning organization, many companies have rushed to become this latest corporate species. Businesses that once fancied themselves process-driven, virtual, networked, or team-based now want to become learning organizations. Senge's ideas have struck a resonant chord with many managers who tire of a business's tendency to repeat its old, failing ways. Staff positions dubbed Vice President for Learning have been created, and many training and development budgets have received well-deserved boosts.

Senge and his colleagues at Innovation Associates, the firm he co-founded, deserve great praise for melding the ideas of MIT's Jay Forrester on system thinking with those of Harvard's Chris Argyris, the original organizational learning guru. Senge made these academics' insights accessible to many managers in ways their originators were never able. These ideas probably have more pressing relevance to Improvisers than to companies on any other growth path. For many businesses, mastery of the process of knowledge creation and learning will pay back in better prospects for long-term growth. Improvisers, however, will see the results much sooner; for them, the ability to detect and correct mistakes is central to ongoing survival. It is a necessity, not a luxury.

Improvisers, though, cannot spare the time necessary to follow any guru's ten-step program to transform themselves into a trendy learning organization. Most Improvisers have gone through enough change and zigzags to last a corporate lifetime. The last thing they need is a new business role model requiring yet another shift in direction. Nor can they afford the overhead expense from adding new "learning expert" staff positions. Improvisers cannot be distracted becoming *learning organizations,* but they must practice *organizational learning*.

This is not just a matter of semantics. Becoming a certain kind of organization implies reaching an end point, achieving a definable objective. It is something acquirable, a quality that can be coupled with whatever a company is already doing. *Doing* organizational learning is different. It is an ongoing process, a way of managing the business, not something added on or changed to. It is something ingrained in every employee and manager. It is what separates perpetually struggling Improvisers from those able to thrive and grow in a hard-to-pin-down business environment. Organizational learning is a strategic imperative, not an overhead expense. Is your company trying to become a learning organization? Or, alternatively, are you practicing *organizational learning?*

A No-Fault Corporate Culture

The Naskapi Indians planned their hunts in a way that ensured survival but not necessarily growth. Their random course-setting process, though, sets the stage for learning to happen. The Naskapi's "corporate culture" is a *no-fault* one. While mistakes do happen—no game may be found in the direction chosen by the hunters on a particular day—they avoid the time-consuming, energy-draining process of searching for scapegoats and targets of blame. They just pick up the pieces the next day and try again, which is the essence of good improvisation.

Pull back from some of the conceptual hype about learning organizations and ask what, concretely, do they do when they are doing organizational learning. It has little to do with sending armies of employees off somewhere to be trained. Instead, other practices dominate the company's management style. Reduced to its core, organizational learning occurs when

- new knowledge is *generated* or *acquired;*

- its insights are *spread widely* throughout the company;

- there is *change* in what employees and managers are *doing* as a result of the new insights; and

- these changes are made in the spirit of *experimentation,* not 100 percent sure-fire certainty.

Improvisers acting along these lines have many balls in the air at once. Rather than rushing to implement any single solution, they mimic the scientist and launch multiple attacks on each problem. **Improvisers are good at creating variations, wary of ultimate solutions.** They realize that just because one approach succeeds today, there is no guarantee it will prevail in tomorrow's changed market.

Look for Productive Failures

Improvisers take to heart Xerox's distinction between productive failures and unproductive successes. *Productive failures* are those that generate new insight and understanding. They are mistakes that are not buried or orphaned but are mined for all they are worth. They may lead to short-run write-offs but pay for themselves in increasing a firm's net intellectual capital. *Unproductive successes,* on the other hand, are positive results that nobody understands from where they came. Although these results are icing on the cake, there is no guarantee of their future performance.

Where does all this new knowledge come from in the first place? Mistakes—when turned into productive ones—are one key source. Insights can also be generated from existing information in the business's databases when the techniques of "knowledge discovery" are applied. Using artificial intelligence software and Silicon Graphics–type data visualization equipment, previously unknown information can often be extracted from a company's records and files. Also important as a source of "new" knowledge is a careful reexamination of a business's history, conducted in light of its current most pressing needs.

A fourth, often neglected, source of business insight is a periodic gathering of a cross section of the company's employees to "put on the table" for discussion all the firm's current assumptions about its customers, competitors, technologies, and management practices. Which beliefs still hold up, which are leading the business astray, and which need some mid-course correction? Such meetings—held in a "no-fault" spirit—are unnatural acts in most companies, but they are vital if "learning" is to be a practice with real teeth to it. If these meetings were held every two years, it would not be too often.

Successful Organizational Learners

Improvisers need to put teeth into what has become, for some companies, today's flavor of the month. Learning is a way to rebound and make money, not just acquire new skills and knowledge. It is what Toyota did in the late 1960s when it shipped its first cars to America, only to see them sitting on the docks because they were too boxy to attract tail fin–weaned auto buyers. Honda suffered a similar experience when its early cars were laughed at by 1970s consumers as looking like two motorcycles bolted together. Honda's vehicle size, in a market where good cars were called "boats," kept the cars from being taken seriously until the first Arab oil embargo. But chance favors the prepared company. Both Japanese car makers—once floundering Improvisers—rethought what they were making and adapted the vehicles to the American market. Their Detroit competitors responded by doing what most successful companies like to do: more of what had always made them successful.

Boeing, the leading American airplane builder and a star Improviser, mimics the Japanese car makers in systematically learning from its past successes and problems. After difficulties arose with the introduction of its smallest and largest planes, the 737 and 747, Boeing set up a high-level review group dubbed "Project Homework" (as in what the company forgot to do in the first place, its "homework"). The group's charge: examine closely the details of how Boeing's two earlier, and most profitable, planes, the 707 and 727 models, were developed. After three years of analysis (plane makers have more breathing room than most Improvisers) and an inch-thick list with hundreds of recommendations, the team felt it had a good grasp on the lessons to be learned. Then several group members were transferred to guide the start-up of the next Boeing aircraft families, the 757 and 767. These, in turn, were the most trouble-free product launches in Boeing's history. Buoyed by this success, Boeing is keeping up its use of organizational learning, drawing from all experiences with past jet development programs to introduce, in record time, the 777 two–engine intercontinental plane. While the 777 project used state-of-the-art digital design technology—no paper drawings or mock-up models were ever made—the human side of its creation was guided by insights gleaned over several decades.

Look back in your company's history. What were your 707s and 727s? What lessons do their success offer for today's generation of new products? How can your 737s and 747s become "productive failures"? What steps will your company's leadership need to take to be sure these lessons are surfaced and put into practice?

Staying Alive and Growing

The role of top management in guiding an Improviser's renewal and growth cannot be underestimated. In a meeting in St. Louis held just after he was appointed chief executive of Monsanto, Robert Shapiro tried hard to get across the point that this chemical maker's days of tranquil growth were over. He feared that, in the wake of a major company-wide restructuring, many managers were now *waiting for things to settle down* so they could get back to business as usual. This attitude, Shapiro lamented, was completely off the mark. There was no reason to expect that the old, calmer times would ever return. Instead, Monsanto needed a way to structure itself to accommodate ongoing change and regular reorganization.

No More Steady State

What Shapiro realized was that the model of change many managers were taught in business school did not hold up any more in his and other turbulent industries. This once-useful formulation said that companies and the people working in them went through three steps when dealing with change. First, they "unfroze" their old ways of acting; then went through some sort of transition process; and finally ended up in a new, steady state. This is nice, neat, and simple but no longer very relevant to the Improviser's situation, one that never really settles down in phase three.

Sustained improvisation requires an organization that is trim, fit, and flexible—a structure able to reshape its form with a minimum of turmoil. And it needs, as Shapiro is starting to shape at Monsanto, employees with expectations appropriate for a company in ongoing metamorphosis, not settling into a new form of homeostasis.

Organizations with these attributes have more in common with biological organisms than with architectural structures. For example, insects have external skeletons. When they grow, they first discard their old skeletons and then secrete new ones to support their enlarged bodies. This is not unlike what Shikhar Ghosh, once chief executive of a clearinghouse that processes cellular phone bills, did when he took charge of the business.

Discarding Old Skeletons

Ghosh's first structure was a Japanese-like set of *concentric circles*, with himself in the center. It was great for blurring boundaries between groups, and it allowed for quick response to market changes, but it also blurred accountabilities and relied on informal communication—two features that caused trouble as the business grew. So after six months, he reorganized. A more *traditional functional structure* was created, complete with two tiers of managers. It lasted a few more months, dealing well with the accountability problem, but soon employees began to identify more with their function than with the overall company goals. Next change: *cross-functional teams*, one for each line of business. This approach lasted for seven months but was very dependent on a limited talent pool available to serve as general managers for the teams. Eventually, the teams were consolidated into *self-contained divisions*, better able to accommodate increased business growth.

Companies Are Organisms, Not Machines

Ghosh's basic principle is to treat a company like an organism, not a machine. An organism *reacts* when something happens to it. A machine just sits still and, if perturbed enough, eventually breaks. **Ghosh kept changing his division's form, observing the ensuing reactions, and took them into account in planning his next change. No single form was right or wrong, each was just a tool to create a temporary balance between conflicting needs.**

At some point in all this reorganization, Ghosh feels that his employees caught on to the reasons behind the changes, and some even started to look forward to them. Ghosh feels that employees learn a lot from experiencing the pros and cons of different configurations and that the learning stays with them long after the old structure is history. Ghosh also suspects that the constant changes force people to relate more to broad company objectives—they no longer have time to establish a power base within any particular structure.

Amoebas Outlast Dinosaurs

Other Improvisers have taken the amoeba as their prototypical form. Amoebas reorganize themselves every time they move forward. Digital Equipment Corporation keeps trying several approaches to creating mini companies around hot product lines to help find a way out of its doldrums. IBM is doing the same, including a willingness to swallow, amoeba-like, Lotus Development Company to add key groupware products to its multi-billion-dollar software unit. Madison Avenue ad agencies, like McCann-Erickson, are subdividing themselves into independent satellite operations that mimic the small, creative boutiques that have been stealing away many of their long-established clients.

These companies are, at least implicitly, aware of a principle of geometry that drives the shape of most biological organisms: in any structure, *bulk increases much faster than surface area.* A company's surface area consists of the employees on its periphery—those keeping in direct contact with customers and suppliers. **The larger an organization becomes, relatively fewer people are spending time connecting the business with the outside world,** a dangerous situation for a company whose survival depends on quick reaction time.

What to Avoid

Sustaining an Improviser's growth involves doing some things and undoing others. Improvisers should work hard to avoid the following:

- *Too many organizational levels.* All growth-oriented businesses need to minimize the levels of management between senior executives and everyone else. For Improvisers this is a necessity, not just another trendy practice. Tall management hierarchies add overhead expense and, even more deadly to Improvisers, distort information flows. Improvisers cannot improvise unless key decision makers have timely, unfiltered information about the company's situation. De-layering is a must; few global corporations require more than six levels of management. Most Improvisers can function well with three or four tiers, maximum.

- *Too much headquarters staff.* High overhead is toxic to an Improviser. In addition to minimizing "checkers of checkers," Improvisers need to find alternatives to traditional staff departments, such as outsourcing, using networks or designated gurus instead of bureaucratic units, and establishment of internal service businesses. At Improviser Pacific Telesis, all in-house attorneys have to bid for the company's legal business in competition with outside law firms. Improvisers have no room for internal monopolies;

growth requires that all employees share a common entrepreneurial bent.

■ *Swiss cheese–looking organizations.* At most Improvisers, downsizing just comes with the territory. Improvisers that emerge from these staff cuts stronger, not weaker, are those that went into them with a clear idea of the kind (not just the number) of people they will need in the future. They avoid untargeted early retirement windows and across-the-board involuntary layoffs, knowing these almost inevitably result in a company losing the people most essential to rebuilding and renewing growth.

■ *Matrix structures.* Dual-reporting relationship, matrix organizations are good when the job is to put a person on the moon, cost being no object. For most businesses, they are of more questionable value, and for Improvisers, they can be fatal. A key part of Robert Palmer's renewal effort at Digital involved abandoning a costly, consensus-driven matrix management philosophy. Instead, division managers call all their own shots, living or dying by the results they achieve. For years one of Digital's most promising product divisions, its networking operation, shared a sales force with other parts of the company. Its revenues grew minimally, if at all. In the first year, Palmer assigned the division a dedicated sales group, and network products sales increased at double-digit rates.

■ *Self-managing teams.* These sound like the organization form of the future, but they are destined to fail in the fast-paced uncertain world of the Improviser. Keeping on track in the short run and adjusting quickly to changing circumstances require strong leadership. Never assign work to a team in an Improviser without designating its leader and clearly laying out the ground rules in advance. Leave self-management to the slower-paced, less anxiety-ridden paths of the Game Players and Specialists.

Practices to Follow

There are some management practices that, on the other hand, should be second nature in growth-oriented Improvisers:

- *Cultivate pragmatism.* Improvisers chart a middle course between the Prussian determinism of Peter Drucker and the laid-back looseness of Tom Peters. Pragmatism is America's unique contribution to philosophy, and nineteenth-century pragmatist William James is its greatest exponent. For James, an idea was to be judged by its practical consequences—what it allows someone to get done—not its theoretical correctness. Pragmatic managers, according to Harvard Business School researchers Nitin Nohria and James Berkley,

  > adapt their actions to the specifics of the situation in which they find themselves;
  >
  > creatively find ways to make do with what resources they have;
  >
  > focus more on results than the processes used to achieve them; and
  >
  > avoid wasting time running from uncertainty—**change, for pragmatic Improvisers, is a welcome source of unexpected opportunities.**

- *Set the right kinds of goals.* The rougher the seas, the more a ship needs a clear idea of where it is going. Improvisers need goals, but not the lockstep, rigid objectives that drive Rule Makers and Specialists. An Improviser's goals should be sufficiently broad as to allow a lot of room for flexibility and opportunistic maneuvering. Goals should also be far enough away in time so that it makes sense to develop more than one option for achieving them. Finally, an Improviser's goals should not be imposed from a distance by top management. They have a much greater chance of being achieved if they are set to reflect what already seems to be an emerging consensus by employees throughout the business.

- *Provide lifeboats.* Do not assume all the survivors of the reorganizations and downsizings will be necessarily happy or content in the change-prone structure of an Improviser. Allow employees to opt out of the new organization without committing career or economic suicide. Provide self-assessment, outplacement, and financial assistance to employees who know where the company is headed and know that they do not want to go along for the ride. These programs cost money, but in the end, everyone benefits.

- *Use sunset laws and half-lives.* Every policy and procedure in an Improviser should be assigned a half-life—the date when each needs to be reconsidered. This applies especially to organization charts. Somewhere on them should be indicated an "effective as of" date, but they also need to be stamped with a future date on which they are no longer valid.

- *Give assignments, not jobs.* Many Improvisers will be best able to accommodate Monsanto's Robert Shapiro's idea of a structure in continual flux by replacing all jobs with portfolios of assignments for each employee. A job is usually defined by a laundry list of activities; an assignment is more focused. Assignments have clear beginnings, middles, and ends: resources, measurable results, and deadlines. Jobs, on the other hand, have an implicit expectation that they will go on the way they are forever. This approach is also a great way to accommodate demand for flextime and telecommuting, practices that can significantly contribute to an Improviser's adaptability.

- *Establish term limits for managers.* One of the greatest mistakes many companies make is to keep managers in place long after the reason they were originally selected disappears. Prespecified, well-thought-out terms can also slow down the too-fast, fast track common in some Improvisers. This dangerous form of management by musical chairs rotates managers before they have had a chance to make a real contribution or to clean up the consequences of a bad decision. Matsushita has applied the term idea to its top R&D performers. Each scientist is given a renewable five-year contract to replace the old Japanese lifetime employment doctrine. Hefty performance bonuses are paid at the end of the term, based on the individual's contributions (which are difficult to judge over shorter periods).

- *Don't let employees get too settled in.* After a few years Shikhar Ghosh left his cellular job to co-found Open Market, a company helping businesses set up shop on the Internet. Open Market's conference rooms are chairless to discourage long meetings, and all job titles have been abolished. Instead, each employee has three responsibilities: (1) the work he or she was hired for, (2) a personal development assignment (learn Spanish or a new programming language, for example), and (3) take on a share of the office administration (keep the coffee pot full, handle timecards, etc.).

- *Manage people flow.* Cash is not the only critical flow in Improvisers. Often, the best way to move ideas from one part of the company to another is by moving the people who practice them. Time-Life moved the manager of its high-growth music division, skilled in innovative approaches to marketing, to its book division where profits were flat and market methods traditional. General Motors learned little from its Fremont, California joint venture with Toyota until it began to transfer intact teams from Fremont to key positions in more traditional GM plants. Practice inplacement as well as providing outplacement. Set up "organizational holding patterns" or internal temporary services units to provide homes for high-potential employees between assignments.

- *Celebrate successes!* Improvisers should not allow Game Players to have a monopoly on all the hoopla and partying. The best way to combat burnout and low morale is to provide careful attention to communications and recognition. Provide awards for employees, teams, and groups, for both absolute performance peaks and for those "most improved." The once-every-Friday celebrations of the Silicon Valley Rule Breakers is just about right for Improvisers that need to keep everyone focused on the here and now.

A Path for Individuals as well as Companies

The path of the Improviser is a route to growth for individuals as well as corporations. Considering the seemingly never-ending waves of cutbacks and reorganizations in many American businesses, the roll-with-the-punches flexibility of the Improviser may well be today's most commonly practiced career strategy. The *Specialist* orientation is a good model for many ex-corprocrats who have spun off and gone into business for themselves; the *Improviser* serves a similar purpose for those who have remained in large organizations and want to thrive amid the chaos and uncertainty.

A Combination of Courage and Spirit

In times of major business turmoil, managers are often asked to think about the Chinese ideogram for the word "change." In Chinese the same symbol is used to denote both the ideas of crisis and opportunity. This dual meaning may be a fitting motto for Rule Breakers, companies that excel at deriving growth opportunities by creating crises for more established businesses.

What symbol is most appropriate for Improvisers, those more on the receiving than the initiating side of change? For them, a different language may provide a better role model, perhaps one with more of a guttural sound. Michael Spindler, chief executive of Improviser Apple Computer, is a German native. His English is fluent, but in meetings with Apple's managers in Cupertino, California, Spindler is frequently heard to use the German word "mut." Like the Chinese word for change, this also has two meanings: courage (Spindler's stock in trade as he restructures and brings order to this ex–Rule Breaker) and spirit (the sense of excitement and direction he is working hard to restore). Mut may not be a very pretty-sounding word, but it embodies the blend of pragmatism and imagination that abound in every successful Improviser.

What Is It Like Working for an Improviser?

This is the BEST place in the world to work.

Here is the last set of pro-and-con face-offs about work life in a growth company. Listen to this pragmatic, action-oriented VP describe herself and her company.

■ ■ ■

When I was a kid, I always loved roller coasters. This company certainly has its ups and downs, but at least we're moving forward.

I'm tired of hearing all the old-timers griping. I wish somebody would pull the plug on the water cooler. For me, this company's excitement city. I know I'm further along than any of my business school classmates who took jobs at safe and stodgy blue chips.

I'm the only female officer here, but I won't be for long. We've just brought in two honchos, one from American Express, the other a veteran of Apple. Both are female, and both are likely to make officer by next year. Our brush with near-bankruptcy five years ago shattered whatever glass ceiling was once in place.

The company used to be the hottest thing going in our industry, and it's going to be—with my ideas—there again.

I'm pragmatic. I make do with what I got. I know what resources are available, and I know what to do to round up more on short notice. That doesn't mean I'm conservative. I know it's unrealistic to try to avoid uncertainty, especially in our business. Every time we try to do that we end up missing something important that a customer wants or something that a competitor is doing.

I've come to welcome sudden changes. They are just unanticipated opportunities, waiting for me to capitalize on them.

I've given up wasting time looking for the best solutions. I want ones that work and work here. Fast. These are my biggest complaints

Improviser   about benchmarking. I tell my people to adapt, not adopt, ideas from elsewhere. I'm tired of all the money we used to spend benchmarking. Just because something works somewhere else doesn't mean squat about it taking off here.

The only time I do any soup-to-nuts benchmarking is when I need some political ammunition to help me sell an idea I already know is the right thing to do. Benchmarking just gives some of my weak-kneed colleagues the prop they need to do what they should have done anyway.

You know how Jack Welsh was so praised for getting his money's worth out of all that quality and reengineering stuff. He customized it to fit GE's uniqueness, creating what he called "work-out." Well, I'm going to do him one better. I'm going to adapt his adaptation to my division.

Things are always a little out-of-date here. That's fine. Staying trendy takes a lot of two things we don't have much of: time and money.

I've seen so many companies go overboard with the latest fad. Take teams. In a lot of places they've become ends unto themselves. Everything that comes up has to be run through a team. Teams end up reporting to teams. "Whoever dies with the most teams wins" I guess is the logic.

I've seen a reengineering project in one of our competitors where the self-managing reengineering team is reporting to a leaderless sponsor team. Now, whom on earth will they blame when the thing gets screwed up?

I like clear accountabilities. Here nothing is assigned to a team if an individual can be found to do it, or else we give it to a department already in place. You don't need an expensive cross-functional, cross-level team to decide what color to paint the walls (assuming we've got any money for the paint).

No flavor-of-the-month management here. Everything is changing so fast in our market that the last thing we need is a new management philosophy every quarter. I can still get a lot of mileage out of what I know already. I didn't learn to be a take-charge boss in business school, anyway.

This is the WORST place in the world to work.

What you see usually depends on where you sit. Here are some musings from a middle manager working in the same Improviser.

■ ■ ■

We've given up on writing new MBOs. What's the point? The plans here keep changing every couple of months. Annual budgets and performance targets are wastes of time. I don't know why we still waste the time going through the motions. And the performance reviews are beauty contests. Who you know is a lot more important than what you know.

I hardly ever see anyone in senior management. They seem to spend most of their time closeted in meetings, with each other. The rest of us are working just as hard just trying to keep our heads above water.

The net result: no clear forward direction. The business keeps zigging and zagging, and our market share shows it. We've confused our customers so much that from once owning a quarter of the market, our share has dropped to 12 percent—on a good day. . . .

Once we come up with a good idea I wish we could just get out there and run with it, but we've got so many priorities—half of them in conflict with each other—that we seem to keep running like crazy but never get anywhere.

The internal competition here is fierce. The way we operate is like a road race where two runners, both on our team, hear the starting pistol go off and then spend the next ten seconds beating each other up. The winner is whomever limps across the finish line first.

We're too busy fighting ourselves to give serious attention to the real battle, regaining market share from the upstarts who have taken over this industry. All this infighting is killing off our future. The way we jerk around priorities and set up multiple teams with the same goal eventually just wears people out. A lot of talented people feel they've been driven out of the company—and into the arms of our kinder, gentler competition.

Improviser   My boss has so many small product development projects going that you can never get a clear sense of what her priorities are.

We practice management by rumor. No one believes much of what they hear from their boss or what they read in the company policy memos anyway. Even the annual report reads like it's a work of fiction—or wishful thinking.

I've had four bosses in the past three years. Top management keeps bringing in people from outside, usually from even outside our industry. If I'm asked to break in another new boss, I will quit.

I call it the "messiah" complex. Our CEO keeps looking for new heroes to bring in and supply the vision he seems to lack.

I really miss the old days. We once owned this market. Our founder's picture was on the cover of every business magazine. Wall Street analysts worshipped the ground he walked on. I was set to retire at age 40 and live on what I'd make cashing in my now deeply underwater stock options.

I'm basically a happy guy, but this place is depression city. I'm convinced the solution to our problems is a good long-range plan. My only problem is that I'm too frantically busy to put any time into writing one.

I better face up to reality: I'm never going to have that kind of time working here. And nobody would probably pay any attention to the plan, anyway. Every time I bring the idea up my boss starts muttering something about the Naskapi Indians. What do a bunch of Indians have to do with us?

Looks like it's time to start looking elsewhere. That shouldn't be hard. Every headhunter in the country knows about our problems. They all call here first when any openings come in . . . I think it's time for me to start returning some of those calls.

Sustain Success

Avoid Becoming Yesterday's News

CHAPTER 9

Keeping the Focus on Growth

A few years ago, bread lines were common in a well-off Washington, D.C. neighborhood, but they had nothing to do with the recession or cutbacks in federal jobs. Politicians, bureaucrats, lawyers, and the occasional media celebrity lined up daily outside a small store on Connecticut Avenue, a few miles north of the White House. On Sundays the crowds would reach 250 to 300, and Art Buchwald was known to stop by and entertain the patient shoppers.

The store was called Marvelous Market, and the wait was for an opportunity to purchase one of its speciality breads. Its baguettes, boules, and sourdough loaves were, in 1990, the talk of the city. Made from a special, time-consuming process involving fermented dough paste starter and imported ovens, the store's products were praised by every Washington food critic. The town's top chef, Jean-Louis Palladin, allowed only Marvelous Market breads to be served in his elite Watergate restaurant. Demand was so strong that customers were rationed, Moscow style, to no more than two loaves a visit. The bakery was a dream come true to its owner, Mark Furstenberg, but its rapid growth was to become his worst nightmare.

Meeting High Demand with High Capacity

Furstenberg coped with high demand the way most business people do: he added capacity. Additional retail stores were opened throughout the city and suburbs, one even in Baltimore, 50 miles away. One hundred new employees were hired, and an 11,000–square-foot building was leased in a nearby industrial park and was converted to a bakery. A fleet of colorfully painted trucks were acquired to shuttle the bread from ovens to stores and downtown restaurants. More people were added to drive the trucks.

In 1993, Game Player Starbucks began to saturate the Washington area with coffee shops and, naturally, wanted Marvelous Market to supply all their breads and pastries. A million-dollar–plus deal was signed, which, in retrospect, was probably the straw that broke the camel's back. Furstenberg was initially skeptical, but Starbucks' business proved necessary to provide the level of sales needed to keep the central production facility running economically. Growth tends to breed the need for more growth. Soon Furstenberg started feeling as though he was running a trucking company, not a bakery, and began worrying about the vast quantities of cash all this growth was consuming.

In addition to managing a mini-logistical empire, Furstenberg—a stickler for total quality—spent every available hour in the centralized bakery, brooding over the vagaries of his customized baking processes. As a result of these preoccupations, he had no time to visit stores or keep in direct contact with customers (the original store featured ovens just behind the sales counter). Furstenberg once wrote a chatty, recipe-filled newsletter welcomed by his customers almost as much as his bread, but the demands of growth left no time for it either.

A "Marvelous Bankruptcy"

Finally, with links to loyal customers strained, quality slipping, and a severe icy winter keeping customers away, cash ran out. Less than four years after opening, Marvelous Market filed for bankruptcy protection. Furstenberg immediately scaled back operations. The central bakery was abandoned, all but a handful of stores closed, and both trucks and employees were downsized. Deliveries are now made in trucks leased from Ryder.

Furstenberg had no illusions about his situation. In a *mea culpa* newsletter to customers, he confessed to being drawn in to premature expansion. **What was not realized, he admitted, was how much that growth would change the character of the company.** "Business failure," he wrote, "is a powerful teacher. Nothing succeeds like failure." Now Furstenberg's efforts are directed "to the principles on which we started this business." He calls it "a great step backward." I call it growth.

Four Growth Paths in Five Years!

In only a few years, Marvelous Market changed from

- *Rule Breaker* (no bread anything like their bread existed east of California), to

- expansion-driven *Game Player,* to

- improvising survivor.

And, most recently, the business is showing signs of settling down as a *Specialist,* focusing on selling a limited range of breads and (higher margin) prepared foods to eat with them. Had it started on this path to growth originally, it most likely would have met escalating demand with higher prices and only gradually expanded its scope, probably including bread-baking ovens in each new store, paid for out of the increased margins.

Marvelous Market's experience is a near-classic example of growth getting out of hand, which is probably why so many other businesses have had similar rapid expansions followed by even more abrupt declines. An almost identical story could be told of People Express airline, with a less hopeful ending. It was merged out of existence into Improviser Continental Airlines, never making it to the Specialist stage.

No Path Goes On Forever

Neither Marvelous Market nor Microsoft has reason to expect its growth path to continue indefinitely. The marketplace equivalents of potholes, fallen power lines, and detours are unpredictable but inevitable. Travelers on a path need rest stops; roads require routine maintenance and periodic repaving. When paths become more heavily used, lanes are widened and one-time rural routes become interstate highways. Old, once-vibrant routes, like the Erie Canal, fall into disuse or are recycled into bike paths. And just as canals were supplanted by railroads, many rail lines have fallen victim to trucks and planes and have been abandoned.

Similar dynamics characterize business growth strategies. Some end because they are successful: companies following them reach their growth objective and need to find another. In other situations, the path is less fruitful because of an unexpected shift in market dynamics, or the business lacks the requisite skills to successfully continue in that direction.

How Do You Measure Growth?

Understanding what is behind these failures can provide good clues about what is needed to sustain growth. *Success at growing a business has multiple definitions*, depending on which path is being followed:

- For *Rule Breakers*, growth is measured in revenue increases from new products. These businesses take an "us against them" approach to their markets, with success frequently defined as how big a mark they leave and how much new demand they create.

- *Game Players* are more straightforward: growth implies market share gains, relative success against like competitors. Game Players grow in turbulent, high-growth markets. Absolute targets mean less than ones that reflect relative standing.

- *Rule Makers*—the undisputed industry leaders—focus on a range of objectives, especially profit growth and expansion of their dominion. But often their most important goals are defensive: success at fending off rivals who want to destabilize or dominate the market.

- Some *Specialists* are like mini–Rule Makers in their particular domain and have similar performance measures. Many more are concerned about the extent they have penetrated their particular niche. Most Specialists judge themselves through a rear view mirror: doing better than they did last year is what counts most.

- Most *Improvisers* are just glad to be able to wake up each morning and find themselves still alive. Positive cash flow bears heavily on the minds of some, while all should be equally concerned about their performance in learning and generating new insights about rapidly changing customer needs.

No single measure of growth is appropriate for all businesses. Growth in size can be counterproductive for Improvisers, some of the most successful are ones that have cut revenues. Large sales increases can give false comfort to a Game Player if its peers are enjoying even larger revenue growth. Obsessive attention to profitability can easily stunt a Rule Breaker's growth. Considering this need for variable measures of success, what can be safely said to apply across all growth paths about why some companies fail to thrive?

Why Does Growth Stop?

Growth slows when either of these happen:

- A company's *outside world* changes in ways such that what the business is especially good at no longer provides significant advantage.

- A company's *inner world,* its organization, loses its sharp external focus.

Both reasons go back to the relation between a business and its environment, customers, suppliers, technologies, and competitors. Thinking about a company without simultaneously examining its surroundings is pointless.

Growth stumbles when companies become over adapted, either to yesterday's market realities or to the internal struggles that take place within every organization. In the words of Canadian business professor Danny Miller:

Organizations lapse into decline precisely because they have developed *too sharp* an edge. They amplify and extend a single strength or function while neglecting most others. Ultimately a rich and complex organization becomes excessively *simple*—it turns into a monolithic, narrowly focused version of its former self, converting a formula for success into a path toward failure.

Firms whose performances are poor or whose intervals of success are interrupted by occasional shocks of disappointment are more apt to preserve a healthy balance of doubt, debate, and diversity.

Success Sets Up Failure

Success, as Mark Furstenberg observed, leads to failure. Professor Miller came to the same conclusion, something he calls the "Icarus Paradox" in his studies of the track records of several hundred companies. His research finds that *success sets up* failure by fostering the following:

- overconfidence;

- intolerance;

- a "culture of busyness" not open to distraction and new inputs;

- egocentric managers, only able to see the world through their own perspective; and

- programmed behaviors, where the ability to shock a competitor with surprise is lost.

Does your company have any of these characteristics? Eventually companies with these "early warning signs" become rigid and myopic. They gravitate to market segments where they are most comfortable, not necessarily the segments richest in growth opportunities. Both Furstenberg and Miller have the right diagnosis. The important issue, though, is what to do about it.

Anticipating, and then avoiding, growth stoppage requires a degree of courage, and the foresight and strength to know *when* to stop plunging ahead with the success formula of the past. Instead, the particular bottlenecks or limiting factors to growth must be identified early, company by company, situation by situation. These are the points of greatest leverage in the business.

Growth Is a Juggling Act

Companies with the special skill of sustaining growth first *expand in place*, then they *change course*. The purpose of the descriptions in the past five chapters was to lay out alternative paths to growth, ways to expand in place. Each has pros and cons, each requires certain kinds of people and organization, and each is best in differing types of markets. After a path is chosen, the issue becomes how to run with it. For this, the business organization has to be internally *aligned* with the growth strategy. This is the subject of several forthcoming sections.

Some market situations do not fit neatly into one of the five paths, and some individuals are able to contribute to more than one growth strategy. For these companies, a *blending* of paths provides the best match to reality. Eventually, with either a "pure" or "hybrid" strategy—for the reasons outlined earlier—growth slows. This is a signal that either the elements of the "blend" need adjustment or the time to *change course* completely is at hand. Skill at managing on a hybrid path can be very useful when the time comes for a complete change of direction. This is how seeds for renewed growth are planted.

Growth failures frequently occur when, rather than moving toward other paths, a company meets adversity with a renewed commitment to do more of the same. Bausch & Lomb (Chapters 1 and 2) and Louisiana-Pacific (Chapter 5) both suffered from this problem. Short-term growth can also cover up serious underlying weaknesses. Many companies have multiplied their size and earnings through aggressive acquisitions, while at the same time allowing these new streams of profits to mask management's inability to continue growing the core business. These situations ultimately unravel but often not until serious damage has already been done to the company's capacity for continued growth.

Sustaining growth over the long haul, across decades for example, requires skill at changing course. The company's structure will most likely go through several transformations to keep pace with its markets. **Growth during the medium term, a stretch of time ranging from 5 to 15 years, can be accomplished for many companies through a combining of paths. In the short run, over the next year or two, assuming a good match has been made between path and situation, the primary growth issue is one of focus.** Here is when it pays to ignore Danny Miller's advice and *get simple.*

All three of these time frames must be managed *simultaneously* if future growth is to be assured. This is a difficult juggling act. The ability to pull it off is what has made companies like 3M, Hewlett Packard, Motorola, and Proctor & Gamble a breed apart from their competitors.

Keeping an Eye on the Ball

As important as legendary performance over decades is, the future will be unreachable if the business has no way to keep attention focused on the needs of the here and now. Change over the long run is something best seen in retrospect. Managing is something, even when directed toward future aims, that only happens in the present.

A company's growth path is largely shaped by market demands. Employees—the only real driver of growth a company has—are a product of genetic makeup, past experiences, current knowledge and skills, social environment, and ability to adapt as circumstances change. In the short run, *neither path nor people are easily changeable.* **What can more easily be manipulated is the link between the two; a company's organization.**

What Is Organization?

The word organization is used with increasing frequency in discussions about competitiveness and growth, but its nature is still commonly misunderstood. Ask an executive about his organization, and most likely he will show you some sort of chart with boxes representing people and lines connecting them, indicating who is accountable to whom. If you probe for more detail, he may hand you a fistful of job descriptions. Talk to a more perceptive manager, and she might try to describe the rich array of informal relationships within every company: who talks to whom, who likes whom, who trusts whom. These are the all-important "glue" that really holds a business together and often determines what can or cannot happen. Meet with a leading-edge academic, like University of Chicago's Ron Burt, and he is likely to quickly engage you in a discussion of "social capital." This is his unique way of measuring the ability employees have, through the networks they belong to, to get real leverage from the "human capital" they represent.

More cynical business observers see organization as what gets in the way of people otherwise trying hard to do their jobs. Organization, they feel, is an overhead cost, something to be minimized. It reflects history more than promise and showcases past strategies instead of today's basis of competition. Organization, according to some wags, is what blinds a company to its future opportunities. Few structures seem to be effective power bases for the capabilities critical to future growth.

Organization Is a Vehicle for Business Growth

Each of these perspectives adds to our understanding, and each is also incomplete. Growth-oriented managers shy away from such conceptual formulations and theoretical debates. They prefer simple, action-oriented ideas. They like to talk about what they can directly manipulate. For them, if a growth strategy is a path, then organization is what they will use to travel along it.

Organization is the vehicle for a business's growth ambitions. That's all. It is a vehicle that travels somewhere, not a machine that runs. When it works, it focuses everyone's efforts toward growth. Organization is what links employees with the company's growth path.

An **organization works the same way a vehicle does. It performs three critical functions:**

- Sets a *Direction.*

- Has a means of *Propulsion.*

- Provides a sense of *Stability.*

There are many kinds of vehicles, just as there are many types of companies, but they all have these three attributes. Reduced to its simplest form, a sailboat has a sail for propulsion, a rudder for steering, and a hull and keel for stability. Planes and autos have their counterparts to these: steering wheels, engines, fuselages, and the like. What about businesses?

Organization Provides Direction

Corporations set Direction through their *top management group* and the *planning process* these executives put in place to involve the rest of the company in the process. Setting a course is more than a one-time event. Just pointing a vehicle in the direction intended is no guarantee it will reach there. *Control and information systems* must be in place to monitor forward movement and provide timely information about deviations from the plan so adjustments can be made to either the company's actions or plan. These three components of business organization need to operate in a tightly coordinated fashion for the business to effectively proceed on any of the five growth paths.

One Leader Is Not Enough

The idea of a "group" setting direction is vital. *No* single chief executive, regardless of talent or past performance, is able to set a sustainable growth course unaided. Never. Just as a company is prisoner of its past successes, any individual's ability to see into the future comes along with that person's unique set of biases and blinders. It is just part of the territory of the human psyche. These limitations can never be entirely eliminated, but they can be balanced and supplemented by others on the team. Strong growth company executives surround themselves with a broad range of personalities and perspectives. Court jesters, devil's advocates, and iconoclasts abound.

The best defense against myopia is diversity. Systems theorists have developed what they call "the law of requisite variety" to explain why this is so important. This principle implies that, if a company is to grow in anything but a monolithic marketplace, there must be at least as great a variety of perspectives inside the organization as there are a variety of complications in the market.

A few doors down from Mark Furstenberg's Marvelous Market on Connecticut Avenue is another Washington institution, the Politics and Prose Bookstore. This store, founded by his sister, celebrated its tenth anniversary the year the bakery declared bankruptcy. Politics and Prose has had a less meteoric path to growth, but it is nonetheless a business that has thrived with a history of near-steady progress. And it has done so in the face of strong challenges to the ongoing existence of other independent bookstores and the rise of the game-playing superstore chains like Borders Books and Barnes & Noble.

Cultivate Diversity of Opinion

Facing these challenges, Politics and Prose, a store already well stocked with comfortable arm chairs and staff who actually read what they sell, refined its approach to specialization. Book groups, interactive CD-ROMs, and arguably the city's best coffeehouse were added. And when Marvelous Market was pruning back its bread selection to regain a high-quality focus, Politics and Prose expanded by taking over the retail space next door.

The bookstore's growth direction is set by a team of two: founder Carla Cohen (nee Furstenberg) and store manager Barbara Meade. Together they model the blending of perspectives that is just as essential in a growth-minded Fortune 500 company as in their 30-person business. They are both very different, and they know how to use their differences to the store's best advantage. Barbara is a morning person, coming in before the store opens to review the previous day's sales and process book reorders. Carla comes in later and stays in the evening to host the store's frequent author talks and readings.

They do not quarrel, but they frequently disagree. Business issues are seldom left unaddressed, according to Barbara. Their personalities complement each other in ways that contribute to each other's growth as well as the business's. Barbara likes being an expert and is an experienced avoider. Carla is more direct and a skilled confronter. In spite of contrasting styles, their staff seem to continually call both Barbara and Carla by each other's name. They have no visible physical resemblance, so this is most likely a symptom of the cohesion their skill at diversity management has brought to the store. (Both Coca-Cola and Disney's greatest growth periods also occurred when these companies were led by similarly complementing duets: Roberto Goizueta and Donald Keough at Coke; Michael Eisner and Frank Wells at Disney.)

As in businesses of any size, the personal values of top management play a big part in direction setting. When some of the large chain booksellers refused to carry Salman Rushdie, Politics and Prose's owners put a big poster of *Satanic Verses* in the front window, reminding customers what an independent bookstore is really all about.

Laying the Groundwork for Growth

Preparing a top team for their direction-setting task is also essential. Some large businesses encourage individual senior executives to independently commission partially overlapping consultant studies of future prospects. Then the team takes it upon itself to pool the outside insights with their own.

Korea's $54-billion growth giant Samsung is led by a chief executive with a strong sense of personal direction and a keen ability to help his top managers develop their own. Lee Kun-Hee knows how to encourage individuality in a culture rife with Asian consensus and conformity. When he became aware of how many American retailers were not taking Samsung's products seriously—something only vaguely appreciated by his inward-looking management team—he flew the entire group to Los Angeles so they could see for themselves how poorly the products were positioned. Then the group returned to Seoul to debate a problem they *all* now knew first hand, rather than meeting to devise a strategy to respond to their "boss's problem."

Samsung's CEO School

Lee is good at aiding others to share his perspective by setting them up to learn for themselves. Recently he launched what is dubbed "CEO School" for Samsung's 850 top managers. Abandoning the two-day, come-if-you-have-time, golf resort, motivational speech pump-up approach to executive education favored by his Western competitors, CEO School lasts for six months. Half this period is spent in classes in Korea; the rest, abroad. Ground rules for the time overseas include no air travel. His executives must use car, bus, or train transportation so they can better see the human side of the countries they visit. One executive crisscrossed the United States learning about leadership by studying the American revolution. Others have backpacked through Egypt and Jordan and explored rain forests in Malaysia.

Why is Lee going to so much trouble to "organize" the experiences of his management team? He wants Samsung to grow, and he knows—traditional Oriental logic aside—that growth has little to do with chance or luck. "Any attempt to strengthen one's competitiveness," he says, "by making temporary adjustments without having the fundamentals in place is similar to building castles in the sand."

Avoiding Self-Management

Effective top management teams *cannot* be self-managing. Their ability to cast far and wide for creative approaches to growth and their ability to confront current problems is highly dependent on the strength of the leadership provided by the chief executive. No strong leadership equates with no good growth plan. **Sound plans are the result of intensive fact-based debate about alternative courses of action.** The confrontation this requires, the willingness to bring forth information that may not flatter the status quo, and the generation of out-of-the-box thinking about future possibilities, all tend to generate heated conflict. Containing and channeling this conflict is one of the most important things a chief executive can do to promote growth. The absence of this kind of leadership ability results in teams that either join in passive lockstep behind the chief executive's solo vision or behave like warring feudal kingdoms.

Too Important for Techies and Bean Counters

Information systems are far too important to any business to be the responsibility of the computer technology department. Likewise, control systems that only serve the needs of the accountants and their auditors are unlikely to promote business growth. Both mechanisms for feedback and midcourse correction must be guided by the group responsible for setting the corporate direction.

Organization Provides Propulsion

Once a direction for growth is set, energy must be marshaled to move the business forward. This is the second critical role of every organization. Companies have a variety of ways to motivate action, such as the following:

- Appeal to employees' sense of identity and idealism by using *a widely shared common vision* of where the business is now and where it is going.

- Select appropriate growth-oriented *performance measures* and couple them tightly to the *incentive and reward programs* that are in place. Managers who enjoy making things happen through carrots and sticks tend to like this approach.

- Ensure that the *"rules of the game,"* both written and unwritten, are in accord with the business's growth plan. This approach works for both managers that are comfortable with the more Machiavellian side of organizations and those who believe that most employees want to do what is expected of them but often find expectations unclear or conflicting.

The Vision Thing

Getting what President George Bush called "the vision thing" right was a challenge for him, many other presidents, and most corporations. Consider the struggles of Prudential Insurance Co. In 1988, the Prudential vision statement was revised to state its first priority, which was the Rule Maker–like intention of remaining the number-one life insurance company in the nation. The next year rival Metropolitan Life pushed Prudential out of first place with the industry's greatest amount of insurance in force. In 1991, Prudential stressed to employees and customers alike that it was the strongest insurance company in the United States. The Moody's rating service disagreed, taking Prudential's top rating away because of too many investments in junk bonds and real estate.

The next year, the company promulgated an update of company values. Topping the list was the importance of the Pru being "worthy of trust." Within months the securities arm of the company found itself embroiled in its worst-ever scandal involving sales of oil, gas, and real estate limited partnerships. And to add insult to injury, the company's symbolic logo, featuring the "rock," was revealed to be a sketch of an outcropping in the Jersey Meadowlands, not the Mediterranean's famous Rock of Gibraltar.

Vision statements should be aspirational, but they also need to be strongly grounded in current reality. Consider the zigzags Xerox took to become more realistic about its corporate identity.

From "Designing the Information Age" to "Processing Documents"

During its golden age, the 1960s, Xerox was the Rule Maker of the copying industry, and every investor was searching for "the next Xerox." The business was moving so fast that growth seemed to be in the air and breathed by every employee, and the business purpose was strong and implicit. Then disaster struck. Japanese competition stole the low end of the copier market, Kodak briefly rediscovered its rule-breaking roots and introduced the first plain-paper copier, and the Xerox product quality plummeted. Market share in 1970 was 95 percent of copier units produced; by 1982 it had fallen to 13 percent.

The initial response of Xerox was a new mission statement. The company would become, CEO Peter McCullough declared, a business built around a vision of "the architecture of information," a company dedicated to providing products for the vaguely defined "office of the future." Catchy phrases, but only loosely linked to Xerox's market reality. McCullough also launched a Rule Breaker–like attempt to invent new technologies in a Silicon Valley–based R&D center. To fund the effort, several cash-rich insurance businesses, with minimal relationship to Xerox's core operations, were purchased.

Soon bad turned to worse. The ideas Xerox's collection of brilliant researchers developed found easier expression in other company's products, especially Apple Computer's Macintosh. The financial service companies ate more cash than they threw off. Several reorganizations and two chief executives later, Xerox narrowed its focus to a more achievable mission: "to be the preeminent *document* company," signaling that a heavy dose of reality had returned.

Stirring People to Action

Missions are only worth having when they are able to stir people to action, the equivalent of the cry of nineteenth-century French revolutionaries, "Aux Barricades!" Spirited feelings of a shared mission spurred Komatsu's growth plan to dethrone the one-time Rule Maker of the tractor and construction equipment industry, Caterpillar. When Martin Luther King led a civil rights revolution, he understood well the ability of language to mobilize activity. He never announced, "I have a strategic plan." Instead, he said, "I have a dream."

When a business is able to couple employees' personal values with those of the company, an incredibly strong motivator is created (and a very cost-effective one, also, considering all the money wasted on expensive executive compensation programs that provide generous rewards for middling, dispirited performance). Employees are much more willing to give up some of their autonomy and make some personal sacrifices when they feel bound through a leader in a shared enterprise. The less this is felt, the more concerns about individual welfare and personal entitlements become paramount.

Put Missions in Writing Only When It's Time to Change Them

It is possible, even preferable, for employees to feel a widely shared sense of common purpose, without any mission statement ever having been drafted. This often occurs during a Rule Breaker's start-up period—everyone there knows what the company is trying to achieve, why waste scarce time writing it down? As businesses mature, writing it down has more utility, as long as the purpose of the codification is to allow the mission's relevance to be questioned.

Never carve a mission statement in stone. Companies that have made especially effective use of these tools, Hewlett Packard and Johnson & Johnson (J&J) for example, have reviewed and revised them many times. The J&J "credo" is subject to periodic "challenges" by thousands of J&J managers. The statement of the "HP Way" originally coined by the company's founders has been revised at least four times. The purpose of these confrontations and changes is not so much to craft an "optimum" statement (words seldom get a business anywhere) but to generate energy and excitement about the course revision the company is about to take.

Making Visions Work

Visions can be tricky tools to use well. Most corporate mission statements are, at best, verbal platitudes. Many companies would be better off with no formal statement than one whose primary impact is to encourage growth-defeating hypocrisy. "If you don't have something to say, don't say it" is probably the best operating principle here. Be patient, wait until the right time comes.

The best time to draft a corporate mission is immediately after a major business victory. Significant growth-inducing events— the launch of a new product, the upset of a longtime rival, or the receipt of a sought-after quality certification from a big customer—can anchor the aspirational tone of the vision to a concrete reality experienced throughout the company. Write the mission when the taste of victory is still fresh. The mission-setting process can then foster learning aimed at discovering the following:

- What was done right and how the company can keep doing this.

- What went wrong, and what can be learned from that.

Missions Don't Set Direction, People Do

Mission statements are not tools for setting direction. If a business needs to keep returning to its statement of purpose to resolve questions about future strategy, it may find itself in the same trouble the Walt Disney Company's managers got themselves into by, after Disney's death, constantly asking "What would Walt do now?" instead of getting in practice thinking for themselves.

Visions come alive the easiest when they reflect an emerging or existing consensus throughout the company. **Mission statements can be most effective for communicating and reinforcing a direction already chosen.** In many circumstances, a company's compensation system can be even more effective.

Compensation Is Too Important to Be Left to Experts

Like mission statements, pay is frequently mismanaged. Harry Pearce, a General Motors executive vice president, once observed that GM's managers were always grateful when they received large bonuses, but they seldom knew what they did to earn them. Pearce called it a system set up to distribute gratuities to those in most favor, not necessarily to reward those most contributing to growth. At GM, and many other major companies, compensation has been for too long the concern of professional experts, rather than a tool used by managers to propel growth. Discussions about pay have long centered on questions such as the following:

- How *much* is appropriate—an issue on which many hours and dollars are spent in exhaustive surveys (the net result of which is to drive industry pay levels higher—few companies want to pay at or below "average").

- How *fairly* is it being doled out—an important concern that if not addressed will lead to internal dissension and distraction from the real purpose of the business. However, establishing pay equity, a threshold requirement for every company, will not by itself drive growth.

- What *forms* of pay are best—an issue that can never finally be resolved but that leads to countless studies as innovative forms of compensation keyed to the latest tax law changes or newest management fads.

Unfortunately, from a growth perspective, all the heated debate that has gone into issues like these has distracted attention from a more strategic concern: *what is the tangible impact of compensation on the people the business depends on for growth?* Managers have for too long become the prisoners of their compensation experts.

Look at the Impact of Incentives, Not the Techniques

Incentive and reward systems need to be "read," not from the perspective of technical or legal requirements or concerns of administrative ease, but to answer the following questions:

- To what are they actually encouraging people to *pay attention?*

- What are they actually encouraging people to *do?*

Keep the technical experts far away until managers are comfortable with their understanding of these issues and can also clearly articulate the following questions:

- What *will* the business need attention directed toward if it is to grow?

- What actions *will* growth require on the part of employees and managers *that are not currently happening?*

The gap between answers to these sets of issues should, then, set the agenda for the most productive use of compensation professionals.

What Really Counts?

Despite all the clutter from feuding top management groups, technician-driven systems and off-the-mark vision statements, most employees eventually find some way to sort things out and get on with their day-to-day jobs.

After a few months in a new job, most alert, career-minded people have some fairly good idea of what it *takes to survive, get things accomplished, and gain—should they want it—influence or advancement* within their new employer. This understanding may be based on what is read in the company's official policy statements or what is heard in orientation and management development programs, but it is more likely gleaned informally from personal experiences and interactions with new colleagues and friends.

Arthur D. Little's unwritten rules expert, Peter Scott-Morgan, calls these "the secrets that everybody knows." Decoding them, he believes, is the first step to any successful change effort. This involves talking with the people most essential to the business's growth plan and understanding:

- *What* is most important to each?

- *Who* in the organization can most help them achieve what they want?

- *How* do they feel they need to behave to get what they want?

Propel Growth by Changing the Unwritten Rules

Uncovering the conflicts and mismatches between the dictates of a company's growth path and the "real" unwritten rules that guide employees is an aspect of organization that is usually neglected or only considered after problems arise. The "rules of the game" lie just under the surface of most businesses. Pull them out, weed out the conflicts, and make use of an underleveraged tool to remove barriers to growth.

Samsung changed the official rules to deal with an unwritten rule that limited its employees' ability to be productive and grow. As in Japan, typical office work hours in Korea were from nine in the morning to eight at night, followed by the unofficial practice of rounds of late-night drinking with work colleagues. Now employees start work at seven in the morning and must finish by four in the afternoon. Morning productivity has soared, and employees looking for early-evening activities are "informally" expected to spend their freed-up time in foreign language or self-improvement courses.

Organization Provides Stability

The third attribute of all organizations, Stability, is the one that usually first comes to most people's minds. This is the realm of organization charts, head counts, and committees. This is what *is to be* given Direction and what *needs to be* Propelled. Businesses derive their stability from the ways jobs, teams, and departments are structured. This is usually a process of dividing the labor.

Pulling the Business Together

These divisions, usually necessary to allow for a measure of specialization and focus, then need to be pulled back together through a repertoire of coordinating mechanisms. Some of these linking pins are easily apparent:

- Cross-functional teams and special coordinating groups.

- Permanent brand or project manager jobs.

- Temporary trouble-shooter or "czar" positions.

- The management structure itself.

Other forms are "organizational glue" and are less obvious but just as effective:

- Training and other forms of managed socialization—especially effective when customized and done internally, with "role model" managers as the faculty.

- Shared incentives and bonus pools between employees, between members of functional departments that need to collaborate, or among team members.

- Information networks (interconnected personal computers are one approach; traditional bulletin boards and large charts indicating progress toward goals can also serve this purpose well).

- Planned rotation of key employees to spread new techniques and perspectives.

None of these structures and techniques will, by themselves, promote growth. For that to happen, programs must be in place to invest in people.

Invest in Growth by Investing in People

Samsung, the 120,000-employee Korean conglomerate that put almost 1,000 executives through a grueling six-month CEO School, does not limit its investment in leadership to those currently in positions of authority. Every year the company selects from among its employees with at least three years of service 400 to be sent overseas for a year, all expenses paid. Their assignment is to do whatever they want, but they must return armed with an intimate knowledge of the culture and language of wherever they went. After returning, they spend several years in assignments in Korea, readjusting to Samsung, and then are sent back to the country they visited, this time to sell their company's products. This effort will involve at least 2,000 employees and is expected to cost over $100 million.

Many companies talk about preparing employees for globalization and the challenges of finding future growth in off-shore markets. Samsung is one that is doing something about it. This company knows what many other growth-minded businesses keenly appreciate: **the more people there are in a company who can imagine what it can become, the more likely it is to get there.**

Eskimos Seldom Buy Refrigerators

It is not enough just to train people and send them overseas. They have to be *listened to* back home, also. Kids 'R' Us, the clothing offshoot of retail powerhouse Toys 'R' Us, was prepared for rapid growth when it opened its first three stores in Puerto Rico. It expected sales to be propelled by back-to-school clothes purchases, and its New Jersey–based centrally run marketing operation shipped thousands of these garments to the Puerto Rican stores. To headquarters' great surprise, almost none sold. Had Kids 'R' Us involved its local store managers in the stocking decisions they quickly would have found that all Puerto Rican children wear uniforms to school! By the time this information reached the home office, the damage was done, the Puerto Rican growth plans were shelved, and the existing stores had to be closed.

Overstaffing Hurts Productivity, but Understaffing Limits Growth

Listening to the wrong people can block growth, and so can not having enough of the right ones. Chrysler has experienced years of strong sales from its minivans, providing its balance sheet with a generous cash cushion. Even though ample investment capital is now available, Robert Eaton, Chrysler's chief executive, complains that the company's major constraint expanding globally is a shortage of skilled engineers and managers.

This talent shortfall is a problem its competitor, Ford, has worked hard for over a decade to avoid. While Chrysler's total employment in the 1980s rose and fell like a roller coaster, Ford avoided the peaks and valleys by a gradual, decade-long plan to, quarter by quarter, reduce the size of its white collar staff. Since this was done slowly, Ford was able to target its cutbacks with voluntary terminations offered only to employees with skills the company predicted it would not need in the future. Chrysler overstaffed when times were good, then downsized deeply when business soured. Short-term morale, naturally, suffered. But so did Chrysler's long-term growth opportunities.

This is a problem plaguing many companies in addition to Chrysler. Arthur D. Little, Inc. consultants interviewed over 300 senior executives from a cross section of American industry. They talked with managers from manufacturing and service companies and found that both groups had a similar lament: *difficulties in hiring and retaining employees* were among the most serious obstacles to growth they faced.

Most of the best business growers recognize the vital importance of people in the growth mix. Some, like Federal Express and Southwest Airlines, go so far as to make sure management recognizes that most of its time, after setting a direction, is to be spent supporting the development of human resources. This is another job that in growth companies is too important to be left to the experts. Herbert Kelleher, Southwest's CEO, says his philosophy is that "**our employees are the customers of our management,** and that we are here to serve them," not the (too common) other way around. Managers need to behave more like coaches if the quarterbacks are to do their quarterbacking.

What about Culture?

An organization is defined by how it handles the basic tasks of direction setting, motivation, and providing needed stability. The idea of "corporate culture" is missing from this definition. Why? **Culture is something that managers cannot put their hands around. It is not something that can be directly managed.**

Recall business meetings of a decade or two ago. Most likely, more than half of those attending were smokers. By the meeting's midpoint, a cloud of smoke filled the conference room. The cloud was real. It was visible; it could be smelled (and inhaled). But it was not something anyone could directly manipulate or "get their hands around." Its nature was too elusive for direct management, but it could be changed. Windows and doors could be opened and an exhaust fan turned on, but these, like many contemporary changes in management programs, were only temporary in effect. Turn off the fan, and the cloud quickly returns. The only way to change the nature of the smoke cloud in a lasting way is to change the nature of what is being smoked. Substitute, say, pipes for cigarettes and cigars; ban Gaulois, and issue sweeter-smelling Kentucky tobacco; or prohibit smoking altogether.

The same is true with corporate culture. Its nature is like a cloud that surrounds a business. It is real. It does affect behavior. Corporate culture is a good indicator of the inner working of the business, but it seldom succumbs to a frontal assault. Changing culture, in a lasting way, requires changing the nature of what produces it: the structures and management practices that direct, motivate, and stabilize the business.

Getting Your Ducks in Order

Direction, Propulsion, and Stability—vehicles require all three. Forward motion, though, also requires these functions to work in reasonably close harmony with each other. Otherwise, ships go around in circles, planes take nose dives, and corporate structures become very inefficient.

A company is positioned for growth when its people are. A growth-oriented organization is one in which its three functions are working in tandem to focus employees' attention on and direct actions toward the requirements of the path it has chosen.

Half a century ago, during the company's first golden age, the founder of Chrysler commented on the nature of the company he created. He thought first of the people that worked with him, not his cars: "When all these minds, through organization, are made to function as a single intelligence, each member of which is a special gifted part, why then you can expect to produce magic." That is a lofty aspiration for any organization—*all its minds functioning as a single intelligence*—but it is a target worthy of a business searching for growth.

Identify the Disconnects

Reality is usually a lot more diffuse. Try this: Identify a representative sample of your company's employees. Include people at all levels of the hierarchy, newcomers and old-timers, and employees based in each function and division. Ask them "Where are we trying to get to?" and you are likely to hear a customized version of the old story of what happens when a group of blind men each try to describe the nature of an elephant. Many employees, outside top management, will provide only vague generalizations of what they understand the corporate strategy to be. Most can speak only about the immediate objectives of the work group in which they are a part. Few will be able to clearly relate their job and their department's goals to the overall growth direction of the corporation. There is more to this problem than what C.K. Pralahad and Gary Hamel enjoy pointing out: most companies are overmanaged and underled. This is true, but improving the growth prospects requires more than stronger leadership at the top.

It is very common to find that a tightly focused executive team is trying to move a business in one direction, while moving the performance measures and incentives motivating employee behavior in a different direction. It is also common to find that the company's staff share a vision of growth through global expansion, but its structure dictates functional autonomy, and few of the employees have had experience working anywhere outside the United States. **Common visions only come to life when a structure is present to support them.** Otherwise they are merely daydreams. **Structures alone are confining prisons of daily drudgery when they lack a source of direction and energy to bring them to life.**

A Phone Company with All the Wrong Numbers

Companies divided against themselves are so common that this is often taken for granted as the nature of organizations. Middle managers of one large regional telephone company once complained: "We spend so much time fighting each other that no one has any energy left over to grow the business." What should top management do about this intramural civil war—send all the managers to "culture/teamwork school," as one of its sister companies spent hundreds of thousands of dollars trying? Instead, an astute senior officer used a few staff people to do a quick-and-dirty diagnosis to find the root cause behind many of these conflicts.

Following a good hunch, she had the assistants collect copies of all the management-by-objectives targets each member of the senior executive team was expected to be working toward. When she examined them, it was quickly obvious this group was a "team" in name only. The executives as a whole had 58 MBOs. Of this only six objectives were shared among the top managers. The remaining 90 percent were keyed to specific departmental or divisional goals. And, to make a bad situation worse, when the vice president talked to the other officers about the six common targets, she discovered the interpretation of these goals varied widely. When the focus of the group at the top of the hierarchy is this diffuse, it is unlikely those in the middle and bottom will be able to find much in the way of common ground.

You Can Never Change Just One Thing

Many well-meaning, expert-driven change and improvement programs fail because they are intended to optimize one aspect of a business operation—create the best planning process or the most proven approach to performance appraisal, for example. **It is never possible to change just one part of an organization. The three functions (Direction, Propulsion, and Stability) are completely intertwined in the minds and behaviors of most employees. Making changes in a disjoined manner only sends mixed signals that dilute focus.** Improvements efforts, even if centered on a particular aspect of the organization—say devising an effective approach to management development and succession—cannot be carried out without reference to how they will impact every other aspect of organization.

Imagine a house renovation. The master plan may call for a wall to be removed, but before the demolition crew arrives, blueprints must be carefully studied, lest the wall be load bearing or contain wiring to be rerouted or plumbing that cannot be rerouted. Good architects and builders do this instinctively, but many organization change programs are guided more by a narrow engineering mentality. Architects are big picture, master plan–oriented thinkers. Engineers focus on change one component at a time. Architects make the best use they can of the materials they have at hand. Engineers are more attuned to imposing the "right answer" on the immediate problem. Often, in organizational change, the best answer is the one that results in the "best fit" among Direction, Propulsion, and Stability.

Building an organization to serve as a growth vehicle starts with an appreciation of the organic, systemlike nature of how it will affect the people working in it. Create a blueprint first; map out the nature of and the interaction among the business's "rudder," "sails," and "hull" as they are now; then move forward on several change fronts simultaneously.

Marching in Lockstep off a Cliff

Internal consistency is important, but it is not sufficient. Slippages on growth paths occur for two reasons. Organizations can become *unaligned,* and most of the company's efforts are wasted dealing with internal conflict, or, even worse, the forces of Direction, Propulsion, and Stability are all aligned, but in the *wrong direction.* Inefficiency is a serious problem, but **a company with all employees marching forward in lockstep can be a disaster if they are headed toward the edge of a steep cliff.** In 1984, AT&T started down the path of improvisation with the organization of a Rule Maker. Less than ten years later, Apple Computer approached markets appropriate for Specialists with an organization of Rule Breakers.

10

Changing Course to Sustain Growth

While off-road driving is fun in a 4×4, it is torturous in a Lincoln Town Car. A minivan makes great sense when kids and car pools dominate your driving time, but a Mazda Miata can ease the pain of an empty nest. Long, straight western interstates were made for Detroit's muscle cars, whereas the Pacific Coast Highway cries out for a BMW convertible.

Matching the Vehicle with the Path

Different paths require different vehicles. Different strategies for growth require different organizations to carry them out. The previous chapters highlighted the differing organizational characteristics of companies on each of the five growth paths. To summarize these, using the three-part perspective of organization as vehicle, it is helpful to think of each dimension as a side of a triangle.

An Organization for Each Strategy

The left side of the triangle is "Direction." "Propulsion" is the right, and "Stability" is at the bottom. In terms of these three aspects of organization, three growth paths are purebreds and two are hybrids.

- Most Rule Breakers have organizations in which the function of *Direction* predominates. Many are even called "extended shadows" of their founder or chief executive. They still require mechanisms to provide Propulsion and Stability, but these are far less developed, especially those contributing to Stability. This is the way it needs to be for a Rule Breaker to thrive in the environment its growth path transverses.

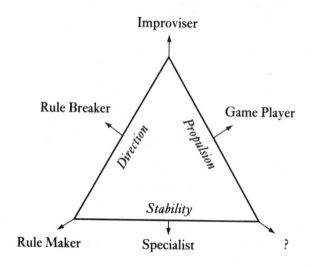

- Game Players do better with vehicles able to steal market share from tough competitors, ones able to do well in double-digit growth rate markets. For them, *Propulsion* is the most vital function of their organizations. Game Players know where they are going; they just need the energy necessary to get there.

- Specialists also overemphasize some aspects of their organizations, but for their slower and focused path to growth, *Stability* is the organizational characteristic that serves them best. Which, again, is not to say they do not need Direction or Propulsion, they just require—compared to companies on the previous two paths—proportionally less to be successful.

- Rule Makers are more complicated. Being a hybrid, they tend to blend strong Bill Gates or Michael Eisner–style *Direction* with well-developed approaches to provide strong internal *Stability*. This combination may even help them carry this sense of Stability to the outside marketplace.

- Improvisers are also a hybrid. Their unique ability to roll with the punches and adjust quickly to chaotic markets is driven by an emphasis on *Direction* (like that provided by George Fisher at Kodak or Michael Spindler at Apple) coupled with strong attention to using the tools of *Propulsion* to rapidly shift course.

Looking at the triangle, one possible combination of organizational characteristics remains. It is the combination of *Propulsion* and *Stability*. Were this vehicle a boat, it would have a large hull and a powerful engine to haul it around—but no place in particular to go. This category, perhaps, should be reserved for one-time successful companies that have lost their will to grow. A number of businesses fit this type; they are just not the subject of this book.

Blending the Paths

Few companies pursue growth on only one of the five paths because few market conditions are so neatly clear cut. Paths can be blended to do the following:

- Best fit the complexities of current industry realities.

- Adapt to changing market conditions by putting out new growth feelers.

- Keep a business from getting "overadapted" to its current situation—always a path to eventual decline.

- Hedge bets—multiproduct, multipath companies tend to last longer than single-focus ones.

Hybrid Growth Strategies

There are increasing instances of businesses following hybrid growth directions:

- For many years Xerox has nurtured its rule-breaking office automation group within a largely Game Player corporate structure.

- More recently Matsushita gave up its rule-making ambitions to dominate the course of the emerging "digital universe" when it sold most of its Hollywood moviemaker, MCA. Realizing it lacked the clear sense of Direction needed by successful Rule Makers, it is refocusing itself to follow a mix of specialization in making electronic components and game playing in the consumer markets it already knows well.

- In the U.S. steel industry, two rivals, Rule Breaker Nucor and U.S. Steel (once an industry Rule Maker, now a hybrid Improviser-Specialist), are following the cooperation-oriented New Rules for Growth. They are setting up a rule-breaking joint venture aimed at revolutionizing the American steel industry by finding a new way to turn iron ore into steel.

- Specialist semiconductor maker, Integrated Device Technology, realizing how hard it is to mix the rule-breaking orientation with its own, allowed its vice president of engineering to "spin off, in place," forming a new semiconductor company right in the middle of Integrated Device's office space. The new company, called MoST, Inc., intends to dramatically speed up how computer screens draw graphics. The parent owns 10 percent of its stock, provides overhead services, and keeps the proximate operations sufficiently blurred so visitors walking through its offices cannot tell where one begins and the other leaves off.

Internal Departments Can Have Their Own Growth Paths, Too

It is even possible to subdivide a business into units according to growth orientation. Functional departments tend to identify with the five growth paths along these lines:

- *R&D* often has many Rule Breaker characteristics.

- *Sales and marketing* departments are classic Game Players.

- *Manufacturing* and many *administrative units* share characteristics with Specialists.

- Most top managements seem to follow either the *Rule Maker* or *Improviser* orientations.

A "Shoeless" Shoe Company

Nike, the athletic footwear "maker," has used this logic to guide its internal organization development. The word maker is in quotes because Nike does not really make shoes, at least few people who work in its organization do. Nike follows a growth strategy that combines rule breaking with game playing and rule making. To keep top management attention on this blend and what needs to happen to keep new product ideas moving into the appropriate marketing channels, Nike outsources manufacturing, distribution, and retailing. These are all provinces of the Specialist, an orientation that Nike feels would dilute its focus on R&D and brand marketing. Nike even encourages its contract factories to make shoes for Adidas and Reebok, two of its strongest competitors. This gives Nike flexibility in not feeling pressured to keep them busy when Nike's marketing focus suggests that products from another source would sell better. Nike believes in the value of organizational learning and wants its suppliers to acquire it, from whatever source is at hand.

Some Combinations Are Easier than Others

Some growth paths blend easier than others. Because of their shared organizational characteristic, Game Player/Improviser and Rule Maker/Specialist pairings can often find some common ground. The general rebelliousness of most Rule Breakers tends to keep companies on this growth path from mixing with others. The visionary Direction inherent in rule breaking is very different from the shorter-term craftiness that Improvisers use to set a course.

Other combinations are possible and can be observed in multibusiness companies like General Electric and Sony that operate in diverse businesses. One principle to bear in mind **when organizing businesses** with diverse growth paths under one corporate umbrella is not to try to tightly integrate things that are not meant to be tightly integrated. This is a sure way to kill off growth potential, as Exxon found when it (a Specialist-cum-Rule Maker) tried to diversify into computer chips and office automation (then dominated by Rule Breakers). The more the businesses resemble combinations of oil and water (Rule Breakers and Specialists; Rule Breakers and Rule Makers) the further apart—organizationally—they need to be. This is when structural forms like autonomous divisions, holding companies, and joint ventures are most useful.

In theory, almost any blending of paths is possible as long as the right organizational accommodations are made. Chemical opposites, like oil and water, can mix if put in a closed container and shaken with sufficient force. This requires the continual addition of energy to keep their molecules in motion, just as **ongoing management attention is required to operate businesses on divergent growth paths under the same corporate structure.** The important consideration here is one of opportunity costs: might not the company's overall performance be better if this management attention were directed elsewhere?

Changing Course

Yesterday's growth strategy is frequently what drives today's organization. What is needed, instead, is *today's organization providing the foundation for tomorrow's growth path.* In business schools, a great deal of time has been spent debating the "chicken and egg" issue of which is more important: strategy or structure, the growth path or the organization that travels it? In the real world, the issue hardly exists. Every established business has both, and each needs to be in sync with each other. The only time strategy is of paramount importance is before the company is launched, when it exists only as an idea in the minds of its founders.

This issue does become of renewed importance, however, when a company reaches the midpoint of its growth path. That is when, assuming the business has been fairly successful, the organization most reflects the requirements of the current growth path. The midpoint is when the company operates most efficiently and when *its sustained growth is threatened the most.*

Rethinking Charles Darwin

Both executives and academics have long tried to apply ideas about biological evolution and concepts such as "genetic mutation" and "natural selection" to help them understand how businesses grow. The most recent of these is highlighted in the popular management book *Built to Last*, by James Collins and Jerry Porras. Their research, a great improvement on the methods of *In Search of Excellence*, suggests that evolutionary processes are a great way to stimulate business growth. They urge companies to follow a "branching and pruning" approach to progress: keep adding variety, branches, to the business while continually pruning the deadwood (Darwin's idea of "selection"). The result, says Collins and Porrus, is a collection of healthy businesses well positioned to prosper in a constantly changing environment. This approach can work well for some companies in the near term (especially Improvisers), but it is based on too flawed an understanding of how evolution really works to be a useful formula to follow to sustain growth over the long haul.

In 1859, Charles Darwin launched a new way of thinking about biological development. He did not answer all the questions about how species evolve, nor are his generalities especially sound when used to describe how businesses behave. More recent research has suggested some better explanations. Darwin's theories imply that there is some long, single chain that connects all species, but studies done since he advanced his ideas have failed to show, for example, how birds descend from reptiles, mammals from simpler quadrupeds, or the four-legged creatures from their assumed marine ancestors. Gaps, more often than not, tend to appear between different species. Some of these may be due to missing, undiscovered biological evidence, but they are sufficiently numerous to suggest that Darwin's paradigm needs some rethinking.

Evolution Is Seldom Evolutionary

Another English scientist, D'Arcy Thompson, spent years applying the tools of mathematics to understand the relationships between biological forms and the processes by which they grew. His bottom line: a biological *principle of discontinuity*. **Some species just cannot turn into others.** Their highly developed forms and process will not allow it. When big variations occur, they are much more likely to be *abrupt*, not orderly and continuous, as Darwin implied. "Higher forms" of life have not necessarily come from ones just below them on some "ladder of development." They are just as likely to have come from the most elementary forms that have always been around. To translate this to the business world, it is still possible for a Harvard dropout to create a multi-billion-dollar, high-growth company from a garage start-up. **After becoming well established, businesses do not grow by successive minor changes in strategy and organization but by large-scale transformations that involve the corporation as a whole.** This is something like the shift, for example, of a Rule Breaker to a Game Player.

Survival of the Luckiest

Harvard paleontologist, Stephen Jay Gould, has even suggested the notion of "survival of the fittest" be replaced by something closer to what studies of fossil remains suggest: "survival of the luckiest." He traces biological history as a story of massive removal of species (from disease, predators, ice ages, etc.), followed by a period of differentiation among the survivors. Growth, from his perspective, is driven as much from events in the surrounding environment than from any code plugged into the genes. Maybe so, but chance still favors the prepared company.

Harvey Golub, American Express's chief executive, is working hard on the preparatory activities. He undid his predecessor's rule-making strategy of attempting to be a "financial supermarket"—a path making little sense in an environment populated with many Rule Breakers and strong and successful Game Players. Instead of variety, Golub selected the company's charge card business as the center of future growth. He has few illusions about the difficulties of this path, considering the already-established strengths of competitors such as Visa, AT&T, and Sears. **Golub believes, for American Express and its competitors, that every business is destined to ultimately go out of business. The only issue, as he sees it, is if the wounds are to be self-inflicted, by American Express changing its product mix, or suffered at the hands of competitors.**

Evolution at American Express

Golub, at least, has American Express's history working in its favor. If he is successful, this will not be the first time American Express has sustained growth through a major course change. The company, years ago, was an "express" company, hauling business freight along the lines of today's Federal Express or UPS.

Golub is attuned to a concept learned in a previous career as a consultant, the "S" curve. Most every product—or new industry, for that matter—goes through a period of development that, when plotted, is the shape of that letter. When the effort that goes into a growth initiative is compared with the return from that investment, three distinct phases are common. First, progress is slow and returns minimal or nonexistent. Then, in the words of "S" curve charter Richard Foster, "all hell breaks loose," and growth runs wild. Then a point is reached when new dollars invested in the growth initiative do not produce the high return of previous investment. Progress in the lab or marketplace becomes more difficult. Golub's American Express is at the upper end of its curve in its charge card and traveler's check businesses. Renewed growth will have to come from paths that begin at the bottom of the curve. Where is your business on its "S" curve?

Successful Course Changers

In looking for these, Golub will have many examples of companies that sustained growth by changing course to consider. These range from package haulers to coffee shop operators and computer makers.

- Emery Worldwide was once a *game-playing* Federal Express look-alike, but its competitive position was weak. Federal Express picked up more packages at Manhattan's World Trade Center than Emery did throughout New York State. It was also plagued by high costs. It cost Emery $16.00 to pick up a one-pound package, for which it only charged customers $6.00. Something had to give, and it was Emery's Game Player growth path. Now Emery refuses to haul letters and small packages. All resources are concentrated on freight weighing over 70 lbs. Changing to *specialization* has brought large increases in revenues and profits, and Emery's share of its market segment is twice as large as its nearest rival (another long-time Specialist, Burlington Air Express).

- Emery's nemesis, Federal Express, has in less than a quarter of a century shifted paths from its *rule-breaking* creation of a new market to, for a brief period, a *rule-making* dominance of its industry. Attempts to sustain its position by reverting to rule breaking—its ill-fated Zap Mail fax delivery service—and emergence of strong competition from UPS, Airborne, and even the U.S. Postal Service, forced it to shift into its current *Game Player* mode.

- Emerson Electric, the manufacturer whose rediscovery of growth was described in Chapter 1, is transforming from a *Specialist* to a *Game Player.* Two well-known consumer beverage makers, Snapple and Starbucks, have made similar changes.

- In the early 1980s, Franklin Computer Company started as a *game playing* imitator of Apple Computer's products. When forced from the cloning business, Franklin repositioned itself as "Franklin Electronic Publishers," a sales leader *specializing* in the electronic language translator and reference book market.

- Apple Computer itself began as a Silicon Valley *Rule Breaker* and for a time attempted to be a *Game Player,* but it was forced by IBM and Microsoft to follow the *Improviser* path. Some industry analysts see a bright future for the company, but it is one that follows the *Specialist's* path.

- American Express's Golub may find it easier learning from others in the financial services industry. Fortunately, examples of growth shifts, both good and bad, abound in banking. Bankers Trust, a once poor-performing blend of *Game Player/Improviser,* dramatically turned its performance around when it shed its branch network and became a *Specialist/Game Player,* focusing on fee-based services for corporate clients. One of these, its derivatives products, led to unexpected consequences for its largest customers, and the bank has moved to the *improvising* path. Bankers Trust's Manhattan neighbor, Citicorp, remained a full-service bank but, during the same period, has gone from *Rule Maker* to near-failing *Improviser* to rebounding *Game Player.*

Change Begins with Unlearning

Radical change, as these companies experienced, does not start with a learning process. Instead, it commences with some serious efforts at "unlearning." When ex–Nissan executive Marvin Runyon became U.S. Postmaster General, he quickly observed that "it wouldn't hurt to lose some of the institutional memory here." Downsizing may be one way to do that, but it is usually self-defeating. The people most needed to grow the business are usually the first to leave.

The Naskapi Indians (chapter 8) had an approach to planning that made it easy to forget old paths. The Spanish explorer Cortez, in the early 1500s, conquered a much larger and better-armed Aztec nation only after scuttling or sending home all the ships that brought him to the New World. His soldiers had no choice: move forward or perish. Compaq Computer's president, Eckhard Pfeiffer, instilled a similar spirit into his employees when he led them to become the world's top PC vendor. He believes in corporate unlearning, the continual replacement of yesterday's wisdom with tomorrow's.

Where does all this new, growth-inducing wisdom come from? A strong-willed executive, coping with a grow-or-perish crisis, is one source. But hard times and survival at stake are not the only ways change happens. Chuck Knight at Emerson moved when profits were strong, as did Federal Express's Fred Smith and many others.

Ed McCracken is no modern-day Cortez, but as chief executive of Silicon Graphics, he has made use of management practices that help employees pay attention to life as it is and what it can become—not how things used to be. **Most major reorganizations—essential in any shift from one growth path to another—are handled very poorly. This is often because all the attention is given to figuring out what comes next, and too little time is devoted to closing the books on the past.**

Before Reorganizing: Hold a Wake

McCracken did not fall into this trap. When growth and new market conditions required a split of two Silicon Graphics divisions into five, McCracken did not just issue new organization charts and job titles and tell everyone to get back to work. He hired a New Orleans band and encouraged employees of the two groups to stage a wake. They did, filling two cardboard coffins with representative paraphernalia from each about-to-disappear unit. They were buried on the company's Mountain View, California campus—visible reference points for employees who might feel a need to mourn the old before getting on with the new.

McCracken believes fun and a little irreverence can make change less scary. He's right.

Avoid Delusions

In addition to burying memories of past successes, successful course changing often requires *giving up some current illusions*. Xerox—a dyed-in-the-wool, sales-driven Game Player—has harbored hopes for many years of finding renewed growth through rule-breaking R&D. Those are two growth paths difficult to blend. **Companies obsessed with winning every game find it very hard to learn a new one.** Xerox may do better reviewing its early history when it came upon the product that obsoleted mimeograph. Xerox did not invent xerography; it bought it from an outside inventor.

Sony is, at times, another corporate wanna-be. It is the world's master at miniaturization and has one of the strongest brand names in consumer electronics, but it also has a history of failing at controlling a market's development. Its pioneering VCR product, Betamax, lacked all the features consumers wanted, and a rival technology (VHS) became standard. Other missteps occurred in software and digital audio standard setting.

A strategy Sony pursued to maneuver around these failures was an attempt to become the Rule Maker controlling both the hardware (Sony's entertainment products) and software sides of the emerging digital entertainment industry. To provide content that can potentially be exclusively adapted for its products, Sony purchased Columbia and Tri-Star studios and entered into the electronic publishing business. Since then, Sony has faced severe challenges combining the rule-breaking electronic path with the game-playing show business. Rule Makers seldom emerge by blending these other two paths.

Sony produces absolutely incredible products; it might benefit if it stops fighting its old battles. Sony can clearly be the 3M of global consumer electronics. 3M has had a much-envied track record of growth—achieved without it ever wanting to be the "Microsoft of abrasives."

Know When to Temporarily Throw in the Towel

Few companies have the patience, or realism, of French clothing maker Devanlay S.A. This company owns the Lacoste brand whose crocodile-crested polo shirts were once fashion icons. Eventually success led to ubiquity, and the crocodile logo appeared on a wide assortment of clothing, much of it not especially well made. With its exclusivity gone and its quality reputation tarnished, Devanlay did the only thing that made any sense: it took the product off the market until consumer memories of the tarnished image faded. Later, it was reintroduced, now only on 100 percent cotton shirts, all made in France, and only sold in carefully selected upmarket outlets.

The lesson: growth-minded businesses sometimes have to face the reality that there are times when "you just can't get there from here." This was an injunction that eluded John Scully, former Apple Computer chief executive. In spite of his game-playing, consumer marketing career at Pepsi, he put a great deal of effort into restoring Apple's growth by attempting to take the company, again, down its original rule-breaking path with the development of the handheld electronic communicator, the Newton.

At times it seems almost every example of success at renewing growth can be countered with missteps or failures. This may be just the nature of business, but there are ways course changes can occur more smoothly and successfully.

Start before You Have To

It always helps to *start before you have to*. Companies able to challenge their own orthodoxies, to do double-, not just single-loop learning, will always come out ahead. Single-loop learning is what is done when a deviation from what is expected is caught and fixed. Double-loop learning, on the other hand, is when **the existence of deviations or performance shortfalls is used to question the original assumptions behind the appropriateness of the performance targets.** Declines in market share may be trying to tell a Rule Breaker it is time to consider becoming a Specialist; surges in demand can tell an Improviser it is time to consider the Game Player's path.

Beware of Too Much Positive Thinking

Behavioral specialist Chris Argyris feels this kind of awareness is unlikely to happen if the company is too committed to the power of positive thinking—always looking for only the bright side of things, killing off the messengers carrying early warnings of change. This kind of atmosphere, common in many businesses, forces managers to censor, hide, or oversimplify problems when they arise. It is also an approach that treats employees condescendingly, by assuming they, as Argyris says, "can only function in a cheerful world, even if the cheer is false."

Sending managers to classes in organizational learning is seldom sufficient to change these inbred patterns. *Structural changes* are also needed to provide power bases for people with insight into the new directions for growth a business may need to consider. This is a role consultants are sometimes asked to play, but they often lack the position and continuity to fight for the changes that need to happen.

Create a Group for Growth

Alternatively, companies may want to build windows to future growth opportunities into their structure by creating a *parallel hierarchy*, mirroring the existing managerial structure. This would be a home for bright individual contributors, people more concerned about the "white space" on the organization chart than being responsible for managing ongoing operations. Getting one of these senior "architects of future growth" positions would be just as difficult as being promoted to top management— only the focus and expectations would be different. **Individuals in these jobs would spend more time worrying about what the company is not doing than what it is doing.** These positions, as a whole, might represent some form of "shadow government," concerned with planting the seeds for and nurturing the business's future.

Levers of Organizational Change

Changing growth paths ultimately requires organizational change. Going back to the idea of organization as a vehicle for growth, what organizational changes can bring the fastest strategic change? In the short run, changes in the composition of the *top management team* when coupled with *new performance measures and rewards* linked to the measures will move a business farthest fastest. However, for the new growth orientation to stick, it needs to be reflected in a *widely shared vision* of where the company is going and in the programs used to *select and develop the people* who will take it there. Then, when these levers for change are in place, does it make sense to adjust the *structure* and the *systems* that support it? There is little point in putting the wrong people in new jobs they are not prepared for and expecting growth to result.

How have companies successfully kept growing over the long haul? They

- become aware of the need for change;

- adapt the vehicle for their growth to the requirements of a new growth path; and

- change, when necessary, from one vehicle to another.

Attention is given to whatever shifts are necessary in Direction, Propulsion, and Stability. Gaps are identified between what is happening now and what will be needed to sustain growth on a different path. On the surface, this is an *analytic* task, involving examination of a variety of important details, including the following:

- the management team's make-up,

- systems in place for planning and control,

- what the business mission is and the extent to which it is widely shared,

- how incentives are tied to measures of growth,

- how the unwritten rules are contributing or detracting from forward movement,

- what kind of structure for what kind of employees has been chosen, and

- what mechanisms are in place to coordinate everyone's activities.

Analysis is important, but, in the end, every one of these issues has a *human side*. What counts the most is the impact each element of organization has on *people*. **The bottom line of any organization is how well it positions its employees for growth. Organizations shape the way people interact.** You can tell that an organization is focused on moving forward when talk about growth permeates conversations throughout the company. No business can "go for growth" unless its employees *want to get there just as much.*

Epilogue

Companies are a lot like sailing ships. Both are essentially vehicles that can take you from one point to another, in a set time frame, and consuming an allotted amount of resources. The integrity of the vessel—its ability to stay afloat and move forward in the desired course—depends on its ability to provide Stability, Propulsion, and Direction. Integrity also depends on how skilled the crew is at performing these functions in a well-orchestrated manner. Different ships are appropriate for different seas; different crews, for different ships. This metaphor sums up many of the ideas in this book. Just as ships are only successful when out in the sea, companies find success in the marketplace, not through cost-cutting or reengineering. Repairs at the dry dock are not what a ship is all about. Ships are meant to sail; businesses, to grow.

The people who "crew" an enterprise have limited resources. They can spend time and money on repair and internal improvements, or they can focus attention on moving forward. Both, of course, are important. The real issue is one of balance, and in recent years, many companies have tilted the balance far inward. It's time to look beyond internal improvements, reengineering, and downsizing. *This is the time to go for growth.*

A Generation of Cost-Cutters

Some companies put considerable efforts into restructuring in hopes of building "a platform for growth." They need to be cautious. Platforms are useless if, in their construction, they absorb all the business's energies. Newark, New Jersey–based First Fidelity Bancorporation followed the industry's conventional wisdom of cost-cutting and operations reengineering, but after the bank was "fixed," little money was available to develop new products to help First Fidelity stand out among its competition. The result: a takeover by First Union, a more aggressive, customer-focused bank.

Kodak's George Fisher likes to say, "Growth is what I am all about." He realizes that cost-cutting and growth are two sides of the same coin. Going for one objective without simultaneously pursuing the other is pointless. He knows only growth can provide a path out of the doldrums for Kodak. "When a company . . . [Kodak's] size doesn't grow," says Fisher, "a kind of atrophy sets in, and then costs become uncontrollable."

Fisher's wisdom is attractive, but putting it into practice won't be easy. The last decade has produced a generation of skilled cost-cutters. Can they—can you—shift gears? **Can you become more of a grower, less of a pruner? What new skills need to be acquired or rediscovered, and which old habits need to be withdrawn from center stage? Spend a minute thinking about where you have most excelled over the past five years. What are the three or four accomplishments for which you have received the most recognition? What is the nature of these achievements? Did your efforts focus on improving the company's inner workings, or was attention directed more outward, at customers, competitors, and markets? How much practice have you had at growing the business, or have you been more of a platform builder? What do you need to focus on now?**

The New Rules of Growth

Keep in mind, as you make future plans, that growth is not what it used to be. It is a seductive objective but one that needs to be approached with caution. What worked in the post–World War II global boom is of questionable relevance to the turn-of-the-century economy. Growth has a new set of rules.

- Real growth opportunities are those a business finds for itself—rising tides seldom lift all boats anymore.

- Find opportunities in places others aren't looking—mature and fragmented markets provide many possibilities for growth.

- Growing a business means making it better, not just bigger.

- Rivals can be your best partners, if you assist each other in making the pool of opportunities bigger for everyone. Growth does not always come at the expense of the competition.

- No-mistakes management eventually leads to stagnation; success does not always beget more success. Today's failures can be the seeds of tomorrow's growth, if properly nourished.

Approaching business along these lines requires less of the mechanistic, lockstep mind-set that worked when the world was simpler and when rising tides *did* lift all boats. The idea now is to operate more like a sailor in uncharted waters and less like a skilled technician running a complex piece of machinery.

Having a growth goal is important, but it is not enough. It is just as important to choose an appropriate path to reach that goal. In most situations, there is more than one way to be successful, but all paths are not uniformly appropriate. Sometimes features from several growth paths must be blended.

Real Advantage Comes from People

Selection of a path, or useful blend, is dependent on the market conditions in which the business operates and on the capabilities of its people. **Employees are linked to market demands through the kind of organization the business has chosen.** Many organization forms are common—functional, divisional, matrix, team, network, and virtual—but all organizations oriented toward growth provide those working in them with a sense of Direction, Propulsion, and Stability.

For many companies, the choice of growth path is predetermined by external conditions. The real edge many businesses have over competitors lies less in strategy than in people and how their talents are utilized. It is employees who make a company grow, not clever, borrowed business ideas or fortunate market positioning. When a business is not growing, the usual suspects are costs, price, overseas competitors, or quality, but the underlying causes are invariably more human in nature.

This idea is given lip service by many companies but taken to heart by those really good at growing. The headquarters offices of many supermarket chains have framed corporate mission statements with paragraphs of glowing prose about the importance of their associates. The walls of their conference rooms, though, are covered with photos of the newest and largest stores. In contrast, a highly profitable and growing Los Angeles–area chain keeps the prose to a minimum ("We are here to make money and have fun"), but every available inch of wall space is crammed with photos of their people. You will see a similar pattern in the airline industry where offices are filled with models and photos of the biggest or latest jets. Southwest Airlines, the past decade's only consistent profit grower, reinforces its philosophy that frontline employees are the customers of management by posting pictures of these "customers" where they will easily be seen by busy executives.

Decoding Growth Problems

Organization serves as the vehicle to move a business forward by keeping everyone focused on the specific requirements of the growth path. Every path has its limitations, pitfalls, and downsides. Effective organizations are designed to anticipate and minimize their impact. When growth problems arise, they can be interpreted in one of two ways:

1. Everyone needs to do what they are doing better, to try harder to resolve inconsistencies between what needs to happen for growth to take place and what the company is currently doing. These problems occur when the organization is sending mixed signals about how people need to behave.

2. The world has changed—and possibly the people within the business have changed—and it is now time to look for a new path.

Paths Have Beginnings, Middles, and Ends

It is important to know where a company is on its growth path. Too many companies stay too long on the path to which they have become most accustomed. Apple Computer loved rule breaking even when its market cried out for game playing and, as a result, missed many growth opportunities. Paths have beginnings, middles, and ends—and a clear destination.

- The *start* of a path is where to get on—it makes little sense to become a Rule Maker in a market favoring specialization. Start by setting an appropriate direction and building the needed capabilities.

- The *middle* is the point of greatest prosperity—and greatest danger. **This is where overly smug managers fail to set aside resources for future growth and are too content with the status quo to prepare the business for renewal.**

- The *end* is the point where the organization's growth objectives have been achieved. It is now time to shift the business on to another path. Successful change is very risky at this stage unless the groundwork has already been solidly put in place.

Arnold Toynbee was a "big picture" historian. He spent most of his career charting why major civilizations all seem to go through similar patterns of emergence, growth, plateauing, and decline. Many of his insights apply to businesses as well:

Insofar as a civilization grows and continues to grow, it has to reckon less and less with challenges delivered by alien adversaries and demanding responses on an outer battlefield and more and more with challenges that are presented by itself to itself in an inner arena. In other words, the criterion of growth is *progress toward self-determination.*

New Paths Require Different Thinking

Businesses also need the ability to determine themselves, to skillfully change growth paths as necessity dictates. New paths almost always require new thinking and different behaviors from managers and executives. People vary in both motivation and ability to make these kinds of changes, so mechanisms for retraining and redeployment, for inplacement and outplacement, are essential to ensure ongoing growth.

The 150-year-old Connecticut Mutual Life Insurance Company understands this truth very well. Recently, David Sams became the first chief executive this company had ever brought in from the outside. To prepare for a much more hostile growth environment than Connecticut Mutual has ever faced, Sams, in turn, put everyone in the company through a radical break with the past. The duties and pay scales for every job in the company were changed. Every one of these new positions was then declared "open," and each employee was allowed to apply for up to three jobs, including their old one, if still offered.

It's amazing how many businesses attempt to make radical shifts in strategy but assume they can leave the team that provided past success in place. In rapidly changing industries, attempts to clone past growth are seldom successful. Amoco, like most major oil companies, realized the limits of cost-cutting-driven growth. Its current focus is to move more products through its efficiently managed system, while selling proportionately more of those commanding higher markups. Robert Rauscher, Amoco's marketing vice president, realized that this path to growth was not one that managers born and bred in the insular oil business knew much about. So he boosted growth by hiring brand managers from consumer product companies instead. At Amoco, ex-managers from Miller Brewing and Quaker Oats are crafting new ways to sell gas, such as applying the cross-branding idea: Amoco now shares sites with Burger King and McDonald's restaurants.

Sometimes sustaining growth requires more than just nonconventional thinking. The job of finding a new growth path for Sony has been given to Nobuyuki Idei, a product design whiz located several rungs below the president whose job he was given. Sony was willing to disappoint several key contributors to ensure that it found the right growth path. AT&T had to bite a different kind of bullet. This company paid a heavy price to keep its growth focus on opportunities in telecommunications when it accepted the resignation of Paul Kahn, one of its superstar managers. Kahn built the Universal Credit Card business from nothing to become the second largest charge-card issuer in the United States, winning a Baldrige quality award on the way. He wanted AT&T to further diversify into other financial services products, something the parent company feared would divert its attention from the growth path it chose.

The Five Growth Paths

AT&T, once an undisputed Rule Maker, has had many characteristics of an Improviser since its 1984 divestiture. Its more recent move, dubbed a tri-vestiture by some, to split into three independent companies, was driven by a realization that sustained growth requires focus. One of these companies, its long-distance and new local calling business, is a Game Player well positioned to battle for market share with MCI and Sprint. Another is a maker of telephone equipment, set to compete with other

Specialists like Ericsson, Northern Telecom, and Siemens. Its third unit, a computer company, is still, Improviser-like, searching for a viable long-term strategy.

Other businesses are making similar growth-inducing shifts. Sony is a returning-to-its-roots Rule Breaker, and Amoco is a Specialist/Game Player hybrid. **These five growth path categories are abstractions.** There is nothing magic about the number five. This book could have been written about four, six, or even a dozen paths. Considering blends, hybrids, and transitional paths, there may be well over 100 ways a business can successfully grow.

The important point is that there is more than one way a company can grow. It is critical to get beyond the "there is one right way for everyone" school of management. Growth is not just a matter of doing the right things and avoiding the wrong. The real world is never that simple.

Five alternatives are offered here as a way to emphasize that there is more than *one* way. There is a long, well-meaning, but dangerous, pattern in business literature to point out a new direction that we *all need to travel,* and then to provide the three, five, or seven key characteristics of that direction. These formulas may make for a quick read and on the surface appear quite logical, but in the end they insult the intelligence of too many managers. They serve an important purpose in helping get across the results of complex research efforts—we all are impatient for the bottom line—but they are dangerous when we start to take them as our sole guides to action.

The purpose of the five is to provide a common language, a vocabulary to label what path is being taken to growth—as well as a way to indicate what is not being done. The idea is to move beyond the simplistic slogans, or exhortations to be "more entrepreneurial" (especially in situations where risky, bet-the-company behavior may be exactly the wrong things to do).

Mental Scaffolding

There is some utility to the five paths. They include most potential growth options and are reasonably mutually exclusive. The paths are also anchored to research done in several business schools (see section on Further Reading) and have proven useful in many consulting situations.

But their real worth lies in how well *you* find them useful in explaining growth situations and in encouraging your thinking about what needs to happen next.

The paths provide a way to typecast some situations, indicating how companies that are seemingly dissimilar actually have a lot in common. The path idea makes it easier to see how Boston Market (formerly Boston Chicken) is following a game-playing approach to growth similar to that of Blockbuster Entertainment, and it is doing it with a top management team that got to know each other when they all worked on the Blockbuster staff. These managers honed their skills on one growth path, and then they fueled their personal growth by migrating this know-how to a different industry where their experience was equally applicable.

Use the five types the way a builder uses scaffolding, as a support to put in place before erecting the actual structure. These are aids in planning growth strategies and in developing the kinds of people and organizations needed to support growth. Like a good builder, never confuse the scaffolding with the actual building. These concepts are supports, not substitutes, for your own thinking. Each path is a caricature, a line drawing. You need to flesh each out from your own experience and sense of what your business needs. When they cease being useful, put them aside. Or even better, invent a set of categories that best fits your own experience.

It All Depends

Many popular management practices have been highlighted here: bringing in outside managers, downsizing, mission statements, outsourcing, reengineering, and self-managed teams. Some were discussed in a positive light; others, more skeptically. As with paths, none of these are inherently wrong, just less suited to the immediate situation. Recall the face-off commentaries at the end of each of the five chapters about growth paths. Each described people almost equally ecstatic or discouraged—with the same company! Truth lies somewhere in the middle of these descriptions.

The practice of requiring all employees to reapply for their jobs may make sense at Connecticut Mutual, but it was disastrous when tried at the World Bank and led to a great deal of disruption at McDonnell-Douglas. **Look hard for the pros and cons of potentially useful** techniques. Both are always present. Then look hard at where the practice worked and understand why it worked in that particular situation. Never try something until you find an example of it failing, and be sure you know what was behind the failure. Then ask how similar—or not—is your business's situation to these others. Finally, list the adjustments you will need to make to the new idea to increase its likelihood of success.

The idea of contingency is one of the most important concepts in management. You have mastered its essentials if you can say "it all depends" without sounding wimpy because you can also describe exactly what the right solution depends on. What management practices are most effective in your particular business? Why? Which are overused or have lost their luster? Why? Which have been neglected but have some promise?

Be Wary of Bandwagons and Exemplars

Be wary of bandwagons, involving either trendy industries or hot business concepts. The fit is more important than the glitter. Be wary also, once a bandwagon has been boarded, of jumping off *too soon* to ride one that looks newer or more attractive. Management by zigzagging around will eventually leave you and your company victims of terminal whiplash, an inability to maintain focus on any growth objective long enough to achieve it.

Successful benchmarking and borrowing is largely a process of customization and fine-tuning. While it is not always necessary to reinvent the wheel, frequently the hub, spokes, and rim need some adjustment.

Many examples, with company names, have been cited here. This is a useful way to communicate and validate new ideas, but these companies' experiences must also be considered with caution. Remember how quickly so many of the *In Search of Excellence* standouts went into the tank. **Don't put any company too high on a pillar.** Examples are used most effectively when they serve to raise *questions* in your mind, not provide answers. Boeing is a good place to see organizational learning in practice, although I'm less certain they have a lock on the best wisdom about cost-cutting.

Think of the corporation you admire the most. What does it do so well that is worth the time to plan how to adapt the practice to your business? Then set aside your favorite company's halo. Find two or three areas in which its performance is not so exemplary. How can you keep these problems from migrating along with the practices worthy of emulation?

Take the Time to Get It Right

Many companies have acquired hard-won experience in making change stick. Arthur D. Little, Inc. consultants talked with several hundred U.S. chief executives and corporate officers about their experiences leading renewal programs. While over half the executives were generally satisfied with the progress their business had made, more than two-thirds also reported experiencing unwanted side effects—low morale, fear and insecurity, and sluggish implementation. The comments of one top energy industry executive, about his business process redesign project, sums up what many felt were behind the unanticipated problems:

> If I had to do it over again, I'd take more time *planning what to do and how to do it*. The doing would go much faster. I'd spend more time on *identifying key work processes* prior to implementation. I'd *increase communication*: it helps settle people.

Your business has most likely been through some type of wrenching change. What would you do differently, if you had to do it over again?

A What-to-Do Book

This is a direction-setting book. The focus is on what to do, not how to do it. My graduate school advisor, Terry Deal, often observed that people tend to use diet books as substitutes for losing weight. Don't let reading about growth replace doing something about it! And don't look here for a neatly packaged, ten-step model of change to take you from here to where you want to be. The most workable processes are those you sequence for yourself. Take the ideas you have read here as inputs for the development of your personal growth strategy, but be sure to start with some sense of direction, some idea about what kind of growth for which you are looking. Without a clear sense of where you are headed, any path is as good as any other.

A clear direction is a good tool to motivate others to join in. Most people are willing to make an extra effort, even uproot old habits, provided they have some idea about where they are headed and what they are likely to find when they get there.

Growth Choices

Going for growth requires making choices. What path is best for me, best for my company? One alternative that is not really available is the "no growth" option. In many industries the reality is that "if you are not growing, you are dying." Is this true in yours?

Norman Mailer observed, "There is that law of life so cruel and so just, which demands that one must grow, or else pay dearly for remaining the same." At some point, as the late Mike Walsh of Tenneco put it, "You either get on with it or you don't." Ask yourself these three questions:

1. Do I need to change myself to meet the requirements of the path I'm on?

Answering this requires absolute candor with yourself. Inputs from others who know you and your work are also essential.

As you read through the descriptions of each of the five paths, you may have felt something that many first-year medical students experience. These doctors-to-be often think they are acquiring the symptoms of each new disease they study. Take this as a clue that the elements of what is needed to thrive on each growth path are present in varying degrees in all of us. The broader your repertoire of skills and behaviors, the less you need to feel condemned to one path when it stops taking you where you want to go.

2. Can I change the company to better match my vision of where it needs to go?

Growth requires

- employees who demonstrate loyalty by their willingness to *challenge* the status quo, and

- managers who understand that the ability to lead business growth is almost completely dependent on how *open* they are to these challenges.

Warren Radtke, a regional manager with the career consulting firm Right Associates, has mastered this approach to leadership. He feels that, in a company constantly reinventing itself, a senior executive needs the view that "I am a rookie in this job. I lead my region, but I make no pretense of attempting to manage it."

A variety of tactics are available for effective challenges:

- Head-on assault: a good approach when the business is in a crisis and doors that were once firmly locked are at least half open.

- Guerrilla warfare: the tactic of shifting the business direction a little each time an opportunity arises. There are often at least two ways to get something done: one is likely to reinforce old habits; the other, to promote change and growth.

- Create an enclave: when it is not feasible to change the entire business, it is still possible to build islands of growth, parts of the company that can serve as beacons for the rest of the organization. When enough of these exist, they can be interconnected to reach a point of critical mass.

3. Do I need to go elsewhere to find a growth path with which I am more compatible?

If your answer leads to considering a job change or to saying no to a great offer, at least you are in excellent company. Before he came to Kodak, George Fisher was approached to become IBM's chief executive. He considered the opportunity and then declined, realizing IBM's situation would require more cost-cutting than he wanted to spend his time doing. He knew his strong points were elsewhere. So did George McKerrow, founder of the Longhorn Steaks restaurant chain. He *fired himself* as chief executive and brought in a team of seasoned industry veterans to take the business to the next level.

All Change Requires People to Change

All change—political, social, or corporate—must ultimately involve people-change. **Choosing the wrong path can lead to ineffectiveness, creating the wrong organization will cause inefficiency, but attempting to grow with the wrong people is likely to result in disaster.** AlliedSignal's chief executive, Larry Bossidy, knows this well. When necessary, he changes executives with the frequency that Abraham Lincoln shifted generals during the Civil War. Bossidy believes that companies operating in drab markets like Allied's auto parts and chemicals need to avoid the "mature market" mentality if they want to seek growth opportunities. According to Bossidy, there are *no mature markets, only mature executives.* Growth fuels the bottom line, but even more importantly, Bossidy feels, it is the best way to attract and motivate the talent on which every business is built. Growth is the only way to guarantee a company's future. It becomes hard wired in a company through the bets the business places on its people.

Companies sustainably grow only when the people who work in them do. Growth happens when you integrate *what you are,* what you *want to become,* and what the *realities are around you.* It is a process that begins with introspection, and then requires information gathering and rolling-up-the-sleeves-style planning. Many choices are likely to emerge. Some will involve hunkering down and clinging to fleeting hopes for stability. Others will involve change and new directions.

Every day thousands of harried commuters rush by a commemorative plaque in the main corridor of Washington, D.C.'s Union Station. It honors Daniel Burnham, the architect of this imposing structure. The plaque includes one of his most famous admonitions: "Make no little plans . . . they have no magic to stir men's souls." Bold growth objectives can energize businesspeople in ways few goals can. But growth is not something that is driven by an autopilot—it only happens when you go for it!

Acknowledgments

Books may have the name of a single author on the cover, but they are never the result of only one person's efforts. This book, which is no exception to that rule, has had a long genesis. Harry Levinson generously helped his former graduate student think about how the psychological makeups of people vary by the businesses they are in. He is also responsible for suggesting the metaphor of organization as a vehicle, with varying types being best suited for different terrains. The ideas in this book would sputter without direction were it not for Harry's kind guidance.

The encouragement of several colleagues helped move these concepts past the infancy stage. Special thanks to Douglas Anderson, Richard Goodale, Stan Halle, Steve Race, Amram Shapiro, and Rob Wilson. Jean-Philippe Deschamps, Nigil Godley, and Richard Stephan provided early opportunities to test this framework outside the United States. Several clients also courageously allowed use of their companies to fine-tune my ideas, including Charles Denny, Daniel Miglio, Michael Waterman, and Jake Wallace.

I am a consultant, not a researcher, so I have been very fortunate to draw on the business school research of several topflight professors whose examinations of the experiences of hundreds of companies have given me confidence to generalize from my personal experiences with dozens. Among the most useful are the studies that have been done by Chris Argyris (Harvard), Paul Lawrence (Harvard), Raymond Miles (Berkeley), Danny Miller (École des Hautes Commerciales), Henry Mintzberg (McGill), and Charles Snow (Penn State).

Harriet Rubin spotted some of my ideas about matching company types with strategies when they were first published in a short article and started me thinking about writing a book. Years later, John Willig, literary agent, picked up Harriet's encouragement and finally got me to go for growth. Considering the turbulence of contemporary publishing, I doubt there's a better guide and source of support than John. He also introduced me to my publisher, Jim Childs.

Jim's authors all praise him profusely, and I agree. My writing abilities are not nearly good enough to outdo their lavish comments, so I won't even try. Let me just say I'm very proud to be associated with him. He is one of the few in business publishing who think with a businessperson's mind-set. Jim has been a hands-on partner in helping shape this book, working relentlessly to turn consultant's babble into business prose. Jim is the perfect editor for someone who has written two books but realizes he doesn't know how to write. If you find this book more readable, or easier to use, than the average management book, credit Jim, not me. Jim Childs embodies the "go for growth" philosophy. If you are one of his competitors, watch out!

As always, the best lessons turn out to be those closest to home. As she did with earlier books, my wife's capable advice kept this one from growing out of control. Brenda Turnbull also unbegrudgingly picked up the parenting slack at home while providing, at her office, one of the best examples I've come across of an executive team with different but complementary perspectives skilled at driving a business forward. And finally, this book is dedicated to our three children, Laura, Julia, and William. Although clients and colleagues have taught me a lot about growth, I don't think I ever understood what that word really meant until I became their father.

Further Reading

If you have enjoyed *Go for Growth,* there are a number of other books that expand on its perspective. Grouped by topic, here are some of the best and most useful.

Strategy and Organization

Go for Growth is one of a long line of books that relates business strategies with the varying organizational configurations needed to carry them out. Business historian Alfred Chandler is the pioneer of this perspective and his *Strategy and Structure* (MIT Press, 1962) is a classic. Two of his Harvard colleagues, Paul Lawrence and Jay Lorsch, fleshed out some of these ideas in *Organization and Environment* (Harvard Business School Press, 1967), with some of the first research on the contingency approach to organizing.

Paul Lawrence has had a lot of influence on me as a teacher also, helping me understand some of the dangers of "one-size-fits-all" management. Paul practices what he preaches. Even though his *Matrix* (Addison-Wesley, 1977), written with Stanley Davis, helped launch the popularity of matrix management, the book begins with suggestions about what situations it is appropriate for and also includes a long list of "matrix pathologies," a level of candor missing from many contemporary business books.

Another important early proponent of the idea that effective companies identify homogeneous segments of their markets and then establish specialized organization units to deal with them was James Thompson in *Organizations in Action* (McGraw-Hill, 1967). This book has many insights that are still fresh today.

Types of Companies

Business school professors and consultants were among the first to apply the contingency idea to discover why some businesses were great successes and others only also-rans. The research of Raymond Miles and Charles Snow in *Organizational Strategy, Structure and Process* (McGraw-Hill, 1978) influenced much of my early thinking about this subject. Their breakdown of businesses into Defenders, Prospectors, Analyzers, and Reactors does not correspond directly with the five growth paths herein, but their work provides great clues about how to start thinking about organizational strategy.

Danny Miller, a Canadian business school professor whose research has been cited at several points in this book, is a not-to-be-missed describer of the dynamics of growth and decline. Read his *The Icarus Paradox* (Harper Business, 1990). Miller's four company types include Craftsmen, Salesmen, Builders, and Pioneers.

Two management consultants have focused on the life cycle approach to characterizing a company's growth stage. Lawrence Miller's *Barbarians to Bureaucrats* (Fawcett Columbine, 1989) is a pleasure to read for those concerned about sustaining growth. Ichak Adizes's *Corporate Lifecycles* (Prentice Hall, 1988) is a more detailed account of what needs to happen when a business grows. . . . Some of the best thinking about organizational life cycles is in Larry Greiner's *Harvard Business Review* (July–August, 1972, pp. 37–46) article titled "Evolution and Revolution as Organizations Grow." Don't attempt to reorganize without reading it!

A number of books describe the stories of companies on each of the five growth paths. Look for some of the recent accounts of Apple, Federal Express, Microsoft, and Wal-Mart. For some reason, Xerox attracts more than its fair share of authors. Read David Dorsey's *The Force* (Ballantine, 1994) to learn what it is really like to work in a Game Player and Douglas Smith and Robert Alexander's *Fumbling the Future* (Morrow, 1988) to understand why Xerox has such a hard time blending the paths of the Game Player and Rule Breaker.

Steven Schnaars's *Managing Imitation Strategies* (Free Press, 1994) is the best guide available about how to be a star Game Player. *Built to Last* (HarperBusiness, 1994), by James Collins and Jerry Porras, provides good detail on the success habits of typical Rule Makers and Game Players. Gary Hamel and C.K. Prahalad's *Competing for the Future*

(Harvard Business School Press, 1994) advises Rule Makers how they can become Rule Breakers.

Applying Psychology to Understand Why Companies Do What They Do

The underlying logic of this book is based on applying lessons from psychology to business. There is a great deal of leverage to be gained by blending insights from these two fields, something most people in business have yet to discover. You could begin by reviewing your college texts, but why not start with what the best author in this field has to say. Harry Levinson's *Psychological Man* (The Levinson Institute, 1976) is the clearest introduction to industrial-strength psychology for managers. If you are serious about wanting to really sort out the inner dynamics of your company, Levinson's 557-page guide is called *Organizational Diagnosis* (Harvard University Press, 1972).

To probe more deeply into personality styles and how they develop, see David Shapiro's *Neurotic Styles* (Basic Books, 1965) and George Vaillant's *Adaptation to Life* (Little, Brown, 1977). Vaillant's book, subtitled "How the Best and Brightest Came of Age," is a great account of how an adult's personality keeps evolving—you'll find some parallels with how corporate "psyches" develop. Both books require some real interest in psychology, but if you have it, you will find good value therein.

Abraham Zaleznik, along with Levinson, is a leading thinker in the emerging field of corporate psychodynamics. Two of his best books are *Power and the Corporate Mind* (Houghton Mifflin, 1975), written with Manfred Kets de Vries, and *The Managerial Mystique* (Harper & Row, 1989). Kets de Vries has followed up Zaleznick's work with a number of excellent books of his own. One of his best for business readers is *Unstable at the Top* (New American Library, 1987), co-authored by Danny Miller.

Several other books sort out managers by personality type or culture in which they best thrive. Michael Maccoby's *The Gamesman* (Simon and Schuster, 1976) is the first to have attracted widespread business attention. Charles Handy's *Gods of Management* (Pan Books Ltd., 1979) is fun to read. Handy names his managers after Greek mythical gods: Zeus, Apollo, Athena, and Dionysus.

Probably the most commonly used application of psychology to business is the Myers-Briggs indicator of personality type. While it is a more limited perspective than some of the others mentioned above, it's a good exercise to try to match these 16 types with the five paths to growth. Otto Kroeger and Janet Thuesen's *Type Talk* (Delacorte Press, 1988) is a good introduction, and Paul Tieger and Barbara Barron-Tieger's *Do What You Are* (Little, Brown, 1992) shows how to apply these ideas to select a well-fitting career.

People Count Most

Most books about how important people are to corporate growth have as much apple pie in them as a typical Sunday sermon. One that gets beyond the platitudes and really sorts out why some companies do a great job of using their employees' talents (and most utterly fail) is Robert Levering's *A Great Place to Work* (Random House, 1988). Levering is the journalist who regularly puts out the list of the 100 best places to work in America. This book tells how to get on his list.

What Is Organization?

My perspective on organization as something that provides Direction, Propulsion, and Stability was influenced by John Kotter's *Organizational Dynamics* (Addison-Wesley, 1978) and Richard Pascale and Anthony Athos's *The Art of Japanese Management* (Simon and Schuster, 1981).

The best all-around thinker on what "organizing" really means is Karl Weick. He tells all about it (including more details on the Naskapi Indians) in *The Social Psychology of Organizing* (Addison-Wesley, 1979). The other thought leader here is Henry Mintzberg, author of a compendium, *The Structuring of Organizations* (Prentice-Hall, 1979).

Organizational Learning and the Hidden Dynamics of Growth

Peter Senge's *The Fifth Discipline* (Doubleday Currency, 1990) has done a great job of popularizing the essentials of organizational learning, a survival necessity for Improvisers and key to any company's ability to sustain growth. If this subject is of interest, you may want to turn to a book by two of the field's founders, Chris Argyris and Donald Schon:

Organizational Learning: A Theory of Action Perspective (Addison-Wesley, 1978).

Some of the best thinking about how businesses use learning and knowledge development to drive growth has been done in Sweden and Japan. One of the most creative books written about the hidden dynamics of corporate growth, especially the political dimensions, is Richard Normann's *Management and Statesmenship* (Scandinavian Institutes for Administrative Research, Stockholm, 1978). It's hard to find but well worth the trouble.

Some of the latest ideas about how companies like Canon, Honda, and NEC grow through innovation and knowledge management are found in *The Knowledge-Creating Company* (Oxford, 1995) by Ikujiro Nonaka and Hirotaka Takeuchi.

Metaphors and Missions

John Clancy has an original discussion of the ways language and metaphors are clues to a company's priorities in *The Invisible Powers* (Lexington, 1989). Mission statements from companies worldwide are dissected in *A Sense of Mission* (Addison-Wesley, 1992) by Andrew Campbell and Laura Nash.

Using Corporate History

Several authors have tackled ways knowledge of history and a company's past can help guide its future. Alan Kantrow's *The Constraints of Corporate Tradition* (Harper & Row, 1988) is a good account of how mind-sets are created; *Scuttle Your Ships Before Advancing* (Oxford, 1994) is Richard Luecke's retelling of several historical episodes along with their relevance to business decision makers. If this is a subject of strong interest, the best how-to book about using the lessons of the past to make better decisions today is Richard Neustadt and Ernest May's *Thinking in Time* (Free Press, 1986).

Change

Change is a subject that runs through all the books that have been mentioned. While business bookshelves abound with books on "change management," one of the best for ideas about how to move a big corporation from one growth path to another is James Brian Quinn's *Strategies for Change* (Irwin, 1980). He calls his approach "logical incrementalism." It works.

The notes that follow are keyed to specific references in the text. Check them for where to find more information about the people and examples used in this book.

Notes

1 The Growth Imperative

PAGE

5   "Most of us": Marc Levinson, "Thanks. You're Fired," *Newsweek*, May 23, 1994, p. 49.

5   "You can't save": Myron Magnet, "Let's Go for Growth," *Fortune*, Mar. 7, 1994, p. 60.

6   "The chain-saw": Steven Pearlstein, "As Firms Go Lean and Mean, Benefits, and Dangers emerge," *The Washington Post*, Jan. 2, 1994, p. H16.

6   Census Bureau: Barbara Presley Noble, "Questioning Productivity Beliefs," *The New York Times*, July 10, 1994, p. F21.

7   studying: Magnet, "Let's Go for Growth," p. 72.

7   Zenith: Elizabeth Lesly and Larry Light, "When Layoffs Alone Don't Turn the Tide," *Business Week*, Dec. 7, 1992, p. 100.

8   Kodak: Ibid.

8   Bausch & Lomb: Magnet, "Let's Go for Growth," pp. 62–64.

9   Emerson Electric: Seth Lubove, "It ain't broke, but fix it anyway," *Forbes*, Aug. 1, 1994, pp. 56–60.

9   Knight pledged: *1993 Emerson Electric Co. Annual Report*, p. 4.

11 Robert Reich, "Companies Are Cutting Their Hearts Out," *The New York Times Magazine*, Dec. 19, 1993, p. 54.

16 Jon Katzenbach and Douglas Smith, *The Wisdom of Teams* (New York: Harper Collins, 1994), pp. 28–40.

2 Growth Isn't What It Used to Be

PAGE

20 Ten years ago: "Stay the Corporate Ax—with Growth," *Business Week*, May 9, 1994, p. 102.

23 Kami: Michael Kami, *Trigger Points* (New York: McGraw-Hill, 1988), pp. 24–28.

24 Harrison: Kevin Kelly, "Who Says Big Companies Are Dinosaurs?" *Business Week*, July 25, 1994, pp. 13–16.

24 Silicon Valley: Bennett Harrison, "Agile, Inventive, Job-Creating—and Big," *The New York Times*, July 17, 1994, p. F11.

26 *Fortune:* Andrew Serwer, "Lessons from America's Fastest Growing Companies," *Fortune*, Aug. 8, 1994, pp. 42–59.

26 research study: "The Growth Imperative," *Mercer Management Journal*, No. 2, 1994, pp. 4–5.

27 "Today's problems": Peter Senge, *The Fifth Discipline* (New York: Doubleday, 1990), p. 58.

27 "The idea": Peter Drucker, *Management: Tasks, Responsibilities, Practices* (New York: Harper & Row, 1974), p. 772.

27 "We don't define": Walter Roessing, "Blue Jean Boss," *Sky*, Aug. 1994, p. 67.

28 "We used to": *Ibid.*

28 "You'll also get": *Ibid.*

29 "If you provide": *Ibid.*

29 *Business Week* investigative reporter: Mark Maremount, "Blind Ambition," *Business Week*, Oct. 23, 1995, pp. 78–92.

31 new schools: Rita Koselka, "Evolutionary Economics: Nice Guys Don't Finish Last," *Forbes*, Oct. 11, 1993, pp. 110–114.

31 Nobel economics prize: Lennart Simonsson, "Game Theory Earns Nobel Economics Prize," *The Washington Times*, Oct. 12, 1994, p. B6.

35 "A mistake": Senge, *The Fifth Discipline*, p. 154.

35 Strauss: Roessing, "Blue Jean Boss," p. 65.

36 Dockers: Roessing, "Blue Jean Boss," p. 68.

37 You can forget: Chrysler Corporation 1993 Report to Shareholders, p. 2.

38 "We're not": *Ibid.*

3   One Size Never Fits All

PAGE

42 Hammer: Fred Bleakley, "Many Companies Try Management Fads, Only to See Them Flop," *The Wall Street Journal*, July 6, 1993, p. A6.

44 Department of Agriculture: *USDA Restructuring* (Washington: U.S. General Accounting Office, August 5, 1994).

47 biography: Jeffery Young, *Steve Jobs: The Journey Is the Reward* (New York: Lynx Books, 1988).

48 Metaphors: Robert Marshak, "Managing the Metaphors of Change," *Organizational Dynamics*, Summer 1993, pp. 44–56.

49 A very bright: Tamara Erickson and David Shanks, "Rethinking Growth and Renewal in the 90s," *Prism*, Second Quarter 1994, p. 61.

50 Flights began: Colleen Barrett, "In Pursuit of Southwest Trivia," *Spirit*, September 1994, p. 161.

4 Breaking the Rules

PAGE

61 Larry Miller: Lawrence Miller, *Barbarians to Bureaucrats* (New York: Fawcett Columbine, 1989), pp. 8–58.

64 James Rogers: Agis Salpukas, "Utility Competition is Coming!," *The New York Times*, Nov. 13, 1994, p. F9.

65 Klein: Tom Peters, "Innovation Myths Destroyed," *Forbes ASAP*, Dec. 5, 1994, p. 184.

66 Sony's rule-breaking growth: Gary Hamel and C.K. Prahalad, "Seeing the Future First," *Fortune*, Sept. 5, 1994, p. 67.

66 Sperlich: Ibid., p. 70.

67 Edwin Land: Danny Miller, *The Icarus Paradox* (New York: Harper Business, 1990), p. 108.

67 "Nothing is more": Mark Maremont, "Kodak's New Focus," *Business Week*, Jan. 30, 1995, p. 68.

68 "Reasonable men": George Bernard Shaw as quoted in Miller, *Barbarians to Bureaucrats*, p. 9.

69 Porsche: Ibid., p. 19.

69 remarkably resilient: Manfred Kets de Vries, *Organizational Paradoxes* (London: Tavistock, 1980), p. 113.

69 Self-destructive: Steven Schnaars, *Managing Imitation Strategies* (New York: The Free Press, 1994), pp. 205–207.

70 He is also reputed: Miller, *The Icarus Paradox*, p. 110.

71 "Computerless computer company": Andrew Rappaport and Shmuel Halevi, "The Computerless Computer Company," *Harvard Business Review*, July–August, 1991, pp. 69–80.

72 Danny Miller: Miller, *The Icarus Paradox*, pp. 114–131.

73 box office hit: Robert Hof, "The Gee-Whiz Company," *Business Week*, July 18, 1994, pp. 56–64.

74 Silicon Graphics: Steven Prokesch, "Mastering Chaos at the High-Tech Frontier: An Interview with Silicon Graphic's Ed McCracken," *Harvard Business Review*, Nov.–Dec. 1993, pp. 135–144.

76 James Clark: Robert Hof, "From the Man Who Brought You Silicon Graphics," *Business Week*, Oct. 24, 1994, pp. 90–91.

77 "Our goal": *Culture, Vision, People, Technology* (Mountain View, CA: Silicon Graphics, 1994), p. 5.

78 "middlemen": Schiller, "Making the Middleman an Endangered Species," pp. 114–115.

79 "first mover" advantages: Schnaars, *Managing Imitation Strategies*, pp. 15–18.

81 Business school professors: Gary Hamel and C.K. Prahalad, *Competing for the Future* (Boston: Harvard Business School Press, 1994).

81 "get to the future first": Ibid., p. 99.

5 Playing the Game

PAGE

90 work hard: Terrance Deal and Allan Kennedy, *Corporate Cultures* (Reading, Mass.: Addison-Wesley, 1982), pp. 107–116.

91 The worst thing: Ibid., p. 114.

91 Nabisco: Scott Ticer, "The Boss at RJR Likes to Keep 'em Guessing," *Business Week*, May 23, 1988, p. 182.

91 small wins: Deal and Kennedy, *Corporate Cultures*, p. 114.

93 Schnaars: Steven Schnaars, *Managing Imitation Strategies* (New York: The Free Press, 1994).

93 Pizza Hut: Myron Magnet, "Let's Go for Growth," *Fortune*, Mar. 7, 1994, p. 72.

93 Bowmar: Ibid., pp. 148–152.

93 DeHavilland: Ibid., pp. 68–74.

93 watchful waiters: Ibid., pp. 11–12.

94 soft drink innovations: Ibid., pp. 87–92.

94 Pepsi executive: Ibid., p. 2.

94 Sam Walton: Ibid., p. 3.

94 worthy battle: Harriet Rubin, "The Revenge of Women," *Currency*, 1993.

95 Louisiana Pacific's: Magnet, "Let's Go for Growth," pp. 64–68.

95 "We just copied": Ibid., p. 68.

97 shadow: Magnet, "Let's Go for Growth," p. 64–68.

99 VF: Joseph Weber, "Just Get It to the Stores on Time," *Business Week*, Mar. 6, 1995, pp. 66–67.

99 MCI: Patricia Sellers, "Yes, Brands Can Still Work Magic," *Fortune*, Feb. 7, 1994, pp. 133–134.

101 long-range planning: Raymond Miles and Charles Snow, *Organizational Strategy, Structure and Process* (New York: McGraw-Hill, 1978), p. 69.

101 Compaq Computer: Gary McWilliams, "At Compaq, a Desktop Crystal Ball," *Business Week*, Mar. 20, 1995, pp. 96–97.

102 rapid growth stumbled: Eric Schine, "The Fall of a Timber Baron," *Business Week*, Oct. 2, 1995, pp. 85–92.

103 Danny Miller: Danny Miller, *The Icarus Paradox* (New York: HarperBusiness, 1990), pp. 133–171.

103 Brand distinctions: Ibid., p. 154.

104 General Motors: Ibid., p. 156.

105 Many find ways: Schnaars, *Managing Imitation Strategies*, pp. 234–237.

106 Publix Super Markets: Matt Walsh, "The Schwarzkopf Gambit," *Forbes*, Nov. 21, 1994, pp. 170–174.

107 Stiritz: Suzanne Oliver, "Out of the Doghouse?," *Forbes*, Mar. 28, 1994, pp. 46–47.

107 Joseph Galli: Suzanne Oliver, "New Personality," *Forbes*, Aug. 15, 1994, p. 114.

6 Making the Rules

PAGE

115 Intel's: Richard Shaffer, "Intel as Conquistador," *Forbes*, Feb. 27, 1995, p. 130.

117 business professors: Gary Hamel and C.K. Prahalad, *Competing for the Future* (Boston: Harvard Business School Press, 1994).

117 the law of diminishing returns: Robert Shapiro, "What DOS Microsoft Want?" *The Washington Post*, April 16, 1995, p. C2.

118 "network" markets: Ibid.

118 Microsoft teamed: Brent Schlender, "What Bill Gates Really Wants," *Fortune*, Jan. 16, 1995, p. 36.

119 Apple's chagrin: Brenton Schlender and David Kirkpatrick, "The Valley Vs. Microsoft," *Fortune*, Mar. 20, 1995, p. 86.

119 software industry observers: Steven Schnaars, *Managing Imitation Strategies* (New York: The Free Press, 1994), p. 3.

121 scenarios: Schlender, "What Bill Gates Really Wants," p. 47.

121 "choke points": Schlender, Ibid.

121 observers say: Shaffer, "Intel as Conquistador."

121 Walt Disney company: Peter Carlson, "More Real than Reality," *The Washington Post Magazine*, May 15, 1994, p. 12.

122 Disney spent: John Huey, "Eisner Explains Everything," *Fortune*, April 17, 1995, p. 52.

122 more real: Carlson, "More Real than Reality," p. 13.

122 Hench: Ibid., p. 14.

123 Eisner: Huey, "Eisner Explains Everything," p. 58.

123 Mickey's head: Ibid., p. 17.

124 Microsoft's new hires: Meyer, "Culture Club," p. 42.

125 Language: James Collins and Jerry Porras, *Built to Last* (New York: HarperBusiness, 1994), p. 128.

125 surly carnies: Carlson, "More Real than Reality," p. 24.

125 boot camp: Meyer, "Culture Club," p. 42.

126 vehicle for the company: Collins and Porras, *Built to Last,* p. 28.

126 inelegant products: Schlender, "What Bill Gates Really Wants," p. 36.

128 Two Canadian: Manfred Kets de Vries and Danny Miller, *Unstable at the Top* (New York: New American Library, 1987), pp. 36–38.

129 a price: Ibid., pp. 49–50.

129 rigid in their thinking: David Shapiro, *Neurotic Styles* (New York: Basic Books, 1965), pp. 54–107.

130 paranoid survive: John Markoff, "The Chip on Intel's Shoulder," *The New York Times,* Dec. 18, 1994, p. E6.

130 Bill Gates . . . is reputed: Schlender, "What Bill Gates Really Wants," p. 63.

131 "Microsoft Way": Meyer, "Culture Club," pp. 40–41.

133 Kodak: Peter Nulty, "Digital Imaging Had Better Boom before Kodak Film Busts," *Fortune,* May 1, 1995, p. 83.

133 Japanese-like system: Subrata Chakravarty and Ruth Simon, "Has the World Passed Kodak By?" *Forbes,* Nov. 5, 1984, p. 190.

134 Britannica: Gary Samuels, "CD-ROM's First Big Victim," *Forbes,* Feb. 28, 1994, pp. 42–44.

134 Western Union: Ibid., p. 43.

135 computer workstations: Alan Deutschman, "The Managing Wisdom of High-Tech Superstars," *Fortune,* Oct. 17, 1994, p. 197.

137 "this is a company...": Walter Roessing, "Blue Jean Boss," *Sky,* August 1994, p. 71.

138 best known package: Maria Mallory, "Behemoth on a Tear," *Business Week,* Oct. 3, 1994, p. 55.

138 Hallmark: Susan Chandler, "Can Hallmark Get Well Soon?" *Business Week,* June 19, 1995, pp. 62–63.

138 "If the competition's . . . :" Michael Flynn and Linda Flynn, "A New Deal at Hallmark Cards," *Hemispheres,* Nov. 1994, p. 34.

139 Harvard Business School professors: Adrian Slywotzky, Benson Shapiro, and Richard Tedlow, *Why Bad Things Happen to Good Companies* (Boston: Harvard Business School, Nov. 29, 1994), p. 8.

140 Mandela observed: "Mandela Says Press Has Vital 'Mirror' Role," *National Press Club Record,* Oct. 13, 1994, p. 2.

141 "I want to maintain . . .": Roessing, "Blue Jean Boss," p. 70.

142 John Aikers: John Byrne, "Be Nice to Everybody," *Forbes*, Nov. 5, 1984, pp. 244–246.

142 Kodak's fall: Chakravarty and Simon, "Has the World Passed Kodak By?" p. 192.

143 New York Yankees: Malcolm Forbes, Jr., "Fact and Comment," *Forbes*, Oct. 10, 1994, p. 26.

7 Specializing

PAGE

148 seal off a portion: Raymond Miles and Charles Snow, *Organizational Strategy, Structure and Process* (New York: McGraw-Hill, 1978), pp. 31–48.

148 Texas Instruments: Danny Miller, *The Icarus Paradox* (New York: HarperBusiness, 1990), p. 19.

149 Batesville Casket: Jaclyn Fierman, "How to Make Money in Mature Markets," *Fortune*, Nov. 25, 1985, pp. 47–53.

149 *mittlestand:* Robert Tomasko, *Rethinking the Corporation* (New York: AMA-COM, 1993), pp. 45–47.

150 Tufte: William Baldwin, "Publish and Prosper," *Forbes*, May 18, 1987, pp. 121–123.

151 General Electric: James Norman, "A Very Nimble Elephant," *Forbes*, Oct. 10, 1994, pp. 88–92.

152 fastest elephant: Ibid., p. 90.

154 makers of drugs: Norm Alster, "A Dry Period," *Forbes*, April 24, 1995, pp. 88–96.

154 Medeva: Peter Fuhrman, "Cheaper to Buy than Invent," *Forbes*, Jan. 16, 1995, pp. 52–53.

155 Forest Laboratories: Howard Rudnitsky, "Sardines, Not Whales," *Forbes*, Dec. 5, 1994, pp. 47–48.

155 "There have always been . . . .": Ibid., p. 48.

155 Midwest Express: Jim Clark, "A Charmed Existence," *Frequent Flyer*, June 1994, pp. 18–19.

155 KLM: Richard Morais, "They Ship Horses, Don't They?" *Forbes*, Nov. 7, 1994, pp. 45–46.

156 MFS: Kevin Kelly, "From Niche Player to Phone Jack-of-all-Trades," *Business Week*, Dec. 12, 1994, pp. 107–109.

156 Benson Eyecare: Andrew Serwer, "A Man with a Vision Consolidates the Eye-Care Business," *Fortune*, April 17, 1995, p. 205.

156 Pahlmeyer: Frank Prial, "What Was That Wine in *Disclosure?*" *The New York Times*, Dec. 18, 1994, p. 77.

157 Codera: Lawrence Fisher, "The Contract Vintner's Motto: What's in a Name?" *The New York Times,* Dec. 18, 1994, p. 12F.

157 Examples of this trend: Shawn Tully, "You'll Never Guess who Really Makes . . ." *Fortune,* Oct. 3, 1994, pp. 124–128.

158 BMW: Alex Taylor, "The Auto Industry Meets the New Economy," *Fortune,* Sept. 5, 1994, pp. 52–60.

159 Caterpillar: Miller, *The Icarus Paradox,* pp. 23 and 40.

159 Strategic Planning Institute: Fierman, "How to Make Money in Mature Markets," p. 48.

162 Hamermesh: Ibid., p. 51.

162 Goulds: Ibid., p. 48.

162 Worthington: Ibid. p. 48.

163 Giant Food: Bill Saporito, "The Giant of the Regional Food Chains," *Fortune,* Nov. 25, 1985, pp. 27–36.

164 Fromm: Erich Fromm, *Escape from Freedom* (New York: Rinehart, 1941).

165 Maccoby: Michael Maccoby, *The Gamesman* (New York: Bantam Books, 1976), pp. 43–44.

166 the world of tomorrow: Miles and Snow, *Organizational Strategy, Structure and Process,* p. 47.

170 Abboud: Manfred Kets de Vries and Danny Miller, *Unstable at the Top* (New York: New American Library, 1987), pp. 91–92.

171 Union Carbide: John Merwin, "Endgame for a Corporate Moonwalker," *Forbes,* May 18, 1987, pp. 130–134.

172 do what it probably should have done: Tim Smart, "A lot of the Weaknesses Carbide Had Are behind It," *Business Week,* Jan. 23, 1995, p. 83.

174 American President Line: James Cook, "Train, Ahoy!" *Forbes,* May 18, 1987, pp. 60–64.

176 "The two quickest ways": *General Electric 1993 Annual Report,* pp. 3–4.

8   Improvising

PAGE

183 Haycock: Catherine Arnst, "Phone Frenzy," *Business Week,* Feb. 20, 1995, p. 96.

185 Naskapi: Karl Weick, *The Social Psychology of Organizing* (Reading: Addison-Wesley, 1979), pp. 262–263.

185 established methodology: Bernard Reimann and Vasudevan Ramanujam, "Acting Vs. Thinking," *Planning Review,* March–April 1992, p. 37.

187 to paraphrase Weick: Weick, *The Social Psychology of Organizing,* p. 263.

190 Spindler's compensation: Kathy Rebello, "Spindler's Apple," *Business Week*, Oct. 3, 1994, p. 95.

190 Spindler has cut: Julie Pitta, "Apple's Mr. Pragmatist," *Forbes*, Mar. 28, 1994, p. 86.

191 John Scully: Ibid.

191 pet ideas: Ibid.

194 Forbes writer: Gary Samuels, "Lord, Make Me Competitive—but Just Not Yet," *Forbes*, Mar. 13, 1995, p. 42.

194 Miglio: Arnst, "Phone Frenzy," p. 92.

194 Raymond Smith: Andrew Kupfer, "The Future of the Phone Companies," *Fortune*, Oct. 3, 1994, p. 106.

199 "detaching": Manfred Kets de Vries and Danny Miller, *Unstable at the Top* (New York: New American Library, 1987), pp. 55–73.

201 Kodak: Mark Maremont, "Kodak's New Focus," *Business Week*, Jan. 30, 1995, pp. 62–68.

202 "to recapture": Alan Kantrow, *The Constraints of Corporate Tradition* (New York: Perennial Library, 1988), p. 192.

202 AT&T: Ibid., p. 183.

203 other practices dominate: David Garvin, "Building a Learning Organization," *Harvard Business Review*, July–Aug. 1993, pp. 78–91.

205 Xerox's: Ibid, pp. 85–86.

206 Boeing: Ibid, p. 85.

207 Ghosh: Julia Lieblich, "Double-Edged Pragmatist," *Harvard Business Review*, Jan.–Feb. 1994, pp. 134–135.

208 Digital: Bruce Upbin, "The Sincerest Form of Flattery," *Forbes*, July 31, 1995, p. 12.

211 pragmatism: Nitin Nohria and James Berkley, "Whatever Happened to the Take-Charge Manager?" *Harvard Business Review*, Jan.–Feb. 1994, p. 131.

211 Improviser's goals: James Brian Quinn, *Strategies for Change* (Homewood, Ill: Richard D. Irwin, 1980), p. 71.

214 "mut": Pitta, "Apple's Mr. Pragmatist," p. 86.

9 Keeping the Focus on Growth

PAGE

221 bread lines: Kim Eisler, "Out of Dough," *The Washingtonian*, Aug. 1994, pp. 157–160.

222 "Business failure": Mark Furstenberg, "A Marvelous Bankruptcy," *Marvelous Market Newsletter*, Nov. 1994, p. 2.

225 "Organizations lapse": Danny Miller, "The Architecture of Simplicity," *Academy of Management Review*, Jan. 1993, pp. 116 and 119.

226 His research finds: Ibid., pp. 121–130.

230 Court jesters: Ibid., p. 134.

230 requisite variety: Ibid., p. 118.

230 Politics and Prose: Politics and Prose Fall 1994 Newsletter, pp. 1–13.

230 blending of perspectives: Ibid., pp. 10–11.

231 Samsung: Laxmi Nakarmi and Robert Neff, "Samsung's Radical Shakeup," *Business Week*, Feb. 28, 1994, pp. 74–76.

232 "Any attempt": Lee Kun-Hee, "Other Comments," *Forbes*, June 5, 1995, p. 32.

233 Prudential: Terence Pare, "Scandal Isn't All that Ails the Pru," *Fortune*, Mar. 21, 1994, pp. 52–60.

234 Xerox: Subrata Chakravarty, "Back in Focus," *Forbes*, June 6, 1994, pp. 72–76.

239 "the secret": Peter Scott-Morgan, *The Unwritten Rules of the Game* (New York: McGraw Hill, 1994), p. 19.

239 Samsung changed the official rules: Nakami and Neff, "Samsung's Radical Shakeup," p. 75.

240 Every year the company selects: Ibid.

241 Kids 'R' Us: Douglas Zehr, "In Puerto Rico, Kids 'R' Not Us," *Business Week*, Feb. 28, 1994, p. 8.

241 Robert Eaton: Marshall Loeb, "Empowerment That Pays Off," *Fortune*, Mar. 20, 1995, p. 145.

242 "our employees are": "Fewer Airlines Seen in Nation's Future," *National Press Club Record*, June 16, 1994, p. 3.

243 "When all these minds": Chrysler Corporation 1993 Annual Report, p. 10.

244 "Where are we": Gary Hamel and C. K. Prahalad, *Competing for the Future* (Boston: Harvard Business School Press, 1994), p. 130.

244 C. K. Prahalad: Ibid.

10 Changing Course to Sustain Growth

PAGE

250 Integrated Device Technology: Edward Gargan, " 'Virtual' Companies Leave the Manufacturing to Others," *The New York Times*, July 17, 1994, p. F5.

251 Nike: Raymond Miles and Charles Snow, *Fit, Failure & the Hall of Fame* (New York: The Free Press, 1994), pp. 102–104.

252 In business schools: Terry Amburgey and Tina Dacin, "As the Left Foot follows the Right? The Dynamics of Strategic and Structural Change," *Academy of Management Journal*, Dec. 1994, pp. 1427–1452.

253 the popular management book: James Collins and Jerry Porras, *Built to Last* (New York: HarperBusiness, 1994), pp. 146–149.

253 English scientist: D'Arcy Thompson, *On Growth and Form* (New York: Dover, 1992), pp. 1093–1095.

254 Gould: William Stolzenburg, "Survival of the Luckiest," *The Washington Post*, Sept. 30, 1990, p. D3.

254 Golub believes: Stephen Soloman, "American Express Applies for a New Line of Credit," *The New York Times Magazine*, July 30, 1995, p. 37.

255 "all hell breaks loose": Richard Foster, *Innovation: The Attacker's Advantage* (New York: Summit Books, 1986), p. 31.

255 Emery Worldwide: Kate Bohner Lewis, "Full Circle," *Forbes*, Mar. 27, 1995, pp. 56–57.

256 Franklin Computer Company: Steven Schnaars, *Managing Imitation Strategies* (New York: The Free Press, 1994), p. 4.

257 "it wouldn't hurt": Speech by Marvin Runyon at National Press Club, Washington, D.C. on Nov. 18, 1992.

257 Cortez: Richard Luecke, *Scuttle Your Ships before Advancing* (New York: Oxford University Press, 1994), p. 23.

257 wake: Steven Prokesch, "Mastering Chaos at the High-Tech Frontier," *Harvard Business Review*, Nov.–Dec. 1993, pp. 142–144.

258 Devanlay: "Anemic Crocodile," *Forbes*, Aug. 15, 1994, p. 116.

260 "can only function": Chris Argyris, "Good Communication that Blocks Learning," *Harvard Business Review*, July–Aug. 1994, p. 84.

Epilogue

PAGE

264 "Growth is what": Peter Nulty, "Digital Imaging Had Better Boom before Kodak Film Busts," *Fortune*, May 1, 1995, p. 83.

265 "When a company": Ibid.

267 "Insofar as a civilization": Arnold Toynbee as quoted in Larry Miller, *Barbarians to Bureaucrats* (New York: Fawcett Columbine, 1989), p. 59.

268 Amoco: Toni Mack, "Catching up to Exxon," *Forbes*, Mar. 13, 1995, pp. 64–66.

272 "If I had to": *Managing Organizational Change: How Leading Organizations Are Meeting the Challenge* (Cambridge, MA: Arthur D. Little, Inc., 1994), p. 5.

273 "law of life": Norman Mailer as quoted in *Going Bonkers*, June 1995, p. 12.

273 "You either get on": Wendy Zellner, "Requiem for a Heavyweight," *Business Week*, May 23, 1994, p. 36.

275 "Make no little plans": commerative plaque in West Corridor of Washington, D.C.'s Union Station.

Index